# Detecting Bull

## How to Identify Biased, Fake and Junk Journalism in the Digital Age

## Third Edition

John H. McManus Ph.D.

THE UNVARNISHED PRESS

ISBN: 1546796835

ISBN-13: 978-1546796831

THE UNVARNISHED PRESS
297 N. Frances St.
Sunnyvale, CA 94086
USA
www.unvarnishedpress.info
408-773-8711

For Laura, always and all ways giving *joie* to my *vivre*

# CONTENTS

# A Confession of Bias

In this book I argue that information-providers should be transparent so you'll know when to power up your skepticism shields.

Nelson Mandela once said "where you stand depends on where you sit." Without being aware of it, we absorb biases from where we are situated in society. Our race, gender, religion, generation, geography, class and nationality each have a great deal to do with how we perceive the world. So let me alert you to where I'm coming from.

With no say in the matter, I was born melanin-challenged to Irish-American parents, a drop in the libidinal tidal wave that followed World War II. My dad was a labor lawyer, a man of stubborn principle who refused to join the country club down the street from our home in the comfortable suburbs of Washington DC until it admitted both blacks and Jews. My mom was a housewife made desperate by five children. I was educated by a tribe of women clad from head to toe in black-and-blue-chadors. Their habits were medieval. Each carried a chain studded with heavy black beads. They called themselves the Sisters of the Immaculate Heart of Mary. Despite their asynchronous appearance, they were wonderful, caring women and master teachers to whom I owe more than I can repay.

I came of age late in the 1960s. I missed Woodstock and the Summer of Love, perhaps because I attended a (then) all-male institution run by men in black dresses, the Jesuits. After graduating from Holy Cross, I headed west to the University of Michigan for a masters degree in journalism (and a minor in rugby) and a decade later to Stanford for a doctorate in communication.

As a child of '60s, I wanted to change the world. And still do. That's why I became a journalist. I worked as a newspaper reporter in the South because what I most wanted to change was racism. In 1983, I resigned from the *Virginian-Pilot*, packed my family and our belongings in a yellow Ryder truck, "the lemon of wrath," and camped from Norfolk, Virginia across the country to Palo Alto, California to finish my formal education. Seduced by weather and surf, I still live in the San Francisco Bay Area.

I left daily journalism partly to report a story about it. In various newsrooms, I kept slamming into commercial barriers that my graduate education at Michigan hadn't warned me about. It was the subject of my doctoral dissertation and later a book about how market forces influence the news – *Market-Driven Journalism: Let the Citizen Beware?*

After Stanford, I taught journalism for a decade at several universities. Naively, I thought I had escaped market pressures, but inevitably I was fired for willfully mistaking my customers for students. I flouted departmental enrollment targets, remorselessly inflicting on hapless students the grades they earned, thus risking their defection to more accommodating majors, or – God forefend – entirely driving away a tuition. I callously returned essays bleeding corrections. I failed to encourage my students' creative spelling, syntax, and grammar. In short, I was a disaster as a post-modern professor.

I left the classroom to design research for the Berkeley Media Studies Group. In 2000, I launched Grade the News, an online effort to do for news in the Bay Area what *Consumer Reports* does for toaster ovens. Attracting funding from the Gerbode, Ford and Knight foundations, I moved it to Stanford and later to San Jose State University.

The idea for this book took shape while evaluating the most popular Bay Area newspapers and TV newscasts at Grade the News. I could see mainstream media deteriorating and the uneven beginnings of a new journalism on the Web. Having been a working journalist, a journalism educator, a media researcher and finally a news analyst, I felt the need to share what I've learned to help others critically evaluate the enormous variety of what now passes for news as well as other information passed along as factual. Today, powerful forces are tearing apart the last century's consensus about what constitutes journalism. And as they do, they are shredding the civic fabric of the nation.

Like most journalists, I consider myself a tough-minded independent. But like most journalists, I lean liberal. I'm convinced that humans depend on each other and need government to brace up the needy and regulate markets so that they work for all. But I also agree with Bill Moyers' analogy: Democracy is like a plane – it requires both a right and left wing. A rational dialogue between liberal and conservative viewpoints yields better results than uniformity on either side.

I remain a practicing Catholic not just because the nuns know where I live, but because I need all the help I can get. My long-suffering wife is Jewish, however, so I get to enjoy two ancient and beautiful faith traditions. (What's not to like?)

I own no shares of media stock beyond a mutual fund. I'm a penny-ante supporter of the Democratic Party, the American Civil Liberties Union, the NAACP, and other non-profits trying to heal the world. In terms of news media, I support my local National Public Radio station, KQED, NPR's On the Media, my local newspaper, the *Mercury News*, the *New York Times* and the e-version of the *Washington Post*. Occasionally I contribute to Democracy Now and FreePress.net. I'm a member of the Association for Education in Journalism and Mass Communication. I subscribe to a raft of professional journals and trade publications.

These comprise most of the perception-bending influences that I am aware of. Now, let's explore how to evaluate news and information!

John McManus

Sunnyvale, California

May 2017

# 1

# Critical Thinking About News

# and Information

*"The responsibility is now on the news consumer.*
*This a caveat emptor world. Let the buyer beware"*

~ Brooke Gladstone, co-host of NPR's On the Media

**W**hy study media, or news, literacy?

News stories, indeed most media messages, are designed to be as easy to swallow as warm honey. The language is simple. Articles are short. So are sentences. Images are dramatic. Key points are trumpeted in headlines and lead paragraphs. Why would anyone need help to figure out the news, or for that matter, any informational media?

The simple answer is that a great deal of what looks like news and factual information on the Web, cable and broadcast TV, the radio, even in newspapers, really isn't. We live in an age when fake news – information designed to mislead – is sowing mass confusion.[1] One recent study showed fabricated news was more "liked" and shared on Facebook than articles reported by professional journalists at *The New York Times* and other mainstream news organizations.[2] Other studies demonstrate that "native advertising" – articles created by real news organizations but to the specs of sponsors – are often mistaken for objective reporting.[3]

Quality journalism is in more trouble than sobriety at a rugby party.

After nearly a century of growth, professional news-gathering is imploding. Tens of thousands of experienced writers, editors and photographers have been laid off and newsrooms are still shrinking.[4] But information is a means to power and digital technologies have made it cheaper than ever to create and distribute. So into the vacuum created by the departing professionals surges a Mardi Gras parade of Instagrammers, Snapchatters, Facebook posters and sharers, Twittering texters, Flik'ring photographers, bloviating bloggers, and YouTubing videographers. There are high-minded – but usually under-trained and under-funded – local citizen and Web journalists. There are advocates of every spot and stripe, corporate and government publicists, and advertisers by the gigabyte. There are fakers – from young men in Macedonia trying to make a buck off Internet advertising to malicious propagandists – out to poison the infosphere. All are providing reports of current issues and events that purport to be true. The Web has become where the wild things are.

"There is an ever-increasing amount of material that flies the flag of journalism, but doesn't qualify by our standards."[5]

~ Nicholas Lemann, former dean of the Columbia University Graduate School of Journalism

In my lifetime and yours, news and information has never been so contested, so up-for-grabs. As a consequence, it has never been so difficult to discern what's reliable from the rest.

Although we claim that others – but not smart people like us – are fooled by ersatz news and "alternate facts," research says different. Stanford University Professor Sam Wineburg tested the information literacy of hundreds of students ranging from middle-school to college. He concluded: "Overall, young people's ability to reason about the information on the Internet can be summed up in one word: bleak."[6]

Fake news came to national attention in the 2016 presidential campaign. But all that's new is how prevalent it's become. Consider this 2008 report forwarded virally through emails:

"**The truth is, in order to get things like Universal Health Care and a revamped Education System, then <u>someone</u> is going to have to give up a piece of the pie so that someone else can have more**"

Michelle Obama

# Oh Really?

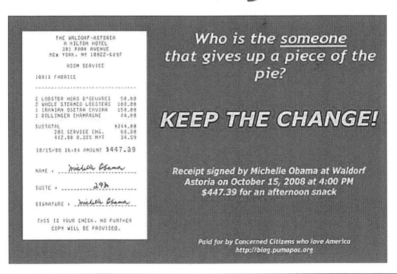

Who is the <u>someone</u> that gives up a piece of the pie?

**KEEP THE CHANGE!**

Receipt signed by Michelle Obama at Waldorf Astoria on October 15, 2008 at 4:00 PM $447.39 for an afternoon snack

Paid for by Concerned Citizens who love America http://blog.pumapac.org

According to multiple news fact-checking organizations, the "receipt" above detailing a mid-afternoon snack with lobster hors d'oeuvres, two whole lobsters, Iranian caviar and a bottle of Bollinger champagne to wash it down is a complete fabrication. Ms.

Obama was not a guest at the hotel on the date the producers of this message claimed she was running up a room service bill. She wasn't even in New York at the time specified on the "receipt."[7] Fiendishly clever enough to have been taken as true by some of my friends, and even by the *New York Post*, such fraudulent fact-claims have become as common as weeds in an abandoned lot.

> "Beware of false knowledge; it is more dangerous than ignorance."
>
> ~George Bernard Shaw, Irish playwright [8]

## The case of the "paid protesters"

While the fake news above was maliciously crafted, simple mistakes in citizen "reporting" can spread like fire in dry grass in today's hyper-connected and highly partisan infosphere.

Eric Tucker, a 35-year-old marketing exec noticed a row of buses parked in downtown Austin the day after the presidential election won by Donald J. Trump. He knew that anti-Trump demonstrations were planned, and familiar with Internet-borne rumors that such protesters were paid rather than authentic, he posted three photos of the buses to his Twitter account with the tweet: "Anti-Trump protestors in Austin today are not as organic as they seem. Here are the busses they came in. #fakeprotests#trump 2016#austin."

The only problem was that the buses were there to transport business people to a convention held nearby. They carried no protesters. Although Tucker only had 40 followers on Twitter, others repeated his tweet. His message was shared at least 16,000 times on Twitter and 350,000 times on Facebook. [9]

*The New York Times* deconstructed the spread of the false report beginning with Mr. Tucker's original tweet on November 9:

> Several hours later, the first important step occurred. Mr. Tucker's tweet was posted to the main Reddit community for Mr. Trump under the heading: 'BREAKING: They found the buses! Dozens lined up just blocks away from the Austin protests.' It quickly generated more than 300 comments, some of which blamed the protests on George Soros, the liberal billionaire philanthropist, who is a frequent target of the group.

> The next morning, the frenzy began. A user on Free Republic, a conservative discussion forum, linked to the Reddit thread about Mr. Tucker's post, increasing the attention and spreading it further into the online world. Later, Facebook pages like Robertson Family Values, which is named for but not affiliated with the stars of "Duck Dynasty," and Donald Trump Commander in Chief 2020, linked to the Free Republic discussion. Those posts were shared more than 5,000 times each, and more than 300,000 Facebook users have linked to the Free Republic thread.

Mainstream news media and Snopes.com checked the story's validity and reported that it was erroneous. Still it spread across conservative bloggers and websites, citing Mr. Tucker as an eyewitness in Austin. The next day, shortly after 9 p.m., Mr. Trump sent this tweet:

> Just had a very open and successful presidential election. Now professional protesters, incited by the media, are protesting. Very unfair! – Donald J. Trump (@realDonaldTrump) November 11, 2016

Although debunked in newspapers and on newscasts, the story and Mr. Tucker's bus photos refused to die:[10] Here's an example from "Right Wing News:"

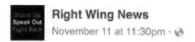

**Right Wing News**
November 11 at 11:30pm · 

Well, well, well...

## Guess Who's Bussing in All of Those Anti-Trump Protesters Who Are Burning Flags & Rioting in the Streets

IHAVETHETRUTH.COM I BY THE CONSERVATIVE MILLENNIAL

It's not just fake news we have to guard against, but half-baked journalism.

### The case of the aluminum tubes

Take the lead article on the front page of the *New York Times* on the second Sunday of September, 2002. Some say it was the most influential story written that year. Here's how it began:

> More than a decade after Saddam Hussein agreed to give up weapons of mass destruction, Iraq has stepped up its quest for nuclear weapons and has embarked on a worldwide hunt for materials to make an atomic bomb, Bush administration officials said today.
>
> In the last 14 months, Iraq has sought to buy thousands of specially designed aluminum tubes, which American

officials believe were intended as components of centrifuges to enrich uranium.[11]

Perhaps the most prestigious and important newspaper in the world was uncritically presenting a string of statements preparing the nation for war, statements that not a single official would take responsibility for.

Even before the *Times* was unfolded at breakfast tables on the West Coast, Vice President Dick Cheney and National Security Advisor Condoleezza Rice appeared on the Sunday morning network political talk shows. They would both point to the *Times* story as confirmation of the Bush administration's claims that Saddam Hussein was trying to make a nuclear bomb.

On Meet the Press, the vice president told Americans, "there's a story in this morning's *New York Times*, and I want to attribute it to the *Times*...."[12] On CNN, Ms. Rice said that waiting for more conclusive evidence of the Iraqi dictator's intentions was risky: "The smoking gun might be a mushroom cloud."[13] Not coincidentally, this was the very same phrase spoken by an anonymous Bush administration source within the *Times* report.

Of all knowledge, news is arguably the most important. That's because we act, not on reality, but on whatever we take to be true at the time. If we believe another nation plans to attack us with weapons of mass destruction, our leaders can generate enough public support to launch a pre-emptive war that kills hundreds of thousands, physically and mentally maims scores of thousands of those who survived combat, and will likely cost three trillion taxpayer dollars before the last bill is paid.[14] By the time we learned that the only weapons of mass destruction were our own, it was too late.

Given such enormous stakes, how can we avoid being misled in real time? Are there techniques we can apply to evaluate news and information purporting to be factual? Are there certain media practices we can identify that routinely obstruct the formation of the informed public that democracy requires? Are there theories that illuminate the vulnerabilities of the emerging digital infosphere;

theories that might guide public policy and enlighten our own information consumption?

This book argues that there are uncomplicated, critical habits of mind we can adopt to reduce our susceptibility to misinformation. Because in a democracy the reliably-informed have no greater say in the voting booth than the un- or misinformed, these sensibilities and skills are necessary tools for a majority of citizens to acquire.

Let's try them out on the most consequential of the misleading reports above. What might a news-literate reader have made of the pivotal *New York Times* article that greased the skids to war?

## The SMELL test

For starters, let's apply what I call the SMELL test to Michael Gordon and Judith Miller's article. Our sense of smell warns us of spoiled food and other things we shouldn't eat. The SMELL test is designed to protect us from foul information. The S in the acronym asks us to consider the *source* of the information. Not a single source is named for the key claim that Iraq's attempt to buy aluminum tubes revealed an intention to build the kind of centrifuges required to purify uranium to bomb strength – merely Bush administration "officials." The administration was happy to leak the story to the *Times*, but not to stand behind it. No one was willing to attach his/er name to the claim.

There are times when reporters legitimately withhold sources' names in order to protect them from retaliation by superiors for telling an embarrassing truth. But there was no embarrassing (at the time) truth here. No angry official denial. Not only was the White House the source of the leak, it booked time on two networks to promote the story. Secondly, in this case the sources were not whistle-blowing underlings, but the superiors themselves, "senior" officials. For a skeptical reader – or journalist – that raises a flag as ominous as the skull and crossbones. The primary reason top officials speak to the press anonymously is to manipulate the public.

Whenever a source, especially one with great power, refuses to be accountable for a statement, we should ask; Why *can't* they take responsibility? What harm would they suffer if the statement were associated with them?

In this case, Mr. Cheney and Ms. Rice would have looked pretty silly portraying the *Times* report of their own leaked claims as confirmation of a key element in the administration's case for war. To be fair to the *Times* and its reporters, the article makes other claims about the aluminum tubes and Iraq's supposed pursuit of nuclear weapons (as well as biological and chemical arms). But every claim about the most threatening of the weapons of mass destruction – the atomic ones – is also anonymous: "American intelligence experts," "Iraqi defectors," "a senior administration official." Not a single source would go on the record.

The M in the SMELL test asks about the source's *motivation*. Is it merely informational? Or perhaps an effort to sell us something? We should elevate our skepticism shields if the latter. People hoping to persuade are more likely to cherry-pick facts to make a case than to dispassionately lay out all of the evidence, including that which might dissuade us from a particular course of action. The language of the anonymous administration officials constitutes an argument rather than a simple description:

> Administration officials also assert that the acquisition of nuclear arms might embolden Mr. Hussein and increase the chances that he might use chemical or biological weapons. The officials contend that Mr. Hussein refrained from using chemical and germ weapons during the 1991 Persian Gulf war because he feared a devastating retaliatory blow from the United States and that he might now conclude that the Americans would not dare strike him if he had nuclear weapons.

> 'The jewel in the crown is nuclear,' a senior administration official said. 'The closer he gets to a nuclear capability, the more credible is his threat to use chemical or biological weapons. Nuclear weapons are his hole card.

> 'The question is not, why now?' the official added, referring to a potential military campaign to oust Mr. Hussein. 'The question is why waiting is better. The closer Saddam Hussein gets to a nuclear weapon, the harder he will be to deal with.'

On the Brink of War

> Hard-liners are alarmed that American intelligence underestimated the pace and scale of Iraq's nuclear program before Baghdad's defeat in the gulf war. Conscious of this lapse in the past, they argue that Washington dare not wait until analysts have found hard evidence that Mr. Hussein has acquired a nuclear weapon. The first sign of a 'smoking gun,' they argue, may be a mushroom cloud.[15]

This is a call to action. The appeal to fear in the final sentence and the argument to act now rather than waiting are routine tools of the pressure sales pitch. This is "a limited time offer."

The E in the SMELL test asks about the *evidence* provided for the claims made in the story. The truth value of a claim rests on either external validation or the credibility of the person making the claim. No effort is made in the article to validate the claim with experts outside of the executive branch of government. And though there was dissent within American intelligence agencies as reported by other news agencies (most notably Knight Ridder newspapers' Washington bureau), it doesn't surface in this article. Of course, the credibility of the sources who *are* quoted can't be assessed because the article doesn't identify them. There were thousands of Bush administration officials, and scores of "senior officials."

The first L in the SMELL test stands for *logic*. The article's premise can be compressed into a syllogism: Iraq is seeking high strength aluminum tubes; one use of such tubes is in the construction of uranium-processing centrifuges; therefore Iraq is seeking to build a nuclear weapon. The first premise is unconfirmed. The second comes from anonymous "intelligence experts," who are said to believe "the diameter, thickness and other technical specifications" make them suitable for centrifuge components. But strong aluminum tubes may have many others uses, such as rocket casings (which was, in fact, their intended use). There are substantial gaps in the logic connecting the purchase of aluminum tubes with the construction of a nuclear weapon, a complex and technically sophisticated process. It's like saying because a man owns a crow bar, he is planning a burglary.

The final L in the test refers to what's *left out* or missing. The most glaring omission is of any source willing to risk being identified with the claims made. The second is the lack of any independent, expert evaluation of the claims the anonymous sources made. Surely there were nuclear experts outside the administration who could have assessed the critical claim that these tubes were designed specifically for enrichment centrifuges. How about officials at the International Atomic Energy Agency, which had inspectors looking for weapons of mass destruction on the ground from 1994 until August of 1998? Or the United Nations Special Commission, which oversaw the destruction of at least part of Iraq's arsenal and the export of its highly enriched uranium.[16] Or nuclear experts in countries not allied with the U.S.? The third was the failure to speak with experts within the U.S. intelligence community who were skeptical of the quality of the evidence the Bush administration was assembling.

When the subject is as momentous as calling the nation to war, the search for essential, but missing, points of view becomes a paramount concern of responsible journalism. It was for this failure more than any other that the *New York Times* later apologized for its pre-war coverage.

Of course, it's much easier to see the problems with this story in hindsight. But a news literate reader in 2002 would have been alarmed by the lack of any named sources *for a story the administration was so eager to promote.* And the narrow range of sources, all answering to the White House, would have added to the skepticism. Finally, the eagerness to persuade, and the tendentious evidence drawing a causal line from the purchase of aluminum tubes to a mushroom cloud rising above an American target would have aroused considerable doubt. Perhaps because it was published by the august *New York Times*, many didn't notice that this emperor of a story was wearing no clothes.

## Unpacking a journalistic failure

How could so flawed a story on so consequential a topic have found its way onto the front page of so prestigious a news organization? When the vice president and National Security

Advisor Rice attempted to portray the *Times* article as independent confirmation of a key claim about Iraqi WMD, those within the *Times* who knew the source of the leaks about the aluminum tubes should have exclaimed "WTF!?* We're being played!"

So why didn't they?

One reason was the strange mélange of practices journalists – rather subjectively – call "objectivity." Objectivity embraces the myths that journalists are unbiased and that news media *reflect* reality rather then *represent* some facet of it under deadline pressure. As we shall see in chapters 4 and 5, both journalists and the news media for which they work are subjective, self-interested agents. Chapter 7 will show how objectivity favors official viewpoints and discourages independent pursuit of what's true. It discourages any public interest advocacy on the part of news media that might lead to rigorous questioning of fact-claims by high government or corporate officials. An "objective" press tends to substitute stenography for skepticism.

A second reason for the failure of the *Times*, and most other American news media, arises from how news is produced in the U.S. There are many theories that attempt to explain why one event is covered or one issue raised while others are ignored. We'll explore four theories that together can help us understand the limitations of mainstream media and the need to search out diverse sources of news.

In their classic book, *Manufacturing Consent*, Edward S. Herman and Noam Chomsky detail a propaganda model of news production. Building on earlier writings of Karl Marx, Antonio Gramsci, Theodore Adorno and more recent political economists such as Peter Golding and Graham Murdock, they propose that the news is tailored to fit the interests of the powerful at the expense of the powerless. From this perspective, American news media collaborated with the Bush administration to make the case for war with Iraq. Both the media and the military-industrial complex make money from wars.

---

* Texters tell me the initials express exasperation.

The second news-selection theory holds that American news media serve the public well when powerful decision-makers in government are vigorously debating policy, but fail when such leaders line up on one side of an issue. Drawing on empirical research by W. Lance Bennett and others showing that the news agenda is defined by the scope of debate among influential politicians, the theory is called "indexing." It holds that news media bracket or limit the range of discussion about public issues to that exhibited by sources with enough power to influence the outcome. In the run-up to the invasion of Iraq, for example, few leading Democrats strongly criticized the Bush administration's case for war. So there was a paucity of skeptical officials to quote.

A third theory holds that the dominant U.S. news media are, at their core, *businesses.* As such, they must compete in the marketplace for audience attention and subscriptions, for advertiser dollars, for access to sources, and for investors on Wall Street. Together, these market pressures conflict more than coincide with the public interest. This economic analysis has been championed by Ben H. Bagdikian, Robert G. Picard, Leo Bogart, James T. Hamilton, C. Edwin Baker, Robert W. McChesney and others, including me.

In the aftermath of the horrific 9/11 attacks on the World Trade Center towers and the Pentagon, the Bush administration commanded wide public sympathy and support for vigorous retribution. News media willing to skeptically assess the case for war, especially against a brutal dictator, risked appearing timid or disloyal. Such a perception can cost audience – customers – as well as the advertising dollars the audience attracts. Further, skeptical "show-me" journalists can alienate the official sources they need to report much of the day's news. That can make gathering news more laborious – more expensive. It can also lead to secondhand coverage of stories broken by more compliant news organizations. Even hours-old news doesn't sell as well as fresh. Reporters willing to suspend their skepticism in return for scoops make easy prey for manipulative sources.

The final theory, the oldest and simplest, is being revived by the rise of bloggers and independent reporters operating on the Web. It holds that what becomes news reflects the personal biases of content-producers who are the gate-keepers for their websites. Even among journalists at the lofty *Times*, 9/11 created a thirst for revenge.

In addition to these theories shedding light on the selection biases of news outlets, we'll explore a common technique described by cognitive scientists such as George Lakoff, that's now widely used by publicists. It's called framing. Skillfully employed, it can skew a public debate without being noticed at the time. We'll see that the subtle shift of frames after the 9/11 attacks led to America's two longest wars. Instead of adopting a criminal justice frame – find and punish the perpetrators – the Bush administration chose – and the press went along with – a much broader frame, a "war on terror" – a war not on a particular enemy, but on a *tactic* as old as humankind.

The purpose of this book is to assemble the best thinking from scholars, civic activists and journalists to help you critically assess fact claims whether presented face-to-face, on Facebook, a blog, a website, or through older media – radio, television and print.

## What's ahead

The next chapter will set the context for the book, exploring how radically our vital infosphere is changing and what that means for the kind of journalism a democracy requires. Then we'll examine the contest our rapidly evolving – or perhaps devolving – information environment has spawned between truth and truthiness. And if we're going to detect bias, we'll need to consider where it comes from, including, dear reader, from you and me. Next, we'll examine the theories mentioned above to understand the weaknesses of mainstream media and their "objective" method. But rather than just carping, we'll look at reachable standards to help the news fulfill its democratic potential.

Because news is moving from paper to pixels and images are becoming as or more important than text, there's a chapter on how to "read" photos and videos. There's also a chapter on the increasingly sophisticated tricks of the misinformation trade. The final chapter details how we can use the Web to its fullest extent both to detect bull and to find alternate sources of information with which to triangulate our understanding of the most pressing issues of the day. There's one appendix, a news scorecard allowing us to identify junk journalism and grade the quality of news against yardsticks derived from the Society of Professional Journalists Code of Ethics.

Join me on an adventure as a news and information detective.

## End Notes

[1] Michael Barthel, Amy Mitchell and Jesse Holcomb (12/15/2016) "Many Americans believe fake news is sowing confusion," Pew Research Center., online at: http://www.journalism.org/2016/12/15/ many-americans-believe-fake-news-is-sowing-confusion/.

[2] Craig Silverman (11/16/2016) "This analysis shows how viral fake election news stories outperformed real news on Facebook," Buzzfeed News, "In the final three months of the US presidential campaign, the top-performing fake election news stories on Facebook generated more engagement than the top stories from major news outlets such as the *New York Times*, *Washington Post*, *Huffington Post*, NBC News, and others.... During these critical months of the campaign, 20 top-performing false election stories from hoax sites and hyperpartisan blogs generated 8,711,000 shares, reactions, and comments on Facebook.
Within the same time period, the 20 best-performing election stories from 19 major news websites generated a total of 7,367,000 shares, reactions, and comments on Facebook." Available online at: https:// www.buzzfeed.com/ craigsilverman/viral-fake-election-news-outperformed-real-news-on-facebook?utm_term=.lkALY39BVm#.hlA2 eNP0vz.

[3] *Editor and Publisher* (January/2017) "Data Page," E&P analyzed 300 respondents who saw four online articles of native advertising in the *New York Times, Huffington Post, Buzzfeed* and *Business Insider*; only 23 percent identified them as advertising.

[4] See the Project for Excellence in Journalism's annual *State of the news media* reports at http://www.journalism.org. Reports of new layoffs of journalists continue to be reported every few months.

[5] Robert Giles (Fall, 2005) "Mainstream media and the survival of journalism," *Nieman Reports*, Nieman Foundation for Journalism, Harvard University.

[6] Sam Wineburg (11/22/2016) "Evaluating information: The cornerstone of civic online reasoning," Stanford History Education Group, executive summary online at: https://sheg.stanford.edu/upload/V3LessonPlans /Executive%20Summary%2011.21.16.pdf.

[7] Angie Drobnic Holan (12/2/2008) "Official looking receipt is a fake," This story merited a "Pants on Fire" designation for extreme falsehood on Politifact, online at: http://www.politifact.com/truth-o-meter/ statements/2008/dec/02/chain-email/official-looking-receipt-is-a-fake/.

[8] George Bernard Shaw, BrainyQuotes, https://www.brainyquote.com/quotes /authors/g/george_bernard_shaw.html.

[9] Sapna Maheshwari (11/20/2016) "How fake news goes viral: A case study," *The New York Times*, online at: https://www.nytimes.com /2016/11/20/business/media/how-fake-news-spreads.html?_r=0.

[10] Maheshwari, cited above.

[11] Michael R. Gordon and Judith Miller (9/8/2002) "Threats and responses: The Iraqis; U.S. says Hussein intensifies quest for A-bomb parts," *New York Times*, p. A1.

[12] Frontline (3/24/2008) "Bush's war," Public Broadcasting System. The "Meet the Press" clip is in Part one, ch. 11, approximately between 3:45 minutes and 5:05; See: http://www.pbs.org/wgbh/pages/frontline /bushswar/.

[13] Bill Moyers (4/25/2007) "Buying the war," Bill Moyers Journal, Public Broadcasting System, transcript online at: http://www.pbs.org /moyers/journal/btw/transcript1.html.

[14] The British scientific journal Lancet estimated in October, 2006, that 655,000 Iraqis had been killed in the initial invasion and subsequent fighting. See "Lancet surveys of Iraq war casualties ," online at: http://en.wikipedia.org/wiki/ Lancet_surveys_of_Iraq_War_casualties. The cost of the war was estimated by Joseph E. Stiglitz and Linda J. Bilmes (2008) *The three trillion-dollar war*, New York: W.W. Norton.

[15] Gordon and Miller, cited above.

[16] Arms Control Association (undated, accessed 6/15/2012) "Iraq: a chronology of UN Inspections," online at http://www.armscontrol.org/ act/2002_10/iraqspecialoct02.

# 2

# The Communication Revolution

*[This is] "the most disruptive transition in the history of mass communications."*

~ Arthur Sulzberger Jr., publisher of the New York Times

Life depends on information.

Without it, even the simplest forms wouldn't exist. They rely on tiny codes of RNA and DNA. The same is true – on a vastly larger scale – for the most complex organisms. Our every thought and action is based on information.

So it's no surprise that throughout history, information has conveyed power. Because we act on what we *think* is real, the most efficient way to control people has always been to control their sources of information, particularly sources of current information about events and issues – news.

"Four hostile newspapers are more to be feared than a thousand bayonets."[1]

~ Napoleon Bonaparte

We are now in the midst of a communication revolution at least as profound as when the printing press broke the choke-hold on information exercised by the church and royal families. As more people gained access to information, they rebelled against the domination of both institutions, greatly diminishing the power of popes and clergy and eventually overthrowing kings, emperors and czars.

The present revolution in communication exhibits a bias similar to the one enabled by the printing press. It radically diffuses control over information. But the pace and volume of change today differs as much from the past as microwave transmission exceeds the speed and capacity of the Pony Express. Johannes Gutenberg invented a press with movable type in the 1440s. But it wasn't until the late eighteenth century, more than 300 years later, that print-borne ideas like liberty, equality, and fraternity were shouted on the streets of Paris — and later across Europe – with enough force to overthrow the kings and queens who had ruled since the middle ages. By contrast, the current revolution began during the final decades of the 20th century, propelled largely by the digitization of information and new means of conveying and processing it.

The electronic manipulation of digital information changed everything, even transforming earlier communication technologies – the printing press, telephone, radio, and television – and it made the Internet possible. Computer-programmed presses eliminated the layout room and streamlined printing. The telephone escaped its copper leash to become a palm-sized computer that goes everywhere and does just about everything, from emailing, texting, finding bargains and Pokémon characters, getting news and directions, reading e-books, and playing music and video, to recording and transmitting images. Some even use it to talk!

Radio has spread from AM and FM to satellite, streaming on the Internet, and podcasts. Television has expanded exponentially from just four national networks to thousand-channel cable and satellite systems. TV is now migrating to infinity and beyond on the World Wide Web. The Web elevated the Internet from a military and research network to an information utility with more than 3.5 billion users around the globe. That's almost half the world's population! From one website in 1991, the Web grew by 2010 to a quarter billion websites. In 2017 there were more than 1.1 billion, with thousands more created every day.[2]

The printing press enabled people to turn society upside down. Legitimate power was once thought to flow from God down through royalty to commoners. But 18th century philosophers argued that legitimate authority traveled upward from the consent of the governed. The present communication revolution is already causing similar upheaval. It has spawned six interconnected paradoxes that are changing the way we live.

**New digital technologies have:**

1.  Given journalists the most powerful tools they've ever had for gathering and distributing news. But they simultaneously stripped news media of billions of advertising dollars, in less than two decades emptying newsrooms of nearly half of their reporters, editors and photographers. Professional journalism is only a shadow of its former self.

2.  Democratized news – allowing anyone with a computer or smart phone both to report and disseminate. We can also now edit – customize our information diet to fit our preferences and biases and then share with like-minded others on social media. But in the process, we are eroding the informational common ground democracy requires to forge the consensus needed to govern. Public and political polarization are tearing the nation apart.

3.  Enabled unprecedented diversity among news outlets. But overthrew the hierarchy and credibility of the most respected American news organizations, which for more than a century had been the gatekeepers of democracy – setting the nation's news agenda and establishing the boundaries of legitimate political discussion. As the signal becomes lost in the noise, we are approaching journalistic anarchy.

4.  Put at our fingertips an informational landscape as vast as the Sahara, but like the desert, full of dangerous mirages.

5.  Enhanced the value of news, even as they drained its resources, by accelerating the pace of change and globalizing the need to know about opportunities and threats.

6. Enabled diverging – even warring – versions of truth, but also gave citizens powerful tools for discovering and sharing which claims rest on the strongest evidence and which are flimsy or fake. There's a silver lining in the digital cloud.

Comparing the infosphere of the late 20th century to that of the early 21st resembles holding a child's balloon up to the Goodyear blimp. The Internet has stitched the globe together with microwaves and threads of copper and clear optical fiber. In less than two decades it has become an indispensable information utility. For those who know how to search and filter it, the explosion of widely available information is exciting and empowering. For those who can't distinguish fact from clever fiction, however, it can be bewildering and misleading, a fun house mirror of the world.

"Information is as vital to the healthy functioning of communities as clean air, safe streets, good schools, and public health. People have not typically thought of information this way, but they should."[3]

~ The Knight Commission on the Information Needs of Communities in a Democracy

## 1. The Web Giveth and the Web Taketh Away

The Web is by far the most engaging, informative and cost-effective technology journalists have ever possessed – better than TV, magazines and newspapers *combined*. It marries reporting in text to photos and video (and increasingly virtual reality), allowing each medium to contribute its unique strengths to a multi-media experience.

On the *news-gathering side*, the Web provides enormous research capability – better than access to the world's largest library – with only a few key strokes. Social media such as Facebook and Twitter also allow reporters to harness the vast expertise of the public. The winner of the 2017 Pulitzer Prize for national reporting, David

Fahrenthold of the *Washington Post*, described how he used Twitter in his investigation of Donald Trump's charitable foundation.

As you may know, laws regulating such foundations require that contributions, to be tax exempt, go to registered charities such as museums, universities and hospitals. Mr. Fahrenthold learned from Trump Foundation tax filings that it paid $10,000 to an artist for a 4-foot high portrait of Mr. Trump. It was important to know whether that portrait had been given to a charitable organization, and was thus legal. Mr. Fahrenthold explained how a nearly impossible search was accomplished in a single day:

> We got a picture of [the portrait] ... but I didn't know where the painting was. On Twitter I post this picture. I say 'this is the portrait I'm looking for.' Now before Twitter, how would I have figured out where that was? I could have gone to all the hotels and golf courses Donald Trump owns and looked in all the corners and nooks and crannies and I still might not have known for sure where it was because maybe it was in his house in Trump Tower and I couldn't get in.

> But by putting it out there, a woman in Atlanta, Allison Aguilar, who follows me on Twitter ... she sees this painting and she has a thought that I didn't have, which was: 'this painting is so ugly that Donald Trump won't put it in his house; he's going to put it someplace where the public has to look at it.' So she goes to the trip advisor page for the Trump golf course at Doral .... There's all these user-generated photos, the hotel bathrooms, the 18th green, whatever, 350 photos, and she finds a picture of this portrait we're looking for, hanging on the wall of this sports bar at the club.... So she tweets it at me.

> So like at 7 o'clock that night I tweet ... 'Oh my God, Allison Aguilar found this picture that shows where the portrait *was*, and where is it now? At that time there was a guy named Enrique Acevedo who is an anchor at Univision, the national Spanish language TV network, and he sees that tweet and he realizes that the Univision studios are four blocks away from Doral.... He goes to the place ... and takes a picture of it. So we went from 10 o'clock that morning having no idea where in the world this thing could possibly be to 12:30 at night, here's a picture of it on the wall, breaking the law. It would have been impossible any other way than social media.[4]

The takeaway? "By using Twitter to ask the public for help," Fahrenthold said, "you tap into all these people who have contacts and knowledge and connections that you could not even imagine."[5]

The advantages of the Internet for *disseminating news* are even greater. The Web is unencumbered by the delay and enormous cost of printing presses, the need to mash forests into paper and buy ink by the barrel, the need to fuel fleets of delivery trucks, and pay paper-flingers. The Web requires no towering, multi-million dollar transmitter nor restrictive government license to operate. It can be carried anywhere in a tablet computer, smart phone or iPod. The cost of publishing news is now almost nil.

The Web turns journalism from a one-way street to a conversational traffic circle. On the Web, you can talk back to the newsroom in comment sections below articles and in online forums.

Unlike newspapers and time-bound newscasts, websites have nearly infinite space for news – breadth *plus* depth – and users can link instantly to other sources and the news organization's own previous coverage, perhaps arranged in an explanatory photo-studded timeline.

The Web enables sharing of news, expanding its impact around the globe. Not least, mistakes – once made permanent as fast as ink dried on paper – can be corrected as soon as discovered.

At long last, journalists possess a news vehicle as awesome as a Ferrari. But there's little money for gas.

That's because this wondrous technology allows advertisers to drive around the toll booth news media were once able to erect between sellers and buyers. That toll funded large numbers of journalists. Before the World Wide Web was invented, retailers had to pay whatever newspapers asked to reach local customers with the kind of price and product detail that print does better than broadcast. For the persuasive ads TV does so well, merchants had to bargain with a handful of broadcast stations, bidding against each other for limited ad time on popular programs like newscasts.

John Wanamaker, who pioneered the department store, once lamented, "Half the money I spend on advertising is wasted; the trouble is, I don't know which half." Ads placed in mass media reach as many – or usually many more – people with no interest in the product advertised as potential customers.

Internet firms help solve that targeting problem. Companies such as Google offer advertisers direct access to potential customers for dimes on the dollar mass media charge. What better place to sell a tablet computer than next to a consumer's search for that term? And then to allow retailers in that consumer's neighborhood to insert an ad. Facebook analyzes the content you post and then tailors ads to match. Craigslist offers for free classified ads that used to cost hundreds of dollars. Firms like Monster.com make it cheaper to list and easier to search for jobs, deleting scores of pages of employment ads that used to enrich newspapers. As empowering as the Web has been for journalists, it's been even more of a god-send to advertisers.

Advertisers had paid for everything in broadcast and once contributed upwards of 80 percent of newspapers' revenue.[6] But their willingness to subsidize journalism has vanished faster than virtue in Vegas.

### The demise of mainstream news

Newspapers constitute the backbone of American journalism. For more than a century they have employed more journalists than all other news media combined. They once had the staff to cover local governments. Newspapers conducted most of the investigative reporting. They dug up the stories that set the agenda for TV, cable, radio, magazine and online news outlets. But like an old spine, newspapers have become brittle and lost much of their substance.

Here's how the Pew Research Center assessed their health in its 2016 report:

> Eight years after the Great Recession sent the U.S. newspaper industry into a tailspin, the pressures facing America's newsrooms have intensified to nothing less than a reorganization of the industry itself... The latest newspaper newsroom employment figures (from 2014) show 10%

declines, greater than in any year since 2009, leaving a workforce that is 20,000 positions smaller than 20 years prior. And the cuts keep coming: Already in 2016, at least 400 cuts, buyouts or layoffs have been announced.[7]

Between 2004 and 2014, one hundred and twenty six daily newspapers shut down. Others merged to increase economies of scale.[8]

"Reporters are the canaries in the mine shaft of our democracy. We lose them at our collective peril."[9]

~ Charles Lewis, founding editor of the Investigative Reporting Workshop and former CBS News "60 Minutes" producer

Although there is no precise count, it appears that about four in ten newspaper journalists have lost their jobs since 2000.[10] At major metropolitan papers, the proportion of empty desks is even higher. The [San Jose] *Mercury News*, for example, went from over 400 journalists two decades ago to fewer than 70 in 2017. In 2009 when the presses of Denver's 150-year-old *Rocky Mountain News* rumbled for the final time, a newly unemployed reporter wrote: "I feel like a blacksmith in 1915. I didn't lose my job; I lost my career."[11] *New York Times* publisher Arthur Sulzberger Jr. described the situation for American newspapers as "the most disruptive transition in the history of mass communications."[12]

Newspaper advertising revenue adjusted for inflation has fallen 70 percent since 2000,[13] despite adding online sales. In 2014, the Newspaper Association of America quit tallying ad dollars.

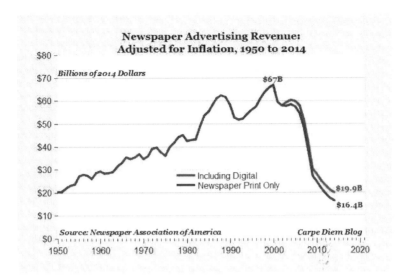

Newspaper Advertising Revenue: Adjusted for Inflation, 1950 to 2014

"The economic foundation of the nation's newspapers, long supported by advertising, is collapsing, and newspapers themselves, which have been the country's chief source of independent reporting, are shrinking—literally. Fewer journalists are reporting less news in fewer pages."[14]

~ Former *Washington Post* Executive Editor Leonard Downie and Columbia University professor Michael Schudson

As advertisers flee, newspapers are relying more on subscription dollars. But as newspapers shrink, fewer Americans are subscribing.[15] With fewer paying for the paper, and more reading online for free or at a great discount, subscription income represents only a trickle compared to the torrent – $47 billion – of lost advertising. Several large newspapers with national scope – *The Wall Street Journal, New York Times* and *Washington Post* – saw online subscription spikes in the last quarter of 2016 continuing into 2017, coinciding with Mr. Trump's rising political fortunes. However, these were not enough to offset longer trends of falling subscription revenue industry-wide.

Advertising revenue, and consequently, journalism employment in network and local TV, and radio has recovered from the Great Recession to levels reached at the turn of the 21st century. However, stations are stretching that staff over more  hours of news programming.[16] The bright spot is an increase in televised political ads, but they appear only during campaigns and are robust only in "battleground" states likely to swing elections. For TV, political campaigns have become as important as Christmas for retailers.

### Resource-poor journalism

As the defection of advertisers empties newsrooms, professionally-produced news content is not just diminishing in volume. The quality is deteriorating. To be sure, some wonderful journalism continues to be broadcast, published, and posted.[17] But there appears to be less coverage of important issues, especially of what state and local governments are doing with our tax dollars. A Pew Research Center survey found 35 percent fewer fulltime newspaper reporters assigned to cover state capitols in 2014 compared to 2003.[18] As newsrooms continue to atrophy, now we would almost certainly find fewer still.[19]

"The future of our self-government, the future of our democracy hinges on having an informed electorate, an electorate with sufficient depth and breadth of information that they can make sense out of all of the complex problems that we face and make intelligent decisions for the future of the country."[20]

~ Former Federal Communications Commission member Michael J. Copps

Given how expensive it is to commit reporters for weeks or months to digging up evidence of official or corporate misdeeds, it's not surprising that investigative reporting is sharply declining.

The *American Journalism Review* reported in 2010:

> Kicked out, bought out or barely hanging on, investigative reporters are a vanishing species in the forests of dead tree media and missing in action on Action News. I-Teams are shrinking or, more often, disappearing altogether. Assigned to cover multiple beats, multitasking backpacking reporters no longer have time to sniff out hidden stories, much less write them. In Washington, bureaus that once did probes have shrunk, closed and consolidated.[21]

From 1985 to 2012, the number of entries for the Pulitzer Prize in investigative reporting dropped 30 percent. For public service, the decline was 42 percent. Even the explanatory journalism category fell 40 percent.[22]

Next to investigative journalism, reporting from abroad is the most expensive kind of news. Establishing bureaus around the world requires large travel allowances, translators, and sometimes body guards. A 2011 survey conducted by the *American Journalism Review* concluded: "Twenty papers and companies have cut their foreign bureaus entirely since AJR conducted its first census of foreign correspondents in 1998." By 2011, only 11 newspapers and chains maintained foreign offices. Network television has also scaled back, AJR found. Only National Public Radio and the *New York Times* had increased its reporting strength abroad.[23] Even though U.S. soldiers were fighting in at least four countries in 2017, the number of foreign correspondents dwindled.

Since 1971, Indiana University has periodically surveyed American journalists. Their most recent poll, in 2013, indicated that 6 in 10 now say journalism is going in the "wrong direction."[24] In 2001, a similar poll conducted by the Project for Excellence in Journalism found only a slight majority, 51 percent, expressing a negative view about the direction of their craft.[25]

In 2014, the union representing staff at the *San Jose Mercury News* paid for a classified ad seeking a new owner more interested in quality journalism.

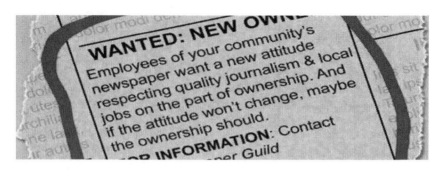

WANTED: NEW OWN...
Employees of your community's
newspaper want a new attitude
respecting quality journalism & local
jobs on the part of ownership. And
if the attitude won't change, maybe
the ownership should.
...R INFORMATION: Contact
...er Guild

## Media consolidation

The management that *Mercury News* staffers complained about, the Bay Area News Group, now operates almost every newspaper within 50 miles of San Francisco, except the *San Francisco Chronicle.* On April 4, 2016, The *San Jose Mercury News* and *Oakland Tribune* printed their last editions. The *Tribune* merged with the *Contra Costa Times*, the *Hayward Daily Review* and the *Fremont Argus* under a new name, the *East Bay Times*. The *Mercury News* no longer bore the name of the Bay Area's largest city, and it absorbed the *San Mateo Times,* 30 miles to the north.[26]

As recently as 2000, reporters for different news outlets competed with each other to report new information in many metro areas. Competing newsrooms are generally more aggressive news-gatherers than monopoly operations. More importantly, the sacred cows and blind spots of one newsroom might be exposed by another. But the drain of advertising dollars has acted like a black hole, sucking once-independent newspapers into thinly-staffed clusters of nearby papers under single ownership that barely emit light.[27] Television stations now cooperate on local news almost as often as they compete.[28] Recognizing the danger of a single company controlling the news, the Federal Communications Commission had long set limits on ownership. But under President Trump, the FCC relaxed those rules, allowing a single company to own more stations than ever. Sinclair Broadcasting Group, which has used its stations to advance conservative causes, grew to 215 stations in 2017, reaching fully 70 percent of U.S. households.[29] While consumers are now able to seek *global* and *national* news online from more sources than ever, mainstream *local* news in most markets has become more of a monotone.

"Newspapers were, for decades, a prime example of a community institution, meant to last through the centuries. A new generation of owners is thinking of them more as something to milk for profit on their way down."[30]

~ Ken Doctor, Nieman Lab

As a result, metro newspapers, the best of which were trusted referees of political disputes, courts of last resort for the powerless, and honesty-inspiring investigators of public and private fraud, no longer possess the resources to guard or guide their communities. Citizens are now more on their own than at any time in the last century.

## 2. The democratization of news and the loss of the civic commons

A.J. Liebling once lamented that "freedom of the press is guaranteed only to those who own one."[31] He should see us now. Anyone with a computer and an Internet connection, can be a reporter, with an audience potentially spanning the globe.

On the positive side, former journalists and citizens can report and edit news outside of traditional media organizations.

Some new journalism outlets emerging on the Internet produce first-rate journalism. Following a nonprofit model, the Voice of San Diego has broken important local stories with a staff of only 13. At the state level, the Texas Tribune has helped fill the journalistic vacuum at the state house. At the national level, newcomers like BuzzFeed, Vox, and Talking Points Memo, have enriched the civic conversation. Foundation-backed Pro Publica in New York City produces investigative reports that it offers for free to traditional news media. Politico.com (www.politico.com) provides insightful original reporting on national politics. So do the Center for Investigative Reporting/Reveal, and Slate, a pioneer of web-based news.

In 2017 Michele McClellan of the Tow-Knight Center for Entrepreneurial Journalism at the City University of New York listed 301 relatively new journalism outlets nationwide, most online only and most focusing on local news. They were supported by local advertising, membership fees, and some had foundation grants or university or public broadcasting affiliations. Many depended on volunteers. Some were run by a husband and wife team — truly mom and pop journalism.[32]

There are also consortia of hyper-local news sites run by profit-seeking corporations such as Patch, which in 2017 boasted a web presence in 1014 communities across 28 states, but had a minuscule staff of fewer than 150.[33] Another company, Nextdoor, operated as a community bulletin board at the neighborhood level.

Only a handful of these newcomers rival even small newspapers in depth, professionalism, or number of journalists. A national study of citizen journalism websites conducted in 2010 by researchers at Michigan State University compared the quantity and quality of their local government coverage — arguably the most important topic of local news — with local weekly and daily newspapers. They found the citizen sites were no substitute for newspaper coverage and that coverage of local government was rare in all but large cities.[34]

The conflicts of interest impinging on established media don't vanish for the citizen journalist, blogger, or local news website. In fact, conflicts may be more intense in hyper-local media where neighbors are writing about neighbors who can respond with more than an angry letter to the editor.

Like traditional news media, these new outlets want to expand their audience, attract and retain advertisers, and have officials return phone calls. But they typically lack the training and resources of professional journalists. They often can't afford editors to check facts or restrain biases. A one- or two-person staff *can't* be diverse. And the person selling the ads is sometimes also reporting the news – cross-purposes that only someone with a split personality could manage.

Conflicts of interest are, in fact, more common when citizen journalists have day jobs and connections with the subjects they report on. And those divided loyalties may not be disclosed. We may not know that the blogger covering the neighborhood school presents the principal in a dim light not for poor leadership but because she disciplined the blogger's son. Larger news outlets can hold their staff to higher standards as well as provide resources, and insulation from the consequences of speaking truth to power.

"I don't think that democratization of news-gathering is necessarily, in and of itself, a good thing."[35]

~ Ted Koppel, former anchor of ABC's Nightline and current NPR senior news analyst

When everyone can be a journalist, anything can become news

The 2016 presidential campaign demonstrated the dark side of the democratization of news – the rise of fake news. The motivation for polluting the infosphere ranged from money made on ads carried on popular fake news websites to political ideology, to countries, such as Russia, interfering in national politics through false reports and selective leaks of stolen information.

Take the case of Mike Cernovich. He has no background in journalism and no respect for its ethics. Sitting on his veranda in Southern Califor23na during the final months of the 2016 presidential campaign, he created videos with his iPad that were long on hatred of Hillary Clinton but short on facts.

Mr. Cernovich was profiled by *The New Yorker's* Andrew Marantz: "Although [Cernovich] doesn't appear on Fox News or syndicated radio shows, he is an expert at using social media to drive alt-right ideas into the heart of American political discourse."[36] He does it with tweets, a blog, an app called Periscope that allows those with smart phones or other video cameras to live-stream events worldwide, and Skype interviews on conservative talk shows.

In September 2016, after Mrs. Clinton fainted at a 9/11 memorial in New York, Mr. Cernovich wrote a blog post suggesting that her health was so poor she was unfit to be president. It received 240,000 page views and launched the meme "Sick Hillary." That month Mr. Cernovich's tweets were seen more than 100 million times. A non-issue – Mrs. Clinton's health – suddenly became a campaign topic for mainstream media. Assessing the phenomenon, Mr. Marantz wrote:

> People have always expressed extreme views online, but for many years there was no easy way for such opinions to spread. The Internet was a vast landscape dotted with isolated viruses. The rise of social networks was like the advent of air travel: a virus can now conquer the world in a day.[37]

Social media such as Twitter and Facebook have made it possible not just to report one's own news, but to easily share news from elsewhere with like-minded others. They act as accelerants. For an alt-right troll such as Mr. Cernovich, social media are like gasoline in the hands of an arsonist.

Perhaps the largest category of new providers of current information purporting to be factual are corporations. "Businesses themselves are rapidly becoming 'publishers,' filling the void with 'news' they generate about themselves and then merrily distribute on the web," according to Ken Doctor, a former Knight Ridder Digital news executive and blogger on trends he calls "newsonomics."[38] (We'll take a deeper look at this category in later chapters, especially chapter 10.)

In 2011, the Federal Communications Commission produced an analysis of the emerging news ecology, "The Information Needs of Communities." Its author, Steven Waldman, said in an interview:

> You have this incredible moment of abundance. There are more stories; there are more media outlets. [But] we're actually experiencing really serious shortages of a certain

type of reporting, which we call local accountability reporting..."[39]

In just three decades, we have moved from an age of news scarcity to abundance as new providers have rushed into the vacuum left by the professional journalists. But the newcomers are often failing to hold government officials accountable for their actions on our behalf. And what's left of the traditional media too often substitute sensation for substance and stenography for shoe-leather.[40] The result is a surfeit of news and information from providers of uncertain reliability coupled with a scarcity of reporting and commentary from trusted brands. This is particularly true at the city and metropolitan level where newspapers that once slammed on front porches now flutter. That's when they arrive at all. In a growing number of American cities, daily delivery has been curtailed to cut costs.[41]

## New communication media as disrupters

In 2011, subjugated masses across the Middle East used new media to stimulate and organize protests against dictators. Social networks like Facebook and Twitter allowed people to plan protests and share an alternative description of events free of government control. That narrative featured satellite- and Internet-borne images from Al Jazeera, documentation of their autocratic leaders' corruption on WikiLeaks, and thousands of images from cell phone cameras.[42] More credible than official propaganda, it electrified a population aggrieved by joblessness, government corruption and rising food prices and urged them into the streets to demand democratic change. Thousands of separate sparks of outrage were suddenly connected into a jolting current of change.

At least for now, the optimism of the "Arab Spring" has been doused in all but Tunisia by repressive state governments. But even police states now have to expend more resources trying to control information.

Like a sword that can be used both to defend and attack, new communication technologies can divide as well as unite. They allow factions on the political left and right to construct alternate versions of news and information. Nowhere is this more apparent than in the polarization of political campaigns.

In the U.S., cable news organizations as disparate as Fox and MSNBC and websites as different as Breitbart News and The Huffington Post empowered competing narratives pitting Democrats against Republicans, liberals versus conservatives, Tea Partiers v. traditional Republicans, Democratic supporters of Bernie Sanders v. Hillary Clinton. Each faction can now claim not merely its own *opinions*, but its own *facts*. At first seen as pillars of freedom, new technologies may be reconstructing the Tower of Babel.

"It's increasingly possible to live in an online world in which you do have your own facts."[43]

~ Eli Pariser, author of *The Filter Bubble*

Americans are rapidly losing the informational commons, the town square, of the late 20th Century. Then nearly everyone in the community read the same metro newspaper and watched national newscasts anchored by Dan Rather, Peter Jennings or Tom Brokaw, all of which were informed by the same principles of journalism. Our opinions surely clashed then, but less often our facts.

"You used to be a consumer of reality, and now you're a designer of reality."[44]

~ Dan Wagner, chief executive of Civis Analytics

For the first time in history, we can fashion our own news diet, rather than some neutral editor. If we wish, we can tailor the news to our own biases and share no common ground for discussion with fellow citizens on the issues of the day. In its effort to bring us relevant search results, Google has installed algorithms that personalize our information searches based on our past preferences. Eli Pariser, former executive director of the liberal lobbying organization Move-on.org, has argued that this leads to informational "echo chambers."[45] Facebook categorizes its 200 million-plus American users' political orientation by what they share, and "like" and then tailors both ads and news to match.[46] Without our knowing it, our informational horizons can be narrowed.

But most of us *prefer* to live in segregated information neighborhoods. Summarizing research in psychology, Cordelia Fine of the Melbourne Business School wrote, "We humans quickly develop an irrational loyalty to our beliefs, and work hard to find evidence that supports those opinions and to discredit, discount or avoid information that does not."[47] That has contributed to partisan gridlock in our politics, an inability to confront the important domestic and international challenges of the day.[48] As former *New York Times* columnist Joe Nocera pointed out, "in Washington these days, there is no such thing as bipartisan. On every major issue facing the country, Democrats and Republicans have competing narratives."[49]

"Giving everyone a voice has historically been a very positive force for public discourse because it increases the diversity of ideas shared. But the past year has shown it may fragment our shared sense of reality."[50]

~ Mark Zuckerberg, founder of Facebook.

In terms of how many will be affected and how adversely, no problem we face surpasses global climate change. We face the prospect of ankle-deep coastal cities, salad-bowl farming regions drying up in prolonged droughts, super storms and floods spawned by the greater capacity of a warmer atmosphere to carry moisture, forests dying off from infestations of insects spawned during shorter winters and oceans absorbing heat and $CO_2$, raising temperatures and acidity faster than fish and plants can adapt.

Perhaps because its impact is so vast, no issue is more subject to "competing narratives." Type the phrase "global climate change" into Google News and you'll see 163 million entries, framing the issue from every point on the compass. The volume alone can be overwhelming, like trying to drink from a fire hose.

"This very expensive GLOBAL WARMING bullshit has got to stop. Our planet is freezing, record low temps, and our GW scientists are stuck in ice."[51]

~ Donald J. Trump (@realDonaldTrump) January 2, 2014

"The earth is warming and human activity is the primary cause."[52]

~ Union of Concerned Scientists

Drawing on parallel but polarized universes of news and comment, Americans can no longer find consensus. Although the scientific evidence for man-made global warming continues to solidify and 2016 was the third year in a row the earth broke the mark for the hottest year on record, Pew's most recent survey of Americans found only 15 percent of conservative Republicans believed "the earth is warming because of human activity." By contrast, 79 percent of liberal Democrats thought so. Even among those who considered themselves moderates in each party, the gap was almost 30 percentage points.[53] With no common ground, Republicans and Democrats can't agree on what's real, much less what to do about it. Congress is no more able to plot a safe course forward than a squirrel caught in traffic.

## 3. Growing diversity of news sources and the rise of journalistic anarchy

Just as the printing press undermined royalty and the church in Europe, new digital technologies are sweeping away the hierarchy of American journalism – and its credibility. The presidential campaign of 2016 overthrew the dominance of elite news media such as the *New York Times, Washington Post,* and the major broadcast networks – PBS, CBS, NBC, and ABC.

Calvin and Hobbes (used with permission)

As recently as 2012, presidential hopefuls approached mainstream newsrooms with reverence knowing they needed the national press corps to make their case to the nation. What the *Times*, the *Post*, or CBS reported set the agenda for smaller news organizations across the land. Sure there was Fox News and Rush Limbaugh. But they were outsiders, voices shouting over the shoulders of traditional news providers. Elite news media set the boundaries of political discourse, and established the factual environment, the common ground for public debate. They acted as filters between candidates and the mass of American voters. For better and for worse, they were the gatekeepers of the democratic process.

No more.

In 2016 Donald J. Trump was able to harness a relatively new tool – Twitter – to get his message to the public *unfiltered*, in punchy 140 character bursts. It was the perfect marriage of candidate and technology. Not only does Twitter provide a direct path from leader to follower, a tweet is a one-way street. No reporter, protester or fact-checker can intrude with questions or comments.

Further, Twitter doesn't allow for detail or nuance; 140 characters is all you can pack in a tweet. Such enforced brevity promotes slogans over substance and provocation over policy. It's ideal for the ideologue, worthless for the wonk. Just as important, each follower can re-tweet the candidate's message spreading it far beyond its original audience almost instantaneously.

A celebrity candidate like Mr. Trump, with more than 20 million followers by the time of his inauguration in 2017, had his own virtual network with almost as great a reach on a typical day as all of the broadcast television networks *combined*. If that weren't enough, Twitter enabled him to set the national news agenda. With a provocative tweet at 3 a.m., Mr. Trump was able to virtually enter the editorial meetings at every national newspaper and network and influence what reporters would cover that day.

Mr. Trump was even able to mock and ridicule journalists at the most respected American news media without risking his candidacy. Already weakened economically, American journalism was sidelined by a candidate able to reach the public without having to endure difficult, but important questions from reporters.

Throughout his campaign and even after he entered the White House, Mr. Trump savagely attacked the national press corps, calling them "dishonest," purveyors of "fake news," and "the enemy of the American people." At his first press conference in February 2017, Mr. Trump spent much of his 77 minutes assailing the press. Ironically, he ended the session with fake news of his own, claiming his margin of victory in the electoral college exceeded any president since Ronald Reagan. In fact, his margin was smaller than all but one president during that period, George W. Bush.[54]

It was not the first time, Mr. Trump was been caught in an obvious falsehood. Pulitzer-Prize-winning fact-checker PoltiFact evaluated 370 political pronouncements of Mr. Trump and found 67 percent "mostly false," "false" or "Pants on fire" false.[55]

> "To hear ... Donald Trump, create a scenario and a rhetoric and a scheme in which the press is the 'other' and 'the enemy of the people' ... should raise the hairs on the back of our neck and should be of enormous concern... for all of us as citizens."[56]
>
> ~ David Remnick, editor of *The New Yorker*

Mr. Trump has praised partisan fake news providers such as Alex Jones of the website Infowars. Mr. Jones has claimed the Sandy Hook Elementary School shooting was a hoax and the 9/11 attacks on the World Trade Centers in New York were an inside job, rather than work of Al Qaeda.

Mr. Jones exemplifies the growth and reach of new media spreading "alternative facts." In the early 1990's, he began with a spare cable channel in Austin, TX. Today Mr. Jones supervises a staff larger than some metro newspapers. Infowars alone boasts some 8 million global visitors a month and its pages have been viewed nearly 50 million times. He also owns 18 YouTube channels, the biggest of which has recorded 1.2 billion views. In addition, he has a nationally syndicated radio program and a popular Facebook page.[57]

"Millions of listeners and viewers tune in to Mr. Jones on his websites, on Facebook and through old-fashioned radio," wrote *New York Times* media columnist Jim Rutenberg. "And their loyalty partly explains how Mr. Trump maintains a hard-core faithful who don't believe a word they read about him in a newspaper like this one."[58]

Going beyond praise of fake news, Mr. Trump elevated Stephen Bannon, the former head of Breitbart News, a highly partisan and often factually-challenged website, to the position of senior White House advisor. While leading Breitbart, Mr. Bannon called it a home for the alt-right, a euphemism for white nationalism.

It is impossible to determine whether the flood of fake news swung the election in Mr. Trump's favor. People are reluctant to admit to being fooled, and they may reject reality when it conflicts with their core biases. In addition, they are not easily able to discern the impact of particular media messages in the formation of their opinions. Much of the process is subconscious.

It's beyond dispute, however, that Mr. Trump seriously damaged Americans' respect for journalism. In 2016 as candidate Trump excoriated the best of American journalism and exalted the worst, the credibility of mainstream U.S. news media was reaching new lows, particularly among Republicans.

The Gallup Organization, which began tracking press credibility in 1972 reported:

> Americans' trust and confidence in the mass media "to report the news fully, accurately and fairly" has dropped to its lowest level in Gallup polling history, with 32% saying they have a great deal or fair amount of trust in the media. This is down eight percentage points from last year. Republicans who say they have trust in the media has plummeted to 14% from 32% a year ago. This is easily the lowest confidence among Republicans in 20 years.[59]

When most people affiliated with a major political party reject reality-based reporting for illusions spread by those with little respect for facts or fairness, the nation is in peril. While it can be denied for a time, reality eventually prevails, often tragically.

## 4. Everyone can access a world of "facts", but many are untrue

When the World Wide Web was invented in 1989 and after companies like Altavista and later Google made it easily searchable, there was enormous optimism about its educational potential. What would have taken a trip to a library, or thumbing through a good encyclopedia, could be located with a few computer strokes, or now, a few taps on a smart phone, or even a question to the knowledge queens, Siri or Cortana. The Internet promised a society where everyone had nearly instant access to facts.

It is truer than ever that you can look up almost anything on the Internet. But much – perhaps most – of the information offered is really trying to sell you a product, service, or point of view. A Website aimed at students, **www.martinlutherking.org**, looks at first like a tribute to the slain civil rights leader. But it's actually a character assassination produced by a white supremacist organization founded by a former Ku Klux Klan leader. A site called **ConsumerNewsReporting.com** mimicked *Consumer Reports*, but was really an advertisement featuring a fictional satisfied customer.

Fake news has gravitated from transparent comedy on Saturday Night Live and the Daily Show and on the pages of *The Onion*, to covert partisan fabrications spewed from an explosion of websites purporting to be truthful. And since the 2010 *Citizen's United* case, when the Supreme Court allowed wealthy individuals, corporations, and unions to sponsor political attack ads without limit or accountability, deceptive messages have spread like a sniffle in a daycare.[60]

With 'round-the-clock cable, 'round-the-world websites, millions of bloggers, Tweeters, Instagrammers, Periscopers, Snapchatters, Facebook posters and sharers, etc. constantly filing reports, even robot trolls programmed to attack political opponents and fake grassroots support for their side's messages, we're drowning in news and views, yet parched for relevant, trustworthy reports of current issues and events. The signal is becoming lost in the noise.

## 5. While resources allocated to news decline, the value of news is rising.

Quality journalism has never been more valuable to the public. News explains change, what's new. And technology is pushing accelerating waves of change through society, shortening the shelf life of every kind of knowledge and altering how we learn, where – sometimes if – we work and what we're paid, even how long we live. Yet, as we have seen, the share of society's resources devoted to the production of reliable news has shriveled in the 21st century.

Not only is news becoming more valuable, its consequence declines less with distance than ever before. In a global economy and ecology, the need to know what's happening farther away has never been greater.

It's not just that a plot hatched on the other side of the world ended in the horror of passenger-laden airliners slamming into the symbols of the nation's economic and military preeminence, the World Trade Center Towers in New York and the Pentagon in Virginia. Nor that we've conducted two of our longest wars thousands of miles from our shores in the 21st century. It's an increasingly competitive global market for commodities like oil, metals, wheat, and corn as developing nations like India, China, and Brazil reach for the lifestyle already achieved in Western Europe, Japan, Australia and the United States. It's events in the Euro zone or China affecting the Dow Jones Industrial Average. It's white-collar jobs following blue to countries where salaries and protections for workers and the environment are minimal. The Internet makes communication with an engineer in India almost as easy as with one in the next cubicle. And a Stanford professor can teach a course for more than 100,000 students spread across six continents online, for free.[61]

We have become *interdependent* as never before. In recent years, we have learned that people around the world must act together, and soon, to prevent cataclysmic changes in our planet's weather. International government coordination was needed to prevent the financial collapse of 2008 from becoming a second Great Depression. If we understand each other and can make sense of change, our planet's problems could create an unprecedented opportunity to cooperate on a global scale.

## In markets we trust

In a rational world as the value of something rises, it ought to attract greater resources. Just the opposite is happening. That's because, especially in the United States, we have entrusted the gathering and dissemination of news to the marketplace. Markets work well matching supply and demand for many goods and services.[62] But not for news.[63]

When news is treated simply as a market commodity, two categories of problems arise. Economists call them "externalities" because they are effects of buying and selling decisions that are *not* taken into account within a transaction. There are two types: positive and negative. Both profoundly affect both the quantity and quality of news.

As the late University of Pennsylvania Professor Edwin Baker has described, good journalism has positive externalities. You may choose to consume quality news for the benefits it provides *you* personally. But it improves life for *all* when voters are informed and therefore able to choose honest, competent leaders. Everyone benefits, even if they pay nothing for news, not even attention. Likewise, even those who ignore the news benefit from the corruption avoided because investigative journalists are hanging around the halls of government.[64]

These public goods – informed voters and honest officials – cannot be monetized by news organizations. They can't charge in the marketplace for the benefits they provide. When news operates under market forces, such public benefits go unrewarded and thus are under-produced. Reporting from abroad is also a public good. But Americans tend to put a low priority on foreign news despite its growing importance. So money spent maintaining bureaus abroad doesn't generate additional profit.

The flip side of the coin describes negative externalities. Businesses compete in the marketplace not primarily to serve the public, but to seek profit. Public benefit occurs by virtue of the "invisible hand," Adam Smith described two centuries ago. It's a byproduct of well-functioning markets. But as we'll see in chapter 5, journalism that maximizes public understanding of current issues and events rarely maximizes return to owners or shareholders. For news, market pressures conflict more than coincide with public service.

The structural defects of relying on markets to produce the kind of news a democracy requires have been exacerbated by the revolution in communication technology. As the Internet has enabled advertisers to abandon their subsidy of news, journalism has been left an orphan in the marketplace.

With only a handful of exceptions, citizens have thus far been reluctant to pick up the slack by paying more for paper subscriptions or for online content. International media economist Robert Picard warns us not to hold our breath waiting for such a rescue from consumers. "The reality," he wrote "is that the average person is not now – and has never been – deeply interested in news."[65] At the 2010 annual convention of the Association for Education in Journalism and Mass Communication, Professor Picard went even further: "Never has news been commercially viable. Never! It has always been funded for some other purpose." In ancient times, he elaborated, that purpose was control, exercised by kings. For the last hundred years, news in the U.S. has been financed by merchants in order to sell products.[66]

If news can't support itself in the marketplace, political economist Robert W. McChesney and others have suggested that some form of government subsidy of journalism is necessary.[67] Although the news media constitute the most important public educators outside the public school system, so far there has been little enthusiasm for spending tax dollars on journalism.

## 6. The digital cloud's silver lining

While the Web enables diverging versions of truth, it also provides powerful tools for discovering and sharing which claims rest on the strongest evidence. It's also makes it easier to unmask fake news and virus-infected emails.

Websites such as FactCheck.org, PolitiFact.com, Snopes.com, CNN's "Keeping Them Honest," and the *Washington Post's* "Fact Checker" can help you separate the signal from the noise. The *New York Times* now fact-checks presidential speeches and tweets, as does National Public Radio,and many major metro newspapers. We've never before had such powerful help in vetting truth claims.

As we'll learn in chapter 11, the Web also puts a virtual reference library at our fingertips 24/7, enabling us to conduct our own fact-checks on virtually any topic in the news. Google offers a suite of vetting tools as extensions on the Chrome browser, such as advanced search, Google scholar, reverse image, and Public Data Explorer. You can also employ Storyful multisearch, and Amnesty International's YouTube DataViewer.

Social media, such as Facebook and Linked-In, plus online discussion groups allow us to take advantage of the much greater pool of knowledge among our friends and student or professional colleagues. The Web can also help us discover alternative sources of news providing a multi-perspectival view of major issues and events. Google Translate can help us understand foreign language news sites to acquire a broader view of international events. Finally, if you're willing to open your mind wide enough to recognize your own biases (everybody's got 'em), there's a website that can help you identify them (in chapter 3).

Our vastly expanded infosphere is a paradoxical place. It offers much more deception and distraction than ever before. But also much deeper educational resources. Learning to think critically about news and information is essential because what James Madison wrote with a goose quill in 1822 is as true as if it were tweeted today:

> Knowledge will forever govern ignorance, and a people who mean to be their own governors, must arm themselves with the power knowledge gives.[68]

---

### Exercises and Discussion Topics

1. How much have newspapers changed in your area? Go to the library and find a copy of the nearest metro paper for this day 10 or 15 years ago. Compare it today's paper, specifically, the number of pages then and now and the size of those pages.

- What else do you notice that has changed? Are the photos larger now? Are there fewer stories on the front page now? More or less local news? More or fewer wire stories (articles written by outside news organizations such as the

Associated Press)? Are there now advertisements on the front page? Are the articles more informative than before, or more entertaining?

- In general, do you feel the paper serves local citizens now as well as it did 10-15 years ago? Why or why not?

2. Look online for local news Websites that are *not* operated by local newspapers or broadcast companies. In other words, look for entirely new sources of journalism in your city or metro area.

- How many did you find?

- Choose one: How many journalists work for this site? (Look for a link to "staff" or "about us." If you can't tell, open some stories and see how many unique bylines you can find on the top stories of the main page.)

- Compare the site to the local newspaper's site: what differences do you notice?

- Are these new sources of local news equal to or better than the newspapers' Websites or those of local broadcast stations?

3. How much do you trust local news-providers – new and old? Which do you trust the most? The least? Why?

## End Notes

[1] Napoleon Bonaparte, https://www.brainyquote.com/quotes/quotes/n/napoleonbo101124.html.

[2] Internet Live Stats, online at: http://www.Internetlivestats.com/total-number-of-websites/.

[3] The Knight commission on the information needs of communities in a democracy, (2009) *Informing communities: Sustaining democracy in the digital*

*age*, "Executive summary," Washington, DC: Aspen Institute, p. 1, online at http://www.knightcomm.org/executive-summary/.

[4] Mina Kim (4/28/2017) "Fahrenthold Investigates Donald Trump One Fact at a Time," Forum, KQED-FM, https://ww2.kqed.org/forum/ 2017/04/27/pulitzer-prize-winner-david-fahrenthold-investigates-donald-trump-one-fact-at-a-time/?a=commentsATag.

[5] Fahrenthold interview cited above.

[6] Robert G. Picard (2010) *Value Creation and the future of news organizations,* Lisbon, Spain: MediaXXi.

[7] Amy Mitchell and Jesse Holcomb, Pew Research Center, "State of the News Media 2016" (6/15/2016) p. 1, http://www. journalism.org/2016/06/15/state-of-the-news-media-2016/.

[8] Michael Barthel, (6/15/2016) Pew Research Center, "Newspapers: Fact Sheet, p. 1: http://www.journalism.org/2016/06/15/newspapers-fact-sheet/#economics.

[9] Charles Lewis (4/25/2012) "Reporting: fundamental necessity to democracy," Investigative Reporting Workshop at American University School of Communication; http://investigativereporting workshop .org/investigations /investigating-power/story/Reporting-a-fundamental-necessity-to-democracy/.

[10] Mitchell and Holcomb, cited above. Also see surveys by the American Society of Newspaper Editors, http://asne.org/.

[11] Lisa Borenstein (2/27/2009) "Rocky Mountain Bye," *Columbia Journalism Review*, http://www.cjr.org/behind_the_news/ rocky_ mountain_bye.php?page=all.

[12] Douglas McCollam (July/August 2008) "Sulzberger at the barricades," *Columbia Journalism Review*, vol. 48, no. 2, p. 26.

[13] Mark J. Perry (5/30/2015) "Creative destruction: Newspaper ad revenue continued its precipitous free fall in 2014, and it's likely to continue," American Enterprise Institute, https://www.aei.org/ publication/creative-destruction-newspaper-ad-revenue-continued-its-precipitous-free-fall-in-2014-and-its-likely-to-continue/.

[14] Leonard Downie Jr. and Michael Schudson (10/19/2009) "The Reconstruction of American Journalism," *Columbia Journalism Review*, http://www.cjr.org/reconstruction/ the_reconstruction_of_american.php?page=all.

[15] Michael Barthel, cited above, p. 10.

[16] See the Project for Excellence in Journalism's annual *State of the American News Media* reports online at: www.journalism.org. These annual reports breakout audience, revenue and employment trends by type of news medium, e.g. newspapers, cable TV, etc.

[17] See, for example, stories awarded the Pulitzer Prize; http://www.pulitzer.org/awards; or http://www.journalism.columbia. edu/cs/ContentServer /jrn/1165270069766/page/1175295284582/JRNSimplePage2.htm.

[18] Jodi Enda (7/15/2014) "At the statehouse, ideological press tries to fill a void in news coverage," Pew Research Center, http://pewresearch.org/author/jenda.

[19] Alas, *American Journalism Review* has ceased publication. *Columbia Journalism Review*, the other magazine devoted to assessing American journalism, now publishes mostly online. With so many fewer journalists to subscribe, these publications have become an endangered species.

[20] Amy Goodman and Juan Gonzalez (1/12/2012) Democracy Now, interview with Michael J. Copps.

[21] Mary Walton (9/2010) "Investigative shortfall," *American Journalism Review*, http://www.ajr.org/article.asp?id=4904.

[22] Charles Lewis (4/25/2012) "Investigating power reporting: fundamental necessity to democracy," Investigative Reporting Workshop, American University School of Communication.

[23] Priya Kumar (Dec./Jan. 2011) "Foreign correspondents: Who covers what?", *American Journalism Review*, http://www.ajr.org/ article.asp?id=4997.

[24] Indiana University, (5/1/2014) "IU survey: U.S. journalists say they are less satisfied and have less autonomy" http://news.indiana.edu/releases/iu/2014/05/american-journalist-in-the-digital-age.shtml.

[25] Project for Excellence in Journalism (3/17/2008) "The Web: Alarming, appealing and a challenge to journalistic values: Financial woes now overshadow all other concerns for journalists," Pew Research Center for the People and the Press, p. 1, http://www.stateofthemedia.org/files/2011 /01/Journalist-report-2008.pdf.

[26] Jennifer Wadsworth (4/5/2016) "Huge media shifts as Mercury News rebrands, KGO cuts staff," *San Jose Inside*.

[27] John McManus (6/5/2007) "Inside the Bay Area's newspaper giant," Grade the News. An interview with John Bowman, former editor of the *Daily Review* in Hayward, CA and executive editor of the *San Mateo County Times.* Article available at: http://www.gradethenews.org /2007/bowman.htm.

[28] Robert Papper (8/5/2010) "The state of the industry: 2010," study presented at the annual convention of the Association for Education in Journalism and Mass Communication, Denver. Professor Papper of Hofstra University found that only 39 percent of local television stations did *not* partner with other local broadcasters or newspapers.

[29] Sydney Ember and Michael J. de la Merced (5/9/2017) "Sinclair will pay $3.9 billion for Tribune," *New York Times*, p. B1.

[30] Ken Doctor (7/16/2015) Neiman Lab, , http://www.niemanlab.org /author/kdoctor/.

[31] A.J. Liebling (1975) *The press,* Pantheon: New York, p. 32. Originally published May 14, 1960 in *The New Yorker* column, "The wayward press," under the title, "Do you belong in journalism?"

[32] Michele McClellan (accessed 2/15/2017) "Michele's List," http://www.micheleslist.org.

[33] Jack Marshall (2/2/2016) "Patch Rebounds after split from AOL," Wall Street Journal, online at https://www.wsj.com/articles/patch-rebounds-after-split-from-aol-1454445340.

[34] Frederick Fico, Stephen Lacy, Thomas Baldwin, Daniel Bergan, Steven S. Wildman and Paul Zube (2011) "Citizen journalism sites as information substitutes and complements for newspaper coverage of local governments," *Digital Journalism* 1(1) 2013, pp. 152-168.

For a more optimistic portrait of non-traditional news media, see Dan Gillmor's 2010 book, *Mediactive.*

[35] Ted Koppel (3/12/2009) "Do News-providers Live Up to News Literacy Standards?", panel held at Stony Brook University; http:// newsliteracyconference.com/content/?p=498.

[36] Andrew Marantz (10/31/2016) "Trolls for Trump: How the alt-right spreads fringe ideas to the mainstream," *The New Yorker*, p. 42.

[37] Marantz, cited above, p. 45.

[38] Ken Doctor (3/10/2008) "Regional Dailies Give Business Away," available online at: http://www.contentbridges.com/2008/03/ regional-dailie.html. His own website is here: http://newsonomics.com/.

[39] Brooke Gladstone (6/17/2011) "FCC report says local reporting in crisis," On the Media, National Public Radio, online at http://www .onthemedia.org /transcripts/2011/06/17/04. For more, see Stephen Waldman (2011) *Information needs of communities: The changing media landscape in a broadband age*, Washington DC: Federal Communication Commission, online at http://www.fcc.gov/info-needs-communities.

[40] Paul Farhi (Spring, 2010) "lost in the woods: Sinking standards, the media and Tiger Woods," *American Journalism Review*, pp. 14-19. More on falling standards in chapter 5.

[41] Christine Haughney (6/3/2012) "Newspapers cut days from publishing week," *The New York Times*, p. B1.

[42] Ben Zimmer (2/13/2011) "How the war of words was won," *New York Times,* Week in Review, p. 4. Also see Nicholas D. Kristof, (2/13/2011) "What Egypt can teach America," *New York Times,* Week in Review, p. 10.

[43] Amy Goodman (5/27/2011) Democracy Now, interview with Eli Pariser, author of *The Filter Bubble*, online at: http://www. democracynow.org /2011/5/27/eli_pariser_on_the_filter_bubble.

[44] Jim Rutenberg (3/13/17) "The choose-your-own-news adventure," NYT, p. B1, online at: https://www.nytimes.com/2017/03/12/business /media/mediator-personalized-feeds-news-choice-jim-rutenberg.html?_r=0.

[45] Goodman interview with Eli Pariser cited above.

[46] Jeremy B. Merrill (8/23/2016) "Liberal, Moderate or Conservative? See how Facebook labels you." New York Times, https://www. nytimes.com /2016/08/24/us/politics/facebook-ads-politics.html?_r=0. To see your label, Go to facebook.com/ads/preferences on your browser. (You may have to log in to Facebook first.) That will bring you to a page with your ad preferences. Under the "Interests" header, click the "Lifestyle and Culture" tab. Then look for a box titled "US Politics." In parentheses, it will describe how Facebook has categorized you, such as liberal, moderate or conservative. If the "US Politics" box does not show up, click the "See more" button under the grid of boxes.

[47] Cordelia Fine (8/31/2011) "Biased but brilliant," *New York Times*, Sunday Review, p. 12.

New research suggests that our selective seeking of news matching our biases may differ from our avoidance of counter-attitudinal news. Also Republicans in the US may be more susceptible to these biases than Democrats. See Hyunjin Song (January-February, 2017) "Why do people (sometimes) become selective about news? The role of emotions and partisan differences in selective approach and avoidance," *Mass Communication and Society* Vol. 20: pp. 47-67.

[48] Michael Dimock, Carroll Doherty, Jocelyn Kiley, Russ Oates (6/12/2014) "Political polarization in the American public," Pew Research Center, http://www.people-press.org/2014/06/12/political-polarization-in-the-american-public/.

[49] Joe Nocera (12/18/2010) "Explaining the crisis with dogma," Talking business column, *New York Times,* p. B1. Other evidence of partisanship: According to *Newsweek* (8/15/2011), in the 1960s, 8% of major bills faced a filibuster. By 2011, the proportion increased to 70%, making it difficult to pass any bill without 60 of 100 senators voting for it; "8 ways to fix our politics," pp. 22-23.

[50] Farhad Manjoo (4/30/2017) "Can Facebook fix its ultimate bug?" *New York Times Magazine*, pp. 38-61.

[51] Donald J. Trump (1/2/2014) Tweet, online at http://www.motherjones.com/politics/2015/06/donald-trump-science-climate-change-vaccines-autism-ebola.

[52] Union of Concerned Scientists, "Global Warming," online at: http://www.ucsusa.org/global_warming/. (Disclosure: I contribute to the Union of Concerned Scientists.)

[53] Cary Funk and Brian Kennedy (10/4/2016) "The Politics of Climate," Pew Research Center, http://www.pewInternet.org/2016/10/04/the-politics-of-climate/.

[54] Nicholas Fandos (2/16/2017) "Trump calls press dishonest, then utters falsehoods of his own," *The New York Times*, online at https://www.nytimes.com/2017/02/16/us/politics/trump-fact-check.html?_r=0.

[55] Politifact (visited 2/20/2017) Donald Trump's File, http://www.politifact.com/personalities/donald-trump/.

[56] David Remnick (3/1/2017) "Trump, Putin and the new cold war," Fresh Air interview with Terry Gross, National Public Radio.

[57] Jim Rutenberg (2/20/2017) "In his volley, Trump echoes a provocateur," p. B1, *The New York Times*, https://www.nytimes.com /2017/02/19/business/media/alex-jones-conspiracy-theories-donald-trump.html?ref=business&_r=0

[58] Rutenberg, cited above.

[59] Art Swift (9/14/2016) "Americans trust in mass media sinks to new low," Gallup Organization, For reference, the high point of trust in news media occurred in 1976, at 72 percent. Online at http://www.gallup.com/poll/195542/americans-trust-mass-media-sinks-new-low.aspx.

[60] Jane Meyer, (2016) *Dark Money*, New York: Doubleday.

[61] Steve Henn (4/18/2012) "From Silicon Valley, a new approach to education," National Public Radio's All Tech Considered, online at: http://www.npr.org/blogs/alltechconsidered/2012/04/18/150846845/from-silicon-valley-a-new-approach-to-education.

[62] Markets have many advantages over other allocation systems. But they work better for non-essential goods and services than for basic human needs. Markets discriminate in favor of the wealthy and against the poor. This may not make a big difference for products such as fancy cars, mansions or diamond rings. But it matters greatly when people are priced out of the market for necessities like healthful food, medical care, clean air and water, safety and security, and educational opportunity.

[63] John H. McManus (1994) *Market-driven journalism: Let the citizen beware?*, Thousand Oaks, CA: Sage.

[64] C. Edwin Baker (2002) *Media, markets and democracy*, Cambridge, UK: Cambridge University Press.

[65] Robert Picard, cited above, p. 11.

[66] Author's notes (8/7/2010) "New Media Economics: In search of viable news business models in a digital media world," panel at the annual convention of the Association for Education in Journalism and Mass Communication.

[67] Robert W. McChesney and John Nichols (2010) *The death and life of American Journalism*," Philadelphia: Nation Books.

[68] James Madison, "Federalist Paper No. 62" in Clinton Rossiter, Ed. (2000, orig. 1822) *The Federalist Papers*, New York: Signet Classic.,

# 3

# Truth vs. Truthiness

*The truth shall set you free.*

~ Jesus of Nazareth (John 8:32)

Jesus, in the Christian bible, says truth leads to liberty, freedom from the trap of being fooled. But Stephen, in the "Colbert Report," says truth is obsolete; the new standard is "truthiness." We live in an era when fake news and partisan propaganda have eroded the informational common ground a democracy requires. So it's essential to understand the nature of truth. This chapter explores four basic propositions:

1. **What we call truth is really a simulation or virtual reality.**

2. **While we can amplify our senses with technology, we can never be sure that the virtual reality within our heads matches what's outside.**

3. **We may think we are in charge of assigning meaning to what we see and hear, but most of our sense-making is programmed by others.**

4. **Despite these limitations, the search for reliable facts is essential to human flourishing.**

When he was a self-professed fake journalist, Stephen Colbert mocked the concept of truth. He described truthiness as a feeling of confidence that something is true that is liberated from any thinking of one's own or reference to others' thinking, such as might appear in an "elitist" medium, like a book. Truth is for those who "think with their heads," Colbert deadpanned. "Truthiness" is for "those who *know* with their hearts."[1]

At the heart of Colbert's humor lies the incongruity of someone dressed in the authority of a dark suit speaking complete nonsense with absolute conviction. But the joke is on us. We've all seen and heard more than enough guys and gals like that at

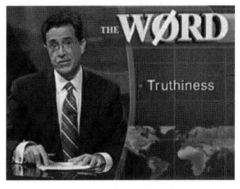

**Courtesy of Thisdayinquotes.com**

school, work, in the marketplace, and in politics. They are frequently in error, but rarely in doubt.

Although Mr. Colbert aimed his jibe about truthiness at President George W. Bush and his vice president, Dick Cheney. For our purposes it refers to any deceptive claim of fact. The presidential campaign of 2016 catapulted truthiness to a new level. Among the fabrications were these: A pizzeria in Washington DC was really a front for a child sex slave operation run by Hillary Clinton; President Obama signed an executive order banning the Pledge of Allegiance in public schools; Mr. Trump was offering free one-way airfare to Mexico and Africa for those who want to leave America; An ISIS leader called for American Muslim voters to support Hillary Clinton; Police found 19 white female bodies in a freezer with "Black Lives Matter" carved into their skin.[2]

Even the pope was not spared.

# WTOE 5 NEWS
## YOUR LOCAL NEWS NOW

HOME    US ELECTION

## Pope Francis Shocks World, Endorses Donald Trump for President, Releases Statement

**TOPICS:** Pope Francis Endorses Donald Trump

photo by Jeffrey Bruno / CC BY-SA 2.0 / cropped & photo by Gage Skidmore / CC BY-SA 3.0 / cropped

Fake news has real consequences. The false report of a child sex ring led a gullible North Carolina man to travel to DC armed with an assault rifle which he fired in the pizza parlor. And while we don't know if fake news swayed the election to Mr. Trump, we do know that various fabrications were widely liked and shared on Facebook.[3] The author of the Facebook study, Craig Silverman, speculated about its political impact: "[T]he performance of the fake stuff on Facebook created so much noise, so much misleading and false information... I just wonder if that repetition of it over time starts to have an effect on people."[4]

Published false political charges go back to the earliest days of the republic. Thomas Jefferson's supporters accused President John Adams of having a "hideous hermaphroditical character, which has neither the force and firmness of a man, nor the gentleness and sensibility of a woman." Adam's boosters called Jefferson "a mean-spirited, low-lived fellow, the son of a half-breed Indian squaw, sired by a Virginia mulatto father."[5]

Mr. Trump, however, has elevated fake news to the highest office in the land, *personally* making fact-claims that defy verification, rather than merely letting *subordinates* publish hyperbolic opinions.

Before 7 a.m. on March 4, 2017 President Trump tweeted:

> How low has President Obama gone to tapp [sic] my phones during the very sacred election process. This is Nixon/Watergate. Bad (or sick) guy!
>
> – Donald J. Trump (@realDonaldTrump)[6]

"This is unprecedented. I have never heard of a president of the United States accusing his predecessor or any other president of the United States of violating the law."[7]

~ Republican Sen. John McCain

Even after the heads of the FBI and the National Security Agency, the Justice Department, and Republican Congressional leaders testified that they knew of no evidence of such surveillance, Mr. Trump refused to substantiate his claim, retract it, or apologize.

The notion that President Obama asked the government to spy on Mr. Trump originated in a rant by a conservative radio talk show host on March 2, It was turned into a story by the right-wing "news" website Breitbart the day before Mr. Trump's tweet.[8] When the president of the United States publishes an accusation of national significance based solely on fake news, truthiness has become more than a gag on Comedy Central. It's become a weapon of mass deception.

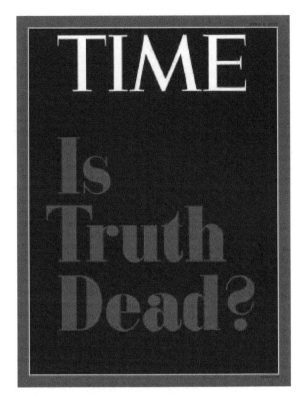

Mr. Trump's repeated falsehoods were the subject of this Time Magazine cover on 3/22/2017

## The nature of truth

Philosophers have long disputed the nature of truth. While those debates are beyond the scope of this book, the concept of truth lies at the very center of our search for reliable news and information. So it's essential to examine it, if only to discover that it differs from what many of us were taught – that truth is self-evident and unchanging.

Perhaps the most common definition of truth is this: a faithful account of what's real. Sounds simple. However it's anything but, as we shall see next.

## 1. What we call truth is really a simulation or virtual reality

The only way we can know truth comes through our five senses and our brain, which interprets those electrochemical neural impulses from our eyes, ears, nose, tongue, and skin. But our senses are only capable of receiving a sliver of what the universe has to offer. Visible light comprises only a narrow range of the frequencies of radiant energy, about 2.5 percent.[9] Similarly, our ears miss tones above and below a thin band of pitches. (Your dog can do better!) Our tongues can only identify five basic tastes. Our skin can sense a traveling ant but not a mite, much less the presence of a germ.

Not only do our senses miss most of what's going on around us, they transform what they do receive. Electromagnetic radiation oscillating at one frequency we call blue, at another, red. A drum makes no sound, only waves of air pressure, until it beats against the tympanum in our ear. Cognitive scientist Robert Ornstein points out:

> The world outside is silent, dull. It could be called odorless, colorless, and tasteless, for there is no color in nature, no sound, no touch, no smell. All these wonders exist inside the shell that the mind creates for us to live in. Out of the few forlorn signals that get inside, we create an entire world in the same way as do architects who create whole buildings using only lines on paper.[10]

Even though our senses miss most of what's going on, they still produce more data than our brains can handle. So our brains have been shaped by evolution to filter out most of this information so they can concentrate on those sensory signals most vital to survival. They are, for example, more attuned to motion than stillness – to the leaping tiger rather than the tree. We notice loud noises more than the background. We are more aware of pain than comfort and more sensitive to loss than gain. We pay greater attention to change than sameness.[11]

Psychologists say we have evolved with two, almost opposite, ways of thinking. Most of the time, we operate in an *automatic* mode: quickly, intuitively, and effortlessly. We're not even aware of it, like how to ride a bike once you've learned. Automatic mode allows us to cope with danger, as well as life's complexity and pace, without conscious effort. But we are easily fooled in automatic mode because we jump to conclusions based on associations rather than logic. If we subconsciously connect pizza with comfort, we may eat it without bothering to consider whether it's healthy.

Only rarely do we engage our brains in the *reflective* mode, the second type of thinking. Reflection requires conscious effort. It's slow. But because we reason deductively from principles we've learned over time, or inductively by generalizing from a range of instances, the results are more trustworthy. Both types of thinking are influenced by our experiences – particularly the most recent and emotional – and our knowledge and beliefs, as well as our purpose at the time.

These limits on our ability to interpret reality should create gradations in what we take to be true. Our most reliable path toward truth arises from reflective thinking. When conducted with others, it's called the empirical method. This is the approach taken by science and to a lesser degree by courts of law. It's a description of reality based on the logical construction of evidence from independent observations that has survived efforts to prove it false.

But we take many things to be true that have not endured so rigorous a test. Most things, in fact. We might accept as true what a website, a TV show, a book, a parent or other authority tells us, what our friends or peers say, or just a rumor. We often draw conclusions from a few haphazard observations. Indeed, some of what we consider true cannot even be subjected to an empirical analysis – notions of God and religion, for example.

## 2. While we can amplify our senses with technology, we can never be sure that the virtual reality within our heads matches what's outside

Because empirical truth is a *description* of reality, it's a human product. It can be written as words or an equation, but either way it's a human invention. Its value is based on how useful it is to help us cope with the world around us.

We've had the most success describing reality when we've relied on the scientific method. That involves careful *observation* by more than one person and the application of *logic* to make sense of what we observe. Science looks for patterns in nature that have a high probability of occurring. Generalizations about these patterns become laws when they have survived enough tests of their validity raised by competing theories.

Science has expanded our ability to sense the world with telescopes, X-rays, and other wonderful instruments. But we still "see" the universe incompletely. As technology has enhanced our senses, some of what we once believed to be true has changed. The first century CE (common era) Egyptian astronomer Claudius Ptolemy's interpretation of the cosmos got the roundness of planets right but portrayed the Earth as the center of the cosmos, circled by the moon, Mercury, Venus, the sun, Mars, Jupiter, and Saturn.

A thousand years ago, everybody "knew" that the sun orbited the Earth. You only had to look to the east in the morning to see the sun rise and track it across the sky until it set in the western sky to "prove" it. Of course, we didn't know then that the Earth was spinning, making the sun only appear to travel across the sky. Most also didn't know that the Earth was round (or as we've learned more recently, slightly ovoid). It seemed so obviously flat.

The truths of those days were in people's heads and bore little relation to the physical universe. As we learned more through the development of better tools – telescopes and ships that could sail around the Earth – what everyone accepted as true became false, even silly.

But even science can't guarantee correspondence with reality. The facts about the physical universe keep changing. The atom ain't what it used to be. Until the turn of the 20th century, it was thought to be the smallest building block of nature. In the virtual reality our minds construct, that's how we "saw" it. Then we discovered electrons, and later neutrons and protons. More recently, we've learned of smaller particles – six "flavors" of quarks, and leptons.[12]

"If you look at the history of science, you'll see that almost every belief that at some point has been proclaimed the truth about the world has at some later point be revealed to be absolutely false. That is, in fact, how science moves forward."[13]

~ Kathryn Schultz, author of *Being Wrong: Adventures in the Margin of Error*

Chastened by new discoveries, scientists consider all knowledge about nature to be tentative – the best we can do right now. We never know what's just around the learning corner that will rewrite our notions of truth.

## 3. We may think we are in charge of assigning meaning to what we see and hear, but most of our sense-making is programmed by others

Because of slight physical differences in our eyes, ears, taste buds, and other sensory organs, we don't all experience the world the same way. And the neurochemical signals traveling from our senses to our brains are interpreted in light of our unique experiences. So some of what we take to be true is unique to us, perhaps stemming from a religious or other deeply-felt experience or an idiosyncratic set of beliefs. Nevertheless, most of what we accept as true or factual is based on a description of reality that *others* agree is true. We are programmed by the culture of our place and time.

Even what we experience directly, we usually interpret as we have been taught. For thousands of years men have experienced firsthand the intelligence, courage, and wisdom of women. But until very recently in human history, it appears almost all men considered women inferior. Not capable of voting in the U.S. until 1920. Not worthy of a university education until late in the 19th Century. Not accepted as rabbis, ministers, or mullahs until very recently. Still not welcome to become Catholic priests. In Saudi Arabia, not yet permitted to drive a car.

Try this thought experiment: You attend a party where the host serves a deep-fried, breaded finger food that looks something like an onion ring. You taste one and find it's delicious. "What is it?" you ask. "Deep-fried worms," the host replies. Would you lose your appetite?[14]

If so, notice that your own judgment of a pleasant taste was overruled by what you had been taught about eating worms. And the discovery that you were chewing on worms affected you not just intellectually – "Oh, that's interesting!" – but as a visceral rejection (maybe even ejection). *Escargot* anyone?

The ideas about what's true exist in our heads, but they are powerfully influenced by others. In most ancient tribal societies, shamans and elders held the authority to say what was true and what was false. Later, religious authorities, kings, queens, and the nobility would claim it. In our day, teachers, scientists, political and religious leaders, and professional news media are the most powerful truth-tellers, at least in developed nations.

Oral, and later written, myths enabled accepted interpretations of basic questions about truth – the nature of humans, the Earth and cosmos, God or gods, order, virtue and vice – to spread through a tribe or a people. *The Iliad*, *The Odyssey*, the Hebrew and Christian Bibles, the Quran, and the Bhagavad-Gita ("Song of God" in Sanskrit) are ancient examples of this. The U.S. Constitution and the United Nations' Universal Declaration of Human Rights are more modern, codified expressions of core values. They form the bedrock upon which societies are built.

Culture comprises all of the stories we tell about ourselves and our environment, in whatever medium. Those stories are grounded in shared myths and beliefs as well as the wisdom and knowledge available at a given place and time. Because so little of what we take as truth arises from empirical investigation, we rely on culture as a social binding agent. It allows our individual reality simulations to sync enough for us to get along within our community. But culture can also be a blinding agent when the cultures of different communities clash. Each community believes its interpretation corresponds to reality, so the other must be in error. As we'll see in the next chapter, even within a single nation there are subcultures which chafe against each other. The misperceptions engendered by those cultural differences breed bias.

## 4. Despite these limitations, the search for reliable facts is essential to human flourishing.

Just because our best claims of truth are uncertain and subject to change doesn't mean they don't matter or shouldn't guide us. We have made great strides in our ability to flourish as a species by following the best knowledge of the day. It's allowed us to make barren deserts flower and fruit, to routinely travel at nearly the speed of sound, to eliminate diseases that crippled our grandparents, to expand our lifespan, and to squeeze thousands of bands – even orchestras – into our iPods!

The inverse is also true. When we have acted on falsehood, we have come to grief. Not long ago we embarked on a war of choice in Iraq based on the faulty claim that it possessed weapons of mass destruction. The war caused hundreds of thousands of lives to be lost, cost the United States as many as $3 trillion dollars, and destabilized much of the Middle East.

### Exercises and Discussion Topics

1. Look for an example of truthiness on the Web or in other media. Describe how it diverges from truth.

2. Consider recent losses and gains in your life. Do you think that you personally are more sensitive to loss than gain?

3. Make a list of five of the most important things you take to be true. How many are based on empirical facts? How many are based on belief rather than empiricism?

4. Find a copy of a newspaper from 100 years ago, either online or in the microfiche section of the library. Examine the stories on the front page. What assumptions or statements are made there that we now know are factually

incorrect? What assumptions or statements are made that would seem out of place in our current culture?

Here's an example. A century ago newspapers described mine collapses and fatal factory or apartment fires as acts of god. They just happened; no one was to blame. Today we look for human causes – was the mine operated safely or the building up to fire codes?

## End Notes

[1] Stephen Colbert (1/10/2007) The Colbert Report, online at http://www.gametrailers.com/user-move/truthiness-the-colbert-report/33403.

[2] Craig Silverman (12/30/2016) "Here Are 50 Of The Biggest Fake News Hits On Facebook From 2016" Buzzfeed, https://www. buzzfeed.com/craigsilverman/top-fake-news-of-2016?utm_term=.mtX219RzLw#.vv4Pq4MoaD.

[3] Craig Silverman  (11/16/2016) "This analysis shows how viral fake election news stories outperformed real news on Facebook," online at: https://www.buzzfeed.com/craigsilverman/viral-fake-election-news-outperformed-real-news-on-facebook?utm_term=.lkALY39BVm#.hlA2 eNP0vz.

[4] Craig Silverman (1/27/2017). Interview with Brooke Gladstone, On the Media,  http://www.wnyc.org/shows/otm.

[5] Kerwin Swint (8/22/2008) "Founding fathers dirty campaign," CNN, online at http://www.cnn.com/2008/LIVING/wayoflife/08/22/mf.campaign.slurs.slogans /. Accessed 3/22/2017.

[6] Michael D. Shear and Michael S. Schmidt (2/4/2017) "Trump, offering no evidence, says Obama tapped his phones." New York Times, online at https://www.nytimes.com/2017/03/04/us/politics/trump-obama-tap-phones.html.

[7] Austin Wright (3/6/2017) "McCain on Trump's wiretap claim: 'I haven't seen anything like this'", Politico, http://www.politico.com/story/2017/03 /mccain-trump-wiretapping-235749.

[8] Peter Baker and Maggie Haberman (3/5/2017) "A conspiracy theory's journey from talk radio to Trump twitter," New York Times, https://www.nytimes.com/2017/03/05/ us/politics/trump-twitter-talk-radio-conspiracy-theory.html.

[9] Molecular Expressions, "Optical microscopy primer: basics of light and color," available online at: http://micro.magnet.fsu.edu /primer/lightandcolor/ electromagintro.html.

[10] Robert Ornstein (2008) *MindReal: How the mind creates its own virtual reality,* Boston: Malor Books, p. 106.

[11] In this paragraph and the next two I'm relying on Daniel Kahneman (2011) *Thinking, fast and slow*, New York: Farrar, Straus and Giroux; Richard H. Thaler and Cass R. Sunstein (2008) *Nudge: Improving decisions about health, wealth, and happiness*, New York: Penguin; and George Lakoff (2008) *The political mind: Why you can't understand 21st-century American politics with an 18th-century brain*, New York: Viking Press.

[12] Wikipedia, "Subatomic particle," https://en.wikipedia.org/wiki/ Subatomic_particle, accessed 3/23/2017.

I know many of you have been warned about trusting Wikipedia. After 2005 it changed its rules for contributors requiring that they cite published materials and barring original research. More recently it's been accused of being too restrictive, requiring too extensive use of footnotes (Noam Cohen, 8/8/2011, "When knowledge isn't written, does it still count?" *New York Times*, p. B4.) I use Wikipedia here only after checking elsewhere. I include it where I think it's reliable because it's online, so with just a click you can go deeper if you're curious. Here's more on atoms, http://en.wikipedia.org/wiki/Atom#History and subatomic particles: http://en.wikipedia.org/wiki/List_of_particles.

[13] Michael Krasny (6/22/2010) Forum, KQED-FM, interview with journalist and author Kathryn Schulz author of *Being Wrong: Adventures in the Margin of Error*.

[14] I adapted this example from Earl Babbie (2007) *The practice of social research*, 11th ed., Belmont, CA: Thomson Wadsworth.

# 4

# Where Bias Comes From

*Why can't they produce a fair, balanced, objective and non-partisan newspaper –
that reflects my point of view?*

~ Classic cartoon caption

We all like to think we see the world just as it is. Those who disagree with us are misinformed, mischievous, morally-challenged or missing a screw. But – alas! – we are all subject to bias. That's because rather than investigating the world empirically, most of the time we rely for our sense of reality on others who are like us. Like a flying wedge of geese in the autumn sky, it takes much less effort to follow in formation than set out alone.

Just as similar types of birds flock together, we form subcultures, tribes, even within one society. From the inside looking out, the lens of culture looks perfectly clear. We don't notice our own group's biases because they are taken-for-granted. But when our views differ from another group's perspective, the "distortions" in *their* cultural lenses are glaringly obvious. "Be reasonable!" we naively plead, "see it my way."

The Christian scriptures quote Jesus telling his disciples, "First take the log out of your own eye, and then you will see clearly to take the speck out of your brother's eye" (Matthew 7:5). It's excellent advice for everyone. When we look for bias in how journalists and other information sources perceive and describe the world, we must also examine *our own* prejudices. Otherwise, we're likely to fall into the cynic's trap of seeing bias in any description or interpretation of reality with which we disagree. As Jesus observed, bias is not something added on to a crystalline perception, it shapes the very act of seeing.

This chapter explores six propositions about our ability to see reality clearly:

1. **Even when we watch the same thing, we don't see the same thing.**

2. **We forget that what we see depends on where we are observing from and when; we treat snapshots as if they were panoramic videos.**

3. **Rather than seeing everything before us, we focus on only a part of it.**

4. **We don't just record what's in focus like a camera; as dot-connecting animals, we unconsciously select just a fraction of what's in focus and impose meaning.**

5. **We are more likely to notice – and seek out – what confirms our expectations than what contradicts them.**

6. **Bias begins with self-interest, but there are other equally subconscious and predictable layers based on race, class, geography, gender, generation, and other cultural groupings.**

Perhaps the best-known study of the perceptual origins of bias was conducted in the fall of 1951 and based on, of all things, a football game: Princeton vs. Dartmouth. From all accounts it was a vicious game. In the second quarter Princeton's All-American quarterback, Dick Kazmaier, left the game with a broken nose. One quarter later a Dartmouth player's leg was broken. Heated words and penalty flags flew back and forth.[1]

After the game, student newspapers on both campuses erupted in outrage.

The *Daily Princetonian* charged: "This observer has never seen quite such a disgusting exhibition of so-called 'sport.' Both teams were guilty, but the blame must be laid primarily on Dartmouth's doorstep." It went on to accuse Dartmouth of "a deliberate attempt to cripple Dick Kazmaier."

The student editors of the *Dartmouth* scoffed: "Kazmaier was the star, an All-American. Other stars have been injured before, but Kazmaier had been built to represent a Princeton idol. When an idol is hurt there is only one recourse – the tag of dirty football." They went on to accuse Princeton's coach of ordering his players to take revenge on Dartmouth's team.

## 1. Even when we watch the same thing, we don't see the same thing

The viewpoints on each campus diverged so widely that a professor at each school agreed to conduct an experiment. They took a film of the game and showed it to students at their university. As students watched the identical film, they were asked to fill in a questionnaire counting the number of rule violations they saw each team commit and characterize each as "mild" or "flagrant."

Although the game took place in broad daylight, following rules of football accepted by both sides and enforced by referees, and both groups of students saw the same action onscreen, the Dartmouth and Princeton students marked their questionnaires very differently. On average, Dartmouth students allocated rule violations evenly between the two teams, while Princeton students "saw" more than twice as many violations by Dartmouth gridders as Princeton players. Each side also regarded the other team's violations as more serious than its own squad's.

The professors concluded that "the 'game' actually was many different games and that each version of the events that transpired was just as 'real' to a particular person as other versions were to other people."[2] In other words, the truth about what happened differed somewhat for each observer. But those observers loyal to Dartmouth green clustered around a different truth than those partial to Princeton orange. The lesson? Our allegiances and associations affect what we see. Notice that this flips the conventional wisdom – "seeing is believing" – on its head. For most of those watching the game film, *believing (in one side or the other) was seeing.*

## 2. We forget that what we see depends on where we are observing from and when; we treat snapshots as if they were panoramic videos

It may seem too obvious to mention, but the fact that we observe from a particular place at a particular time limits our grasp of the whole truth. Our vantage point might not be the best place to see what's going on. And our timing might be off, arriving too early or – as is usually the case with journalists – too late to observe something for ourselves. When that happens, we all rely on sources. But each of those sources suffers the same limitation of a fixed viewpoint at a given time. It's a profound problem for journalism.

Former NBC and MSNBC reporter Ashleigh Banfield explained the limitations of viewpoint experienced by reporters, such as her, who were embedded with American soldiers firing at Saddam Hussein's army in 2003. The coverage, she explained, "certainly did show the American side of things, because that's where we were shooting [video] from." But, she continued:

> You didn't see where those bullets landed. You didn't see what happened when the mortar landed. A puff of smoke is not what a mortar looks like when it explodes, believe me. There are horrors that were completely left out of this war. ...
>
> ... There is a grand difference between journalism and coverage, and getting access does not mean you're getting the story; it just means you're getting one more arm or leg of the story. And that's what we got, and it was a glorious, wonderful picture that had a lot of people watching and a lot of advertisers excited about cable news. But it wasn't journalism.... We got rid of a dictator, we got rid of a monster, but we didn't see what it took to do that.[3]

Ms. Banfield's candor is uncommon in journalism. Executives don't like to reveal how one-sided and time-bound many news reports are.

So three questions we should ask about anyone's description of an event are: *Where were they or their sources watching from? And when? Were they in a position to know what they claim to know? What couldn't they notice from their vantage point?*

## 3. Rather than seeing everything before us, we focus on only a part

Even if we're limited to observing from one spot at any given moment, our five senses take in a great deal of information. More than our brains can handle.[4] So we're forced to focus on a few things rather than the whole panorama.

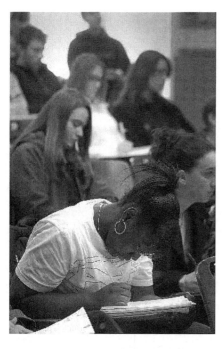

**Image from Wikimedia Commons**

Test this the next time you're in a group of people, perhaps a meeting, class, or religious service. Depending on where you're sitting, within the "screen" of your vision, you may be able to see many people. They may differ from one another in multiple ways: gender, race, ethnicity, body size and shape, clothing, and posture But I'll bet you can't describe the characteristics of each person until you place him/er at the center of your vision. Our vision resembles the focal point of a camera. Our subject is sharply focused, while objects closer and farther away are blurred.

Our other senses are similarly focused. The person who convened the gathering might be speaking loudly, but we can reduce the noise to an incoherent drone as we listen to a friend whisper from the next seat. We notice food smells more before dinner than afterwards. We can eat a sandwich and barely taste it when we're absorbed in a conversation or reading something. We can even turn off our senses and go inside to our imagination or memory.

We might replay a compliment or complaint from a boss or friend, or a passionate moment. And if none of these happened, we can imagine how it would (or should!) have happened. We can be lost in our thoughts and not see or hear the speaker at all. (As a professor, I've stared out at glassy eyes that were pointed my way. But I was only seeing the backs of screens playing an internal movie more compelling than my words.)

Our attention is not like a mirror, capturing everything happening before it. It's more like the narrow beam of a flashlight in the dark, illuminating particular parts of our external environment or the internal landscape of our minds.

So two more questions to ponder are: *What were we or our information-provider paying the most attention to? What might have been missed?*

## 4. We don't just record what's in focus like a camera; as dot-connecting animals we unconsciously select just a fraction of what's in focus and impose meaning

Even when we turn the searchlight of our attention on someone or something, we don't record it the way a camera might. We perceive *selectively* and *imaginatively*. Humans tend to organize the data their senses feed them into patterns. We are dot-connecting animals. Where there is no logical order, we often make one up.

Ancient people would behold a sky bright with stars and "see" a big dipper, a hunter, a bull, a scorpion, or a cross. Believers see the face of a saint in the bark pattern of a tree. When looking at an ink blot, we might see demons or lovers. This happens below the level of our conscious awareness in our automatic thinking mode. If I type a colon then a dash followed by a right parenthesis, you are likely to rotate these three keystrokes 90 degrees, assemble them into a single symbol, and infer ☺ from :-).

The ability to connect dots has obvious evolutionary value. Making connections among pieces of sensory information helped early humans cope with a dangerous environment. Thanks to our automatic mode of thinking, when we experience something, our minds don't dispassionately assemble the data from our eyes, ears, and nose, then logically evaluate it and render a judgment about the reality we face. That would have taken too long to avoid a tribal warrior's hurled spear. We're wired to create a pattern that we can act on in the blink of an eye.

As Malcolm Gladwell described in his book *Blink*, these instant, intuitive patterns remain very helpful. They might alert us to danger by picking up an expression on the face of someone about to attack us. They might cue us to romantic possibilities when we sense someone likes us. They can alert us to fraud when we sense something isn't quite right.

Mr. Gladwell quoted police officers, soldiers, and athletes describing the positive aspects of selective perception. It filters out irrelevant information and sharpens our focus on what we are doing so effectively that time may seem to slow down. He offered this description of a policeman and his partner facing a gunman:

> When he started toward us, it was almost like it was in slow motion and everything went into a tight focus. ... My vision focused on his torso and the gun. I couldn't tell you what his left hand was doing. I have no idea. I didn't hear a thing, not one thing. Alan [his partner] had fired one round when I shot my first pair, but I didn't hear him shoot.[5]

## 5. We are more likely to notice – and seek out – what confirms our expectations than what contradicts them

The selective and imaginative perception of our automatic system of thinking can also get us into trouble. It has at least two known and related biases. First, *it imposes a pattern that's known and familiar on the unknown and unfamiliar.* Second, *it provides a picture more likely to confirm our beliefs (including our prejudices) than to contradict them.*

Experiments have shown that we are more likely to perceive what's familiar to us than what's unfamiliar.[6] So we tend to see something new not as it is, but in terms of something more familiar. When the steam locomotive was new, we called it the "iron horse." The first automobile was a "horseless carriage." The early radio was called a "wireless," because it could receive signals without a telegraph wire. The Internet was introduced as an "information superhighway."

Psychologists say we also notice things that *support* our beliefs more than those that *contradict* them.[7] This is called "confirmatory bias." If we think someone dislikes us, we might notice the person passing on a crowded walkway and perceive a lack of a glance in our direction as a deliberate snub. The person, however, might simply not have seen us. Conversely, if we think someone likes us, we might see a nod under similar circumstances as confirming our belief, even if the nod signals no more than recognition.

Stereotypes often shape these selective perceptions. If we believe women are poorer drivers than men, we notice the woman standing beside the wrecked vehicle on the side of the road, but not the man in similar circumstances. If we believe Islam encourages violence against non-Muslims, we notice the woman at the airport wearing a headscarf, even though no American woman has ever attempted to blow up a plane. If we think African-American men are especially prone to anger and violence we may feel no sympathy for those who protest a white officer's violence against an unarmed black youth. Or we may be surprised when a black leader speaks and acts so calmly he's nicknamed "No Drama Obama."

Historically, stereotypes justified slavery and not so long ago, murderous anti-Semitism and the imprisonment of American citizens of Japanese descent.

This is why stereotypes are so dangerous. They can cause us to misjudge others without even being aware of it. (They can also cause us to devalue *ourselves* when we avoid a challenge because we don't think we're good at something without having given ourselves a fair chance.) So we can add to our questions about our own and other's accounts: *Does it stereotype or discount by gender, race, religion or other type? Whose viewpoints are privileged and whose are marginalized or missing?*

## 6. Bias begins with self-interest, but there are other equally subconscious and predictable layers based on race, class, geography, gender, generation, and other cultural groupings

We have no choice but to make sense of the world from within our own skulls. We are always most aware of our own experience, our own pains and pleasures, our own needs, wants and fears. Evolution has formed us to see the world not as it is, but as it *relates to us*, especially how it might serve or threaten our interests. To survive in a competitive environment humans have had to look out for themselves and their tribe. We are inherently self-interested. This is where bias begins.

Unless we are as empathetic as a Gandhi or Martin Luther King Jr., our concern for, and knowledge of, others falls off rapidly with distance from our own interests. Loving our neighbors as ourselves is a wonderful goal, but almost impossible to achieve. (As for loving strangers, much less our enemies – God help us!)

Our preoccupation with ourselves and those close to us explains why Princeton students saw their varsity classmates performing differently than did Dartmouth students. That's why we identify more easily with those of similar race, class, gender, generation, nationality, religion, or profession and than those who differ from us. It's why men have to be trained to lower the toilet seat. (Where you stand depends on whether you stand or sit!) In addition to misunderstanding, otherness breeds apathy, if not contempt. (What's so difficult about putting the damn seat down?!!)

Don't get me wrong. Self-reliance is a virtue. Though no one can manage it alone, we need to take care of and love ourselves. Moderate self-interest is healthy. But it becomes corrosive when what we do for ourselves harms others. Selfishness is a vice – one we hate to admit.

To maintain our self-esteem even when we are serving our self-interest at others' expense, humans engage in what researchers call "motivated blindness." It's "the tendency to overlook information that works against one's best interest," according to Max H. Bazerman, a professor of business administration at Harvard and Ann E. Tenbrunsel, a professor of management at Notre Dame. They conclude: "Ample research shows that people who have a vested self-interest, even the most honest among us, have difficulty being objective. Worse yet, they fail to recognize their lack of objectivity."[8]

To avoid being fooled, we should examine the predictable, but invisible-to-us, layers of social bias that radiate from our self-interest.

### Social fault lines: Predictable biases in American culture

The late Robert C. Maynard, one of the first African-American reporters at the *Washington Post* and later publisher of the *Oakland Tribune,* had an insight late in his career. The San Francisco Bay Area, where the *Tribune* is located, has a number of earthquake faults. So does society, Mr. Maynard recognized. We are divided, he realized, by subcultures based on race, class, geography, gender, and generation. Much of our misunderstanding of each other, he wrote, arises from these "fault lines." When we peer across one of these fault lines, we might misconstrue what we see because the terrain is not as familiar as it is on our side of the cracks. Or because we've been led to believe certain things about other people and places.[9]

As new media allow us to choose both our facts and opinions, and as we live, work and associate with others like ourselves, these fault lines grow from cracks to chasms. New York University social psychologist Jonathan Haidt observed:

> America has ... become in the post-war world gradually a nation of lifestyle enclaves where people choose to self-segregate. If people are concentrating just where people are like them, then they're not exposed to ideas from the other side from people they can actually like and respect. If you get all your ideas about the other side from the Internet, where there's no human connection, it's just so easy and automatic to reject it and demonize it. So once we've sorted

ourselves into homogeneous moral communities, it becomes a lot harder to work together.[10]

## The fault line of race

The public reaction to the acquittal of O.J. Simpson in 1995 revealed this tear in our social fabric. After a televised, year-long trial and almost obsessive news coverage, the Hall-of-Fame running back was judged not guilty of slashing the throats of his estranged wife and her companion. Two weeks after the Oct. 3 verdict, the Gallup Poll found that 89 percent of black respondents agreed that the jury had made the "right decision," against only 36 percent of whites.[11]

Responding to polar differences in the televised reaction to the verdict between blacks and whites, *New York Times* columnist Anthony Lewis wrote: "We knew we were a divided society. But not before had the depth of that division been so instantly dramatized. It was as if we lived in different countries."[12]

You might think journalists would exhibit a milder version of these divisions; they're always proclaiming themselves "objective," or "fair and balanced." But on the tenth anniversary of the Simpson verdict, NPR's Karen Grigsby Bates asked journalists to recall the day the trial ended:

Judy Muller was in ABC's Los Angeles bureau watching TV monitors as she waited to write a piece on the Simpson verdict that would run on "Nightline." When the verdict was read, Ms. Muller, who is white, remembers that her jaw dropped. "I think the reaction in the newsroom was the same as newsrooms and cafes and diners all across the country. I think the reaction split down racial lines." Other journalists Ms. Bates interviewed responded similarly.[13]

A more recent example concerns Black Lives Matter, the protest movement arising from the police shooting of a young unarmed black man in Ferguson, Missouri in 2014. The Pew Research Center found that 65 percent of black Americans supported BLM, but only 41 percent of whites in a 2016 survey.[14]

We can now ask the following questions: *Is our viewpoint, or the information-provider's, biased by race? Do they quote racially and ethnically diverse sources? Which viewpoints are marginalized or missing?*

### The fault line of class

Have you ever heard someone say, "If you're so damn smart, why aren't you rich?" The saying reflects an article of faith: We Americans tend to believe we live in a classless meritocracy, a country where everyone with talent who makes an effort can land a good job and salary. From this perspective, either the poor lack talent or they are lazy – or both. Any way you slice it, they are seen as inferior to the well-to-do.

But sociologists can provide lots of statistics showing that the American playing field is far from level. The differences in outcomes – such as lifetime accumulation of wealth – can be reliably predicted from differences in inputs, for example, the resources a family can provide for its children.[15] Many were surprised when the Pew Charitable Trust's Economic Mobility Project found Americans are less socially mobile from one generation to the next than Canadians and the citizens of every European nation in the study.[16] We are blind to class bias, yet it alters our perceptions as surely as a magnet bends a line of iron filings.

Sociologists William Thompson and Joseph Hickey wrote:

> It is impossible to understand people's behavior ... without the concept of social stratification, because class position has a pervasive influence on almost everything ... the clothes we wear ... the television shows we watch ... the colors we paint our homes in and the names we give our pets. ... Our position in the social hierarchy affects our health, happiness, and even how long we will live.[17]

We can now ask the following questions: *Is our viewpoint, or the information-provider's, biased by class? Are there sources presenting different class perspectives? Which viewpoints are marginalized or missing?*

### The fault line of geography

The fault line of geography concerns the physical location – nation, region of the country, neighborhood – where we grew up or have lived most of our lives. People who grew up on farms differ in outlook from those who grew up in suburbs, who differ from those who grew up in the inner city. Some in "blue" states would like to secede from "red" states and some in "red" states wouldn't mind if they did.

Geography's impact on reporting can be seen in a study conducted by the Youth Media Council of Oakland, California. The council examined local newspaper coverage of housing issues for three months in 2007. Its report, *Displacing the dream,* shows how differently reporters from mostly middle-class neighborhoods saw housing issues compared to the residents of poor neighborhoods undergoing redevelopment:

> Displacement [of the poor] and gentrification are not portrayed as problems in coverage of housing and development. Instead, housing market issues, including subprime lending and stagnation of the market, were the primary problems raised in coverage. Corporate-driven solutions, including market-rate housing and luxury retail development, overshadowed government- and community-driven solutions, including affordable housing creation and improved social services. The voices of government officials, corporate spokespeople, and other traditional experts dominated over the voices of community advocates and organizers at a rate of six-to-one. Residents appeared in coverage primarily as "scene-setters"... [but not] as experts who voice analysis or solutions.

> Discussion of race and racism was nearly absent from coverage, despite ... statistics showing that San Francisco and Oakland have lost nearly a quarter of their African-American populations in the past five years. [18]

The YMC study illustrates how fault lines can overlap. Divisions based on race, class, and geography frequently reinforce each other.

Geographic biases *within* a nation, however, pale when compared to biases arising *between* nations. That's because every nation has a unique culture: a set of shared symbols, history, myths, language (or at least accent and idioms, mate!), and assumptions about how the world does, and should, operate. Americans, Germans, Chinese, Nigerians, Egyptians, and Brazilians all see the world somewhat differently from each other. (And, of course, all see it differently than the French!)

The nationality fault line is the most important one to take into account when the press interprets world affairs for American audiences. And news from abroad grows ever more consequential as the nation becomes more *inter*dependent on others with the exponential growth of world trade, finance, communication, and travel.[19]

Nowhere is the fault line of nationality wider and deeper than in coverage of war. Despite the First Amendment's specific protection of press freedom, throughout our history government officials have censored dispatches from the front and substituted propaganda. Editors and correspondents have often been happy to go along, mistaking – or more likely, masking – jingoism with patriotism.[20] Even the most professional journalist embedded with soldiers is likely to be swayed, if not by simple camaraderie, by dependence on them for his/er safety. And how about us? Don't we in the audience *want* to hear of valor and victory even though we *need* to know exactly what's going on, including pain and shame.

Coverage of important U.S. allies is also likely to reflect partisan bias when they are in conflict with non-allied nations. The Israeli-Palestinian struggle stands out, perhaps because nationalistic biases are reinforced by ethnic and religious affiliations. Grade the News (a project I directed that reported on news quality in the San Francisco Bay Area) analyzed front-page coverage of the conflict in the *San Jose Mercury News* for six months from April 1 to Sept. 30, 2002. We found that an Israeli death was 11 times more likely to make a front-page headline in San Jose than a Palestinian fatality.[21]

The priority given to Israeli suffering in front-page headlines was reinforced throughout the stories by the order in which casualties were described, and first-person accounts of Israeli deaths contrasted with second-hand and approximate estimates of

Palestinian fatalities. We also noticed that Palestinian forces were consistently labeled as "gunmen" and "militants" – terms with negative connotations in our culture – but rarely as "fighters" and never as "resistance forces," despite references to Palestinian cities as "the occupied territories."[22] (I consider the designation of "terrorist" for those who target civilians appropriate, but it also applies to states when they target non-combatants or kill indiscriminately.)

During the same period, we also monitored headlines of Middle East stories moved by the Associated Press, which most American newspapers relied on to cover the conflict. In its headlines, Israeli deaths were twice as likely to be mentioned as Palestinian ones.

Marda Dunsky, a professor at Northwestern University's Medill School of Journalism, illuminated the disparity in a book, *Pens and swords: How the American mainstream media report the Israeli-Palestinian conflict*. In her view, neutral standards of news judgment are sometimes trumped by three factors. First, Americans tend to identify with Israel and Israelis more than with Arab nations and Palestinians. Israel is a frequent travel destination for Americans, especially Jews and Christians who consider it the Holy Land. Second, she said, Israel comes closer to democratic ideals than Arab nations. Third, because American foreign policy treats Israel as a special ally, Americans tend to as well.

Cultural ties between Americans and Israelis can also affect the language choices reporters make, according to Dr. Dunsky. The name of the Palestinian group HAMAS is an acronym, she explained. The M stands for a word that translates to mean "resistance." Yet Palestinian fighters are almost never referred to as "the resistance."

Elise Ackerman, who covered the Israeli-Palestinian conflict for the *Mercury News* before the study period, elaborated on what she now considers her cross-cultural blindness:

> I couldn't believe that I hadn't used the term 'resistance' in my stories. There's been a resistance throughout the Arab world. It's a resistance to colonizers. I think that whole idea is missing from the coverage of the Palestinian conflict, because there is a resistance of Americans and Israelis to

see the Israelis as colonizers, and that creates a problem with the use of the term.

I do know in hindsight that the Palestinians do see this as resistance. The translator may not have provided the nuances. In hindsight I think I did really get lost.[23]

The fault line of geography helps us inquire whether a story might have been told quite differently by someone from a different place, especially a different nation. We can ask, *Is our viewpoint, or the information-provider's, biased by geography? Are there sources quoted presenting different perspectives based on where people live? Which viewpoints are marginalized or missing?*

### The fault line of gender

If you've ever banged your head against the wall after talking to a colleague or family-member of the opposite sex, you've already stumbled over this fault line. The linguist Deborah Tannen says the differences in the way men and women use language are so great it's cross-cultural, as if an American were speaking with a Japanese.[24]

"Nowhere," Professor Tannen wrote, "is the conflict between femininity and authority more crucial than with women in politics. If a man appears forceful, logical, direct, masterful, and powerful, he enhances his value as a man." If a woman embodies these characteristics, "she risks undercutting her value as a woman."[25]

Gender exerts bias not just in differences in content, but in which topics are considered newsworthy. Domestic and intimate partner violence, for example, has been a more frequent news story as women have increased their numbers and clout in newsrooms. Kim Barker, a reporter for the investigative journalism Website *Pro Publica,* noted that women reporters "do a pretty good job of covering what it's like to live in a war zone, not just die in one." She wrote:

Without female correspondents in war zones, the experiences of women there may be only a rumor. Look at the articles about women who set themselves on fire in Afghanistan to protest their arranged marriages, or about girls being maimed by fundamentalists, about child marriage in India, about rape in Congo and Haiti. Female journalists often tell those stories in the most compelling ways, because abused women are sometimes more comfortable talking to them. And those stories are at least as important as accounts of battles."[26]

So the fault line of gender prompts us to ask, *Is our viewpoint, or the information-provider's, biased by gender? Does their information discount, stereotype, patronize, or belittle women, or men? Do the sources they reference differ by gender? Which viewpoints are marginalized or missing?*

### The fault line of generation

Every generation seems to consider the one before, and eventually the one after, as less informed or at least less sophisticated than itself. (Are you woke?)

The news media seem very aware of generational stereotypes: the selfless "greatest generation," the self-absorbed "baby boomers," "Gen X," "Gen Y," "Millennials," even "Gen Next." Generalizations about such age groupings are often applied to everyone within them, despite great individual differences. *New York* Times technology columnist Farhad Manjoo noted:

> One of the primary functions of the media these days is to traffic in gleefully broad generalizations and criticisms of millennials, the more than 75 million Americans born about 1980 to 2000. Although millennials are now the largest demographic group in the country (sorry, boomers), and though they are more racially diverse than any other generation in American history, they are often depicted on TV, in movies and music, and in the news (including *The New York Times*) as a collectively homogeneous cliché.[27]

The most common generational bias, however, is ageism, the tendency to discount the importance of young people's or old people's points of view.

The fault line of generation encourages us to ask, *Is our viewpoint, or the information-provider's, biased by age? Does their report discount or stereotype the young or old? Do the sources differ by generation? Whose viewpoints are privileged and whose discounted or ignored?*

### The fault lines of other group cultures

I would add a sixth catchall category of perception-benders – group cultures. Political parties, religions, ethnic identities, even professions, exercise a gravitational pull toward group-think – a condition in which those within a group echo and thereby reinforce an interpretation of reality common to the group.

"We tend to be extremely tribal. We tend to like to cohere into groups. And we like perfect group loyalty."[28]

~ *New York Times* columnist David Brooks

In *#republic*, Harvard Law School Professor Cass Sunstein wrote: "Over the last generation, the United States has seen an explosion in 'partyism' – a kind of visceral, automatic dislike of people of the opposing political party." He cited surveys showing that in 1960 just 5 percent of Republicans and 4 percent of Democrats would be "displeased" if their child married someone from the opposite party. By 2010, cross-party antipathy had grown to 49 and 33 percent respectively, more than said they disfavor marriage to a partner of another race.[29] (Some of my Southern conservative friends refer to me as a "Democrap" and a "libtard.")

At the University of California at Berkeley, *the birthplace of the campus free speech movement*, protesters blocked a public speech by a provocative conservative, Milo Yiannopoulos, in early 2017, and then vandalized university property.

Even social scientists suffer tribalism. NYU Professor Haidt described bias in his own community of supposedly objective social psychologists: "If a group circles around sacred values, they will evolve into a tribal-moral community. They'll embrace science whenever it supports their sacred values, but they'll ditch it or distort it as soon as it threatens a sacred value." Dr. Haidt noted that it's easy for social scientists to observe this process in *other* communities, such as fundamentalist Christians who reject evolution in favor of "intelligent design." But academics do the same thing, as Harvard sociologist Daniel Patrick Moynihan found in 1965 when he warned about the rise of unmarried parenthood and welfare dependency among blacks – violating the taboo against criticizing victims of racism.[30]

This fault line encourages us to ask: *Is our viewpoint, or the information-provider's, biased by cultural groupings? Does the news report discount or stereotype cultural out-groups as inferior or even as enemies? Do the sources differ by cultural group? Which groups' viewpoints are privileged and which are discounted or missing, even when the story concerns them?*

Robert Maynard's insights about social fault lines make a compelling case for diversity both of sources quoted in news and among journalists themselves.

Most of the layers of bias outlined in this chapter have been *personal* – belonging to us and those who inform us. In the next chapter we'll examine an even more powerful type of bias – the self-interest of the *institution* providing news or information.

---

### Exercises and Discussion Topics

1. Describe an event that you saw very differently from someone with an allegiance to a group other than your own – perhaps a different college, fraternity, major, or pick-up sports team. Alternately, go online and compare how your college newspaper described a sports contest with another college with the account in that school's student paper. Where did they agree and where differ?

2. Describe an event you saw differently from someone else because you were watching from a different vantage point.

3. When you are in a cafeteria or other gathering place, look at one person and without moving your head or your eyes, see how many people you can accurately describe around that person (by gender, dress, etc.) Next, move your eyes, but not your head. Did the number of accurate descriptions rise significantly?

4. Go online to a news website and pick out a story describing an event in the first screen that interests you. Read/watch the story and note where the reporter focused his/er attention. What else might

the reporter have seen at the event but didn't report on? Use your imagination. Were there questions you feel the reporter should have asked, but apparently didn't because of the angle or focus of the story? List the most significant.

5. Describe a situation that wasn't what you first took it for. Which elements of that situation did you connect into a false interpretation? What misled or threw you off? Alternately, perform the same analysis for a person rather than a situation.

6. Have you experienced differences across race, class, gender, geography, generation or culture between your view of some issue or event and the view of a person on the other side of one or more of these fault lines? If so, describe the fault line and how your views differed.

8. Identify news stories from any medium in which there appears to be a bias based on one or more fault lines. Tell why you think so.

## End Notes

[1] Albert H. Hastorf and Hadley Cantril (1971, original 1954) "They saw a game: A case study," in Wilbur F. Schramm and Donald F. Roberts, Eds. *The process and effects of mass communication*, second edition, Urbana, IL: University of Illinois Press, pp. 300-312.

[2] Hastorf and Cantril, p. 308.

[3] Ashleigh Banfield (4/29/2003) "MSNBC's Banfield slams war coverage," Alternet, online at: http://www.alternet.org/story/15778.

[4] Robert Ornstein (2008) *MindReal: How the mind creates its own virtual reality,* Boston: Malor Books. Dr. Ornstein is a cognitive scientist at Stanford University.

[5] Malcolm Gladwell (2005) *Blink*, New York: Little, Brown and Company, p. 223.

[6] Jack Glaser (2007) "The social psychology of intergroup bias, summary of concepts and research," online at: http://calswec. berkeley.edu/calswec/ 2007_FE_SocialPsychPrejudice.pdf. Dr. Glaser is a professor at the Goldman School of Public Policy, University of California, Berkeley.

[7] Max H. Bazerman and Ann E. Tenbrunsel (2011) *Blind spots: why we fail to do what's right and what to do about it,* Princeton, NJ: Princeton University Press.

[8] Max H. Bazerman and Ann E. Tenbrunsel (4/21/2011) "Stumbling into bad behavior," *New York Times*, op-ed, p. A21, online at: http://www.nytimes.com/2011/04/21/opinion/21bazerman.html?_r=1&scp=1&sq= percent22 Stumbling percent20into percent20bad percent20behavior percent22&st=cse.

Even scientists – those paragons of dispassionate rationality – have to guard against the power of self-interest to distort their perceptions. To be published in a scientific journal, research must be vetted by peers. In many journals, those who fund the research now must be named as a hedge against unconscious or willful tailoring of results to please sponsors. To be accepted as knowledge, studies must be replicated by others. So powerful and subconscious is the influence of self-interest, medical science has adopted as its gold standard "double-blind" experiments in which not even the researchers know which pill is the placebo and which the actual medicine until the study is complete.

[9] Robert Maynard's daughter, Dori, carried on his work at the Maynard Institute for Education in Journalism in Oakland. In 2006 she held a question and answer session with editors to explain fault lines analysis. See: http://www.editteach.org/special/editingthefuture/06_ Maynard/video01.htm.

[10] Bill Moyers (2/3/2012) "How do conservatives and liberals see the world?" interview with Jonathan Haidt, "Moyers and Company," Public Affairs Television Inc., available online at: http://billmoyers.com /episode/how-do-conservatives-and-liberals-see-the-world/. Prof. Haidt's book, *The Righteous Mind: Why Good People are Divided by Politics and Religion* (2012), became a *New York Times* bestseller. He was named one of the "top global thinkers" by *Foreign Policy* magazine,

[11] George Gallup, Ed. (1998) *The Gallup Poll: Public Opinion, 1997*, Lanham, MD: Rowman and Littlefield Publishing Group; available online at: http://books.google.com/books?id=fLGQKjdXJCs C&pg=PA23&lpg=PA23&dq= percent22oj+simpson percent22+and+public+reaction+of+blacks+and+whites&source=web&ots=jmNzrZcsEq&sig=VAi0XxF3oPt0lfuyN6IAH9nem Sw#PPA22,M1.

[12] Anthony Lewis (10/6/1995) "Abroad at home; an American dilemma," *New York Times*; available online at: http://query.nytimes.com/gst/fullpage.html?res=9A0DE4DE1239F935A35753C1A963958260.

[13] Karen Grigsby Bates (10/3/2005) "The O.J. Simpson Verdict, Race and the Media," on Day to Day, National Public Radio; available online at: http://www.npr.org/templates/story/story.php?storyId=4934067.

[14] Juliana Menasce Horowitz and Gretchen Livingston (7/8/2016) "How Americans view Black Lives Matter movement," http://www.pewresearch.org/fact-tank/2016/07/08/how-americans-view-the-black-lives-matter-movement/.

[15] Dennis Gilbert (1998). *The American class structure*, New York: Wadsworth Publishing.

[16] Pew Charitable Trusts Economic Mobility Project (11/2011) "Does America promote mobility as well as other nations?" available online at: http://www.economicmobility.org/reports_and_research/other?id=0017.

[17] William Thompson and Joseph Hickey (2005) *Society in focus*, Boston: Pearson.

[18] Youth Media Council (since renamed the Center for Media Justice) (2007) "Displacing the dream," online at http://www.datacenter. org /displacing-the-dream/. Also at: http://209.85.173.104/search?q= cache :XtmxU8OQHz UJ:cmj.centerformediajustice.org/documents/download/61+ percent 22Displacing+the+Dream percent22&hl=en&ct=clnk&cd=3&gl=us.

[19] Just look at the labels in your clothes, on the back of your computer, or on the frame of your car. Or count the number of nations in the world where U.S. soldiers are garrisoned. Or listen to the accent of the technical support person who assists you by telephone.

[20] Phillip Knightly (1975) *The first casualty: From the Crimea to Vietnam – the war correspondent as hero, propagandist and myth maker,* New York: Harcourt Brace Jovanovich.

[21] John H. McManus (12/18/2003) "The newsworthiness of death," GradeTheNews.org, online at: http://www.gradethenews.org/pages/middleeast.htm.

[22] Some news organizations, notably National Public Radio, have largely discarded the term "occupied territories" in favor of "West Bank," a change that eliminates the moral stigma of military occupation.

[23] McManus, cited above. Both the Ackerman and Dunsky interviews were included in "The newsworthiness of death," cited above.

[24] Deborah Tannen (1990) *You just don't understand: Women and men in conversation*, New York: Ballantine Books, pp. 24-25. In the 1980s feminist scholars such as Carol Gilligan showed that research on moral development and ethics based entirely on male subjects was misleading and incomplete because

of gender differences. See, for example, Professor Gilligan's path-breaking 1982 book *In a different voice*, Cambridge, MA: Harvard University Press.

[25] Tannen, p. 241.

[26] Kim Barker (2/20/2011) "Why we need women in war zones," *New York Times*, Week in Review, p. 11.

[27] Farhad Manjoo (5/26/2016) *New York Times*, "Corporate America Chases the Mythical Millennial," p. B1, online at: http://www. nytimes .com/2016 /05/26/technology/corporate-america-chases-the-mythical-millennial.html.

[28] Michael Krasny (3/23/2011)Forum, KQED-FM, interview with David Brooks about his 2011 book *The social animal: The hidden sources of love, character, and achievement,* New York: Random House.

[29] Cass R. Sunstein (2017) *#republic*, Princeton, NJ: Princeton University Press, p. 10.

[30] John Tierney (2/7/2011) "Social scientist sees bias within," *New York Times*, p. D1, online at: http://www.nytimes.com/2011/02/ 08/ science /08tier.html?scp=1&sq= percent22liberal percent20bias percent22&st= cse.

# 5

# The Covert Bias of Institutions

*The press ... is caught between its desire to please and extend its audience and its desire to give a picture of events and people as they really are.*

~ The Commission on Freedom of the Press[1]

When I was a young journalist I worked for a newspaper in the red-clay foothills of western South Carolina – cotton mill country in the mid-1970s. At one end of the mill, walnut-sized cotton balls were separated from their dried husks and combed into thread that was then woven by hundreds of clanking looms into the towels and sheets that probably graced your parents' home. The air was hot, humid, and thick with dust and lint. It settled on the looms like a downy coat, making them look like frantic birds. It nestled in the hair of the workers, who were sometimes derided as "lint heads."

Over years, the finer particles of cotton dust accumulated in workers' lungs causing in many a disease called "brown lung" – more formally, byssinosis – that shortened the breath and lives of millworkers. Consulting the Occupational Safety and Health Administration, OSHA, I discovered that not a single mill in the region my newspaper served was even close to healthy air quality standards. But none were penalized as South Carolina had only one lawyer working part-time enforcing OSHA standards. It seemed like a pretty important story. Indeed, it won the coveted Pulitzer Prize for Public Service in 1981.

But I didn't get to write the prize-winning stories. My first investigative article was my last. The editor who put it on the front page was fired the following week.

The publisher never said why he killed the series. But textile manufacturing was the dominant local industry, employing almost 400,000 people in the piedmont of the two Carolinas. If a newspaper made a public issue of unhealthy mills, OSHA might demand a healthy factory environment. Many of the once-stream-powered red-brick mills of the South were old. The cost of cleaning them up might have exceeded the cost of abandoning them for modern mills constructed beyond the U.S. border, where labor was even cheaper and health regulations even less binding. Major textile companies were already planning to abandon the Carolinas for foreign sites. But local business leaders hoped to avoid the loss of so many jobs and their aggregate purchasing power. High unemployment would have reduced my newspaper's advertising revenue. Exposing the health risk to so many workers might have been a life and breath story, but it put the paper's considerable profits at risk. Fortunately, a more socially responsible newspaper, the *Charlotte* (N.C.) *Observer*, picked up the story, conducted an extensive investigation and won the Pulitzer Prize and a trophy case of other awards.[2]

There are two lessons here. Information-providers often face a conflict between their self-interest and the public interest. But not all put private profit ahead of public service.

The institutions – governments, non-profits, corporations, and especially news media – that produce most of what we know about current events[3] can mute but not moot most of the *individual* prejudices described in chapter 4 by employing a sufficiently diverse and collaborative staff. But institutions exert their own overarching self-interest, which can be imposed on the behavior of their employees. Particularly for profit-seeking institutions, their short-term self-interest *conflicts* more than *coincides* with serving the common good. Most media corporations seek to maximize profit rather than maximizing public understanding of those current issues and events with the greatest impact on the community served – the definition of socially responsible journalism.[4]

Companies offering shares on the stock market are legally *required* to optimize value for their investors. Privately held media firms – and those with protected classes of voting stock, such as the *New York Times* – enjoy greater flexibility, but *all* institutions look out for themselves. Government agencies, even non-profit organizations, are focused, if not on growth, on their own survival. An institution eager to put itself out of business is as rare as an exterminator who would welcome the extinction of termites.

Institutional information-providers – just like individuals – are loath to admit any conflict between their own self-interest and the audience's interest in obtaining truth, the whole truth and nothing but the truth. Imagine my paper's publisher saying, "We're censoring a story about workplaces that damage the health of thousands of readers in order to protect our extraordinary profits – and my bonus." Such candor would erode public trust. News media that lose their credibility risk losing their audience. So they are forever boasting that they report "objectively," "without fear or favor" or that they are "fair and balanced."[5]

The same conflict applies to advertisers. Commercials are most persuasive when they appear to be purely informational. And to PR; to be believed, press agents present themselves as honest information brokers.

"The language of advertising and public relations is meant to seduce you into buying or believing something."[6]

Steve Inskeep, host of NPR's Morning Edition

No one should be surprised that job #1 for advertisers is to boost sales rather than accurate public knowledge of goods and services, or candidates for office. Nor should it come as a shock that public relations practitioners are advocates paid to make their clients look as good as plausible, not to be impartial fact-finders. When processing ads or PR, our skepticism shields should be set close to 100 percent. We expect more of our news sources. To see how high we should raise our shields for any particular news provider, we'll explore three propositions:

1. **From the *New York Times* to Fox News to NPR, every organization providing news or information suffers from a conflict of interest.**

2. **Market forces encourage commercial bias – subordinating the public interest to maximizing private profit. It's expressed primarily in four ways: (1) pandering to the audience's prejudices or whimsy; (2) displacing substance with sensation; (3) shaping content to suit advertisers or major investors; and (4) letting corporate and government publicists set the news agenda or supply its content.**

3. **Because it's more common and covert than political bias, commercial bias represents the graver threat to democracy.**

Because commercial bias is a taboo subject in American journalism, even in parts of the news literacy movement,[7] it's helpful to begin with some insights from communication theory and microeconomics.

### All communication is based on an exchange

We rarely think of personal communication in economic terms. But when we provide others with news or information face-to-face or at a digital water cooler such as Facebook, whether we're aware of it or not, we are participating in an *exchange*. We provide information we think will interest them. In return, we receive their attention (which humans always crave) and the chance to influence them with what we say, write or share. No money changes hands, but they "pay" attention. So we're getting something increasingly scarce and valuable. Like all voluntary exchanges, neither party would engage if they didn't believe something were in it for them.

In addition to this beneficial side of such exchanges, there can be a downside because most of the time each party is seeking its own ends, not altruistically satisfying the other's needs. While our audience may wish to know the truth in order to make the best decisions, more often than we care to admit, we exaggerate or embellish or selectively inform or flatter. Or worse. In a word, we often try to manipulate our audience, even if only to get and keep their attention.

To see how your self-interest can interfere with factual communication, try this thought experiment: Let's say you're married or living with a romantic partner. Now imagine you're at a party without your main squeeze and an attractive stranger strikes up a conversation. Sensing interest in a relationship, do you alert them to your existing partnership – something they would clearly want to know – or do you kindle the sparks of a flirtation? You may have no intention of starting a fire, but who doesn't want to feel attractive?

Or a police officer pulls you over and asks how fast you were going? Or how much you've been drinking? Or your sweetie pie asks, "Have I gained some weight?" Honesty may be the best policy, but it can cost you. If we're honest with ourselves – perhaps the most painful place in which to recognize truth – we often let our self-interest influence our communications with others.

So do institutions.

## 1. Every organization providing news or information suffers from a conflict of interest

Unlike the exchange between two persons, other unseen parties exert a powerful influence on communication between an institution and members of an audience.

To begin with, a news organization must answer not to a single person, but compete for a *mass* audience in a marketplace. They vie for our attention not just with other news-providers, but with *every other use of our time* – entertainment, work, family, even sleep. Next, commercial media, the dominant type in American journalism, must follow priorities set and enforced not by journalists or professional communicators, but by profit-seeking owners or a board of directors running a corporation competing in a market for investors. (If you think investors don't matter, consider how a single investment manager, Bruce Sherman, vaporized Knight Ridder, then the nation's highest quality newspaper chain.[8]) And because most media still rely on advertisers for a substantial part of their revenue, they compete for the favor of retailers. Finally, every news-provider from the neighborhood blogger to Gannett, the nation's largest newspaper chain, must compete for access to sources of information – those who supply the raw material for the production of news. Together audiences, owners, advertisers and sources influence the news by creating overlapping market pressures.

Am I overlooking individual journalists? After all, they conduct the reporting, take the pictures, and produce the content. What becomes news must pass through their eyes, ears and – one hopes – brains. That does give them a say. But despite their longing for independent professional status, journalists are much more decision-takers than decision-makers.[9] They are cooks, not chefs – employees who do what they're told or risk their jobs. In *Media Ethics*, Professor Conrad Fink gives journalists this blunt advice: "Either you and the hand that feeds you agree on ethics in reporting and writing, or you (not your editor) will be a very unhappy employee – or unemployed."[10]

Thus the news, which seems like the creation of a single journalist, is really an elaborate compromise.[11] It's a bit like a puppet being pulled simultaneously by four puppeteers. Owners, through managers, hold the thickest string, followed by advertisers, sources, and the mass audience. The slack in the strings constitutes the journalist's autonomy.

From each of these four markets a conflict arises between the public interest and the self-interest of the news-provider:[12]

• Rational **owners** seeking to maximize profit should produce whatever content generates the largest audience attractive to advertisers at the lowest cost. But often the information most essential to the public interest is expensive to gather (e.g. investigative reporting). It may offend major employers (such as the textile industry), advertisers, or sources (if their faults are publicized) or alienate some segments of the audience (if it punctures popular myths, threatens a major industry, or exposes a popular leader's flaws). Further, entertaining information often generates more bang for the buck than serious news. News organizations run by or seeking funding from liberal or conservative investors should slant the news to please them, rather than providing the public a more accurate representation of reality. Socially responsible journalism, which maximizes public understanding, tends to *diminish* returns – of cash or partisan political influence.[13]

• Rational **advertisers** seek the largest audience of *potential customers* at the least cost, in a neutral – or better, a favorable context – one that uncritically excites interest in acquiring those goods and services on offer. Political advertisers follow similar logic in selling candidates.

Audiences with money to spend, particularly those in the peak buying ages from 18 to 54, are the most likely to become customers. For political ad buyers, customers are persuadable likely voters. Advertisers pay a premium for their eyeballs. But the common good is not advanced by selecting news designed to appeal primarily to the demographic segments of the community that advertisers value most. News ought to be more than bait.

Democracies require information that's responsive to the information needs of *all* citizens in the community, regardless of customer potential. Nor is the public interest served by content designed to stoke interest in advertised goods, services, or a particular candidate for office. Rather, the public requires trustworthy information about those people, issues and events most powerfully shaping its environment. Such news rarely addresses the thrill of home improvement, dining out, visiting the theater, owning a wall-sized TV, the newest smart phone, or a sporty SUV. It neither demonizes nor canonizes one political side. Content tailored to honestly answer the entire community's questions about current events, rather than to attract the most advertising dollars, generates lower rates of profit.

You might think the influence of advertisers would be waning as they abandon news as a bridge to customers. But the scarcity of ad dollars and the lack of alternative streams of revenue has had the opposite effect. Desperate to hold onto advertising, news media have become more accommodating. In recent years, "native advertising," news-like articles produced by a news organization's journalists, but sponsored by an advertiser and – usually subtly – designed to sell has appeared in news organizations across the land, even the august *New York Times.*

• Rational **sources** – from athletes to business execs to politicians and officials – reward news media that they believe portray them fairly – i.e. uncritically – with scoops and access.[14] (Sources who relish critical coverage are as common as vegetarian sharks.) Sources punish those whom they perceive as unfair by denying or delaying access. They may not return phone calls. When news-providers serve the public interest by holding the powerful to account, they may be making it more effortful – and therefore expensive – to gather news.

• The **audience:** You and I, dear reader, may *not* be paragons of rational self-interest. We may favor softer, simpler stories over more substantive content. Who is not tempted by titillation? Immune from the allure of emotion-drenched tales of violent crime? Unfazed by celebrity? Unexcited by conflict. Unmoved by stories aimed like Cupid's bow at our heartstrings, but bypassing our brains? Who has no fears that can be exploited? Likewise, who applauds coverage of *our* side's faults? Who does not exult at coverage of *their* side's failures? Who favors complexity and nuance over simplicity and brevity? Who has the time and idealism to keep up with news of civic import when we each have only a single vote, one say in thousands at the most local level and in a hundred million at the national? Who needs the trouble? You and I may make it more profitable to provide the news we *want* – or are encouraged to want – than the news we *need.*

Even *non-commercial* news-providers, such as National Public Radio, face three of these market influences. Liberation from the unrelenting pressure to earn the rising profits investors covet is no small thing. But non-profits must more than break even to expand or ensure their future. For that they rely significantly on advertisers (whom they call underwriters). Those advertisers pay based on how many potential customers are attracted to the content, just as they do for profit-seeking news media. Non-profits must also attract a mass of users willing to donate, just as for-profit media seek subscribers. And non-profits face pressure to report delicately about the interests of those who can write big checks, just as for-profits worry about offending major advertisers or investors. Like all journalists, those working for non-profits also rely on access to news-making sources. Regardless of employer, a journalist can only be as good as his/er sources.

> "We need to run our businesses like businesses, even if our goal is public service rather than profitability."[15]
>
> ~ John Thornton, chairman of the *Texas Tribune*, an online non-profit news organization specializing in covering state politics

Some news organizations surrender to these market forces. Most compromise. Some resist. But none can ignore their demands. Nor can we, if we hope to avoid being fooled.

2. Market forces encourage commercial bias – subordinating the public interest to maximizing private profit. It's expressed primarily in four ways:

- Pandering to audience prejudices and whimsy

- Displacing substance with sensation

- Shaping content to suit advertisers or major investors

- Letting corporate and government publicists set the news agenda or supply its content

"It is these forces of commercialism which now provide the greatest obstacle to truth-telling journalism."[16]

~ British journalist Nick Davies, author of *Flat Earth News*

Think of news media as society's headlights. They can't smooth a bumpy road, but they can help us steer around obstacles and avoid plunging off a cliff. That is, if they are bright and aimed at the path ahead. Commercial bias dims the lights so we can't make out ruinous practices on Wall Street before the world's economy crashes, or see through a demagogue's empty promises. Commercial bias also directs the spotlight of public attention *away* from the road, perhaps to illuminate a couple necking in the woods or young men playing with a ball, or it shines in our eyes, on our own sense of grievance and resentment, blinding us.

## Pandering to prejudice and whimsy

The quote at the top of this chapter from the Commission on Freedom of the Press refers to first type of commercial bias in news – slanting the news to maximize audience rather than public understanding. Writing in 1947, the Commission noted that "People seldom want to read or hear about what does not please them; they seldom want others to read or hear about what disagrees with their convictions or what presents an unfavorable picture of groups they belong to."[17] This creates financial pressure to pander to public prejudices rather than challenge them, to turn heads rather than fill them.

The most common and enduring pandering to audience biases is probably geographic. Stories about how lucky local residents are to live in a modern Eden ( as superior to others as Springfield is to Shelbyville). Such puffery is relatively harmless. That's not the case, however, when media play to hurtful prejudices – to our dark side.

A half century ago this destructive type of commercial bias was evident when most newspapers and television stations in the former Confederate states during the struggle for civil rights portrayed African-Americans' campaign for equality as lawless or worse, when they reported on it at all.[18]

From 9/11/2001 to March, 2003 many news outlets, including some of the most prestigious, avoided critical coverage of the Bush administration's case for invading Iraq. The strategy prevented any accusations of being unpatriotic and thus risking loss of audience. In his 2008 memoir, Scott McClellan, the White House press secretary at the time, called the media "complicit enablers" in the administration's effort to sell the war.[19] The Fox News Channel went so far as to brand all of its coverage of the invasion with the logo "Operation Iraqi Freedom," using the Bush administration's partisan label rather than maintaining the independent stance required in codes of journalism ethics.

Despite deep reservations about Donald Trump's candidacy, news media cashed in on him in 2016.

> "It may not be good for America, but it's damn good for CBS. I've never seen anything like this, and this going to be a very good year for us. Sorry. It's a terrible thing to say. But, bring it on, Donald. Keep going." [20]
>
> ~Leslie Moonves, CBS executive chairman

As the head of CBS explained, the sheer unconventionality of Mr. Trump and his provocative daily tweets made him catnip for news executives hell-bent on ratings. He combined the allure of celebrity – thanks to his hit TV show, The Apprentice – with the legitimate news value of consequence, by virtue of running for the most important job in the land. In the primaries of 2015 into the presidential campaigns of 2016, many news media – especially on cable TV and online – couldn't get enough of Donald J. Trump. And neither could we. He thrilled his supporters and made politics into a spectacle. Even his detractors couldn't take their eyes off him.

Both cable and broadcast networks saw their audience and profits soar.[21] The *Washington Post* reported:

> Trump, in particular, seems to have been a magnet for attracting viewers. The first Republican debate in August of 2015, carried by Fox, attracted 24 million viewers, the most ever for an event during the primaries. That was bookended by the first presidential debate featuring Trump and Clinton in late September, which attracted 84 million viewers, a record audience for such an event.
>
> In between, the networks have larded their airwaves with copious coverage of Trump's rallies and events, leading to criticism that all the attention propelled Trump to the Republican nomination.[22]

MediaQuant estimated that by the end of February, 2016, Mr. Trump had received news and commentary about his campaign on television, in newspapers and magazines, and on social media worth nearly $2 billion if it were paid advertising. That was almost nine times the amount of coverage the Republican front runner at the beginning of the party primary, Jeb Bush, received. And it dwarfed Mr. Bush's paid advertising, even though Mr. Bush spent far more than any other candidate in either primary. Mr. Trump's coverage was worth six times more than his closest Republican rival, Senator Ted Cruz. And Mr. Trump received two and a half times more coverage than Ms. Clinton.[23] News coverage can be more valuable than ads because it's more credible.

"Trump couldn't compete with the likes of Ted Cruz, Marco Rubio, or Jeb Bush on the basis of his political standing or following. The politics of outrage was his edge, and the press became his dependable if unwitting ally."[24]

~ Thomas E. Patterson, Shorenstein Center on Media, Politics, and Public Policy, Harvard University

Such a massive advantage in exposure gave Mr. Trump an early edge in the primaries, according to Prof. Patterson. People became familiar with his broad promises to "make America great again" and witnessed the enthusiasm at his rallies. But they heard too little about most of his 16 competitors to form an opinion. Rather than vetting all 17 candidates' records and policy proposals, most of the media followed Mr. Trump – all the way to the bank.

In the final months of the presidential campaign against Mrs. Clinton, coverage of Mr. Trump in elite media such as the *New York Times* and *Washington Post* was quite critical, but Mr. Trump's relentless attacks on professional journalism appear to have inoculated him among his supporters. As he boasted, "I could stand in the middle of 5th Avenue and shoot somebody and I wouldn't lose voters."[25]

### Why pandering is a growing problem

Two recent developments made pandering more prevalent. First, technology has enormously expanded the news and information marketplace by nearly eliminating barriers to entering the news business. Second, the more society separates across the liberal-conservative divide, the greater the demand for narrowly ideological news.

Before the mid-1990s, when there were only four national TV networks, leaning to one side or another of the political spectrum would have made little economic sense. A conservative or liberal slant would have alienated too many viewers. With many more channels, radio was a more natural home for partisanship. Now, thanks to cable and satellite TV as well as video on the Web, which anyone with a smart phone can produce, the market for national news and commentary is crowded. Such markets favor niche programming. A network like Fox can gather more audience by owning the allegiance of conservatives than by competing with CNN, ABC, NBC, CBS, PBS, and video on the websites of the *New York Times*, the *Washington Post* and others for an increasingly small slice of the middle of the political spectrum. Online, the *Huffington Post* appears to be using the same niche strategy on the left; Breitbart on the right.[26]

News critics who used to decry the beige sameness of news reports in the era of media monopoly, now worry about how starkly reports of the same event clash depending on which side of the ideological divide they fall in today's crowded, fiercely competitive market.

The mutually reinforcing combination of new technology and societal polarization has made ideological news and commentary profitable. The ranks of the panderers have expanded, exemplified by talk radio/multimedia personalities such as Alex Jones, Rush Limbaugh, Glenn Beck, Laura Ingraham, Ann Coulter, and digital newcomers such as Mike Cernovich (Danger and Play) and Jim Hoft (Gateway Pundit). Fox News Channel commentators such as Bill O'Reilly (until he was fired in April 2017) Tucker Carlson and Sean Hannity consistently adopt a conservative viewpoint that contrasts with Fox's "fair and balanced" logo. Breitbart News is hospitable to extreme right-wing, even white nationalist viewpoints, but hostile to any news that might cast liberals in a positive light.

There are certainly liberal pundits – columnists at the *Huffington Post*, Markos Moulitsas Zuniga (The Daily Kos), Rachel Maddow on MSNBC, Gail Collins and Paul Krugman at the *New York Times*, Syndicated columnist Mark Shields, and E.J. Dionne of the *Washington Post*, Brookings Institute and the PBS News Hour. However, I don't think these pundits on the left are equivalent to those on the right. In view of my self-professed liberal perspective, you are right to be skeptical. But hear me out.

The *Huffington Post* comes close to being reflexively liberal, as does Mr. Moulitsas. But they make a conscious effort to respect facts. That marks them as different from many of those I named on the right. Most of those named in the previous paragraph work for professional news organizations. Some, such as Mr. Dionne and Mr. Krugman are attached to prestigious institutions, Brookings and Princeton University, respectively.

As for less famous commentators, a BuzzFeed analysis of political reporting on four mainstream, four liberal and four conservative Facebook pages found no mostly or partly false content on mainstream pages; 19 percent fit those categories on liberal sites and 38 percent on conservative websites.[27]

How about Stephen Colbert, Jon Stewart, Samantha Bee, John Oliver, Seth Meyers, and the whole cast of Saturday Night Live? None of them work on news programs. None claim to be journalists. Their satire is transparent. Most of those I named on the right, however, purport to report and/ or comment on the news. Indeed Fox and Breitbart have "News" in their titles. Fox fetishizes neutrality with slogans like "We report; you decide."

Mr. Limbaugh, in a candid moment, described himself not as a journalist bound by a professional code of ethics, but as an "entertainer." However, he reports and comments on current events *as if* he were a journalist. He's certainly not a comic; he elicits more smirks than smiles. When Mr. Hannity was criticized for his blatant promotion of Mr. Trump, he said flatly, "I'm not a journalist," perhaps to defend his violation of journalism's norms of fairness and independence. But he plays one on TV. He comments on *news* events for the Fox NEWS Channel. Mr. Cernovich, Mr. Hoft and Mr. Jones make a pretense of reporting news, but have been widely discredited as frauds.[28]

You might argue that many of the news-providers and commentators above are acting more from ideological than commercial motivations. Not panderers but true believers. You could make a case for Ms. Maddow, Mr. Beck, Ms. Coulter, Ms. Ingraham and Mr. Zuniga. But were any of these to experience a sudden conversion to the alternate pole, there would likely be severe economic consequences. With right v. left polarization pumping up audience at either end of the political spectrum, it can be difficult to disentangle conviction to a liberal or conservative cause from a desire to mine one's point of view for dollars. Ideology can go hand-in-glove with commercialism.

Adopting a liberal viewpoint appears to be financially advantageous in the genre of humor. Stephen Colbert and Jon Stewart made a handsome living, not so much supporting liberals, as attacking conservatives. But in the news genre, taking a strong conservative view appears to be more remunerative. The young Macedonians who spread false news about the 2016 presidential campaign found support for Mr. Trump and attacks on Mrs. Clinton gained more traction – and ad dollars – for their websites than the opposite, though they tried both.[29]

### 'Click bait'

A second type of commercial pandering is apolitical. It gives prominence to whatever catches the public imagination, no matter how trivial. Online editors call it "click candy" or "click bait." Web masters can count their own site visitors in real time and scan Google Trends (http://www.google.com /trends) and the "most popular" or "most shared" sections of major news websites to tailor the news to what's hot at the moment.

Calvin and Hobbes (used with permission)

"Favoring subjects already trending high in online interest is called search engine optimization," explained Bob Garfield, co-host of WNYC's On the Media program. "Another term might be 'autopandering.'"[30] No matter what it's called, advertisers pay more to be seen on sites with lots of visitors. Such sites also come up higher in Google searches, generating even greater popularity to sell ads against.

Newsroom ethnographer Angele Christin spent 400 hours at established online news organizations in the U.S. and France. She outlined several of her findings for Harvard's Nieman Lab:

- **Real-time analytics have become central in the daily routines of all media sites.** Editors check traffic numbers in real-time to manage the location of articles on the homepage and make headlines more appealing.

- **At many websites, writers are directly encouraged to think about traffic.** Editors and data specialists send rankings based on traffic numbers to staff writers on a regular basis.

- **Web metrics are often used as a management tool.** This is sometimes a conscious decision, for example when websites rely on traffic-based financial incentives. In other cases it is less direct, but editors explain that they take metrics seriously when deciding on promotion and compensation.

- **There is often a gap between what journalist say about metrics and what they do.** Many writers express cynical views about traffic and say that they do not care about page views. Yet they almost always check whether they are in the "top ten" most read articles list.[31]

Although the Web makes it easier, playing to the audience's whimsy is nothing new. At a news literacy conference in 2009, the former president of CBS News Andrew Heyward said, "Let's not kid ourselves... there are a lot of examples of journalism that are driven by pure circulation considerations that clearly could be called pandering."[32]

"If you use popularity in any form, surveys or hit counts, for what stories you run, that leads to a universe where we're in two wars and two economic crises and what you see or read is basically about celebrities and political yelling."[33]

~ Radio satirist and The Simpsons' voice actor Harry Shearer

Sensationalism

Closely related to selecting news based on Web hits, sensationalism is a conscious effort to boost audience by choosing – and often exaggerating – events likely to stir emotion – especially fear, surprise, sorrow, anger, or titillation – at the expense of more newsworthy occurrences. Sensationalism can also contaminate *presentation* – focusing on the provocative aspects of important events and issues while ignoring or downplaying the substantive.

Sensationalism has long plagued news media. In 1870 Mark Twain observed that "the first great end and aim of journalism is to make a *sensation*. Never let your paper go to press without a sensation. If you have none, make one." (Emphasis in original).[34] Newspapers became more professional during most of the 20th century, adopting standards of ethics, hiring better educated journalists, and diminishing sensationalism. But since the mid-1980s, greater demand for profit from Wall Street investors and the advent of cable news and the Web have brought sensationalism roaring back.[35]

"The press can hold its magnifying glass up to our problems, bring them into focus.... Or they can use that magnifying glass to light ants on fire. And then perhaps host a week of shows on the sudden, dangerous flaming ant epidemic."[36]

~ Jon Stewart, former host of The Daily Show

## Selecting stories for sensation

The most obvious examples of choosing sensation over substance are stories about celebrities and saturation coverage of shocking episodes of violent crime. In the late 1990s O.J. Simpson's arrest and trial combined the two and dominated coverage for more than a year. Missing blondes and murdered children – especially when the mom is suspected – are popular. So are the peccadilloes of celebrities such as Charlie Sheen and those cleavish Kardashians. Some local TV stations have hired angry shouters such as Bubba the Love Sponge to rant for ratings.[37]

To give a sense of journalism's obsession with celebrities, I conducted a Google News search in April, 2017. I asked for the number of news articles mentioning actress/model Kim Kardashian, Senate Republican Majority Leader Mitch McConnell, and Senate Democratic Majority Leader Chuck Schumer. Check out the results:

**Number of Articles Mentioning:**

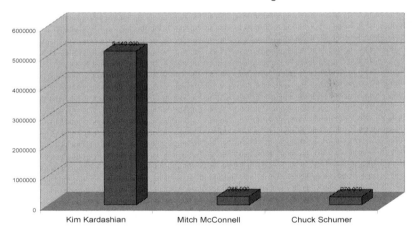

Ms. Kardashian had nearly ten times as many news articles written about her (5,140,000) as Sen. McConnell (285,000) and Sen. Schumer (270,000) *combined*. (Actually, it's worse than it looks because many of the articles mentioning one senator, also mentioned the other. So the combination creates duplicates.) When I restricted my search to the *New York Times* website, however, a very different picture emerged. The actress merited 819 articles while Sen.

McConnell had 5,122 and Sen. Schumer, 1,230. The take-away: Some news organizations are much more responsible than others, but at least among those Google News includes, most find Ms. K to be far more newsworthy than the leaders of the world's most powerful law-making body.

Coverage of celebrities, however, has almost zero value in orienting us to reality or helping us make wise collective or personal decisions – the primary goal of socially responsible journalism. Yes, it may empower chit-chat at the water cooler. But otherwise, such stories are simply nonfiction entertainment. What the Senate does, or fails to do, on the other hand, often has direct bearing on every American's – and many foreigners' – lives.

Calvin and Hobbes (used with permission)

Sex, violent crime and gossip about the famous sell, however, and are usually cheap to report. Publicists promote celebrities, suggesting stories, setting up interviews and providing free photos and videos. Police dig up crime information and provide it without charge. Courtrooms provide a free reality show focused on bad behavior. On cable TV, publicity-hungry, self-proclaimed experts are happy to fill time speculating about events that have sparked public curiosity, for almost nothing. From a short-term economic standpoint, sensation has a great benefit-to-cost ratio.

Several years ago when singer Britney Spears' life was in disarray, *Los Angeles Times* sports columnist Bill Dwyre put the opportunistic nature of celebrity-chasing in perspective:

Our society has a massive appetite for drama, and little for reality. We read about Britney Spears when we need to read about Afghanistan. And the media, which [have] the mandate – and the constitutional right – to lead us from this abyss, are all too often not doing so. Media, which once led public opinion, now all too often follow it.

We aren't just talking celebrity scandal sheets, weekly shoppers and sports-talk radio. Last week, a Los Angeles bureau executive of the Associated Press, no less, put out a memo to staff that said they were to pay more attention to developments about Britney Spears. The message was: She is news.

No she isn't. She is titillation. She is a troubled young woman whom we cover with delight, rather than empathy. She is web hits, the current fool's gold of the newspaper industry.[38]

Coverage of celebrities and episodes of violence, however, represents just the tip of the sensationalism iceberg. Any person or thing that's quirky or elicits strong emotional reaction can become "newsworthy" if it promises to attract mass attention at little cost. Often it's someone from the local community who does something extraordinary or outrageous.

This is not a new phenomenon driven by scarce newsroom resources. Back when the *Mercury News* still had San Jose in its title and hundreds of excellent journalists, it focused readers' attention on one Anna Ayala, a little-known grifter. Little-known, that is, until she found an ingenious use for the tip of a finger her husband had brought home from work, the result of a co-worker's industrial accident. Ms. Ayala submerged the finger in a steaming bowl of Wendy's chili and then feigned visceral disgust. (She hadn't ordered finger food!) Protesting that the fast-food chain had taken a short cut in its preparation of *con carne*, she threatened to file a lawsuit. Lots of money would settle her stomach and quell her anguish.

Thirty-three days passed from the first media report of the finger in the chili to the weekend of her arrest for fraud. At the time, March to April 2005, a violent revolt against American forces was springing up in Iraq as the U.S. tried to establish a government in that fractured land. On the home front, the Bush administration was attempting to privatize Social Security. Congressional Republicans were crafting an energy bill giving massive subsidies to oil companies that were already reaping record profits. The controversy over U.S. soldiers torturing and sexually humiliating Iraqi prisoners at Abu Ghraib was at full boil. North Korea was building long-range missiles and boasting of nuclear weapons. A would-be Al Qaeda airline hijacker, Zacarias Moussaoui, was being tried. In short, lots of newsworthy stuff was going on.

How often do you think the two-time Pulitzer Prize-winning *San Jose Mercury News* chose the finger-in-the-chili-bowl story for its *front page* during those 33 days? Eleven. It was in the paper a total of 23 times, including an editorial.

How often did the increasingly bloody war crack the front page during that 33-day period? Once. How about the attempt to form a new Iraqi government? Abu Ghraib? Social Security privatization? The energy bill? North Korea? Moussaoui's trial? *Nada.* Not once in 33 days.[39]

Why tell people so much about something so insignificant on the most-read page of a newspaper that was once rated among the top ten in the nation? Because the story had "buzz." Editors could tell from counting website hits on its articles about the scam. It was also cheap. Not only were police providing most of the information, but reporters from other news organizations – operating on commercial logic similar to the *Mercury's* – were finding out tidbits about Ms. Ayala's colorful past. Once reported, other media could use them for free.

There's no question the finger-in-the-chili case was bizarre and interesting. It deserved some coverage. But putting it on the front page so often pushed far more consequential stories to inside pages or entirely out of the paper.

"If your goal is to return a profit to a shareholder, it's going to take you down a different path than if you are really looking at your work as enlightening, inspiring, educating the public."[40]

~ Paula Kerger, president of the Public Broadcasting System

### Sensationalism in crafting the story

Even if a news organization selects important topics, a conflict between public service and media self-interest can still arise from *how the story is told*. Two related techniques predominate: exaggeration and over-dramatization.

*Exaggeration*

To boost audience, news tellers are constantly tempted to make more of the available facts than they merit. Have you ever come away from the evening newscast preparing for a flood only to experience a seasonal sprinkle? TV weathercasters trained at the "Chicken Little" school of meteorology have become commonplace on local newscasts. (Of course, global warming threatens to make such forecasts more accurate!)

"The press is our immune system. If it overreacts to everything, we actually get sicker...."[41]

~ Jon Stewart, former host of The Daily Show

When I was a reporter, I used to try to write stories to the hilt, getting every bit of larger meaning out of whatever I was covering. That's what I told myself. But I was also trying to get on the front page as often as possible to advance my career. Reporters' reputations – and salaries – are based on how often their stories are judged worthy of page one. And, of course, the more startling the news, the more people feel they have to read or watch to be in the know. Overplaying the news is more profitable for both the journalist and the news firm than underplaying it.

*Over-dramatization*

Journalists are taught that the best way to make the important engaging is to inject human interest value in the news. "People-izing the news," they call the technique in local television newsrooms. News told with empathy makes us care about the people in the spotlight. It humanizes them, helping us see ourselves in them, and thus it can build community as well as audience. That's all to the good. The danger arises when dramatic storytelling overwhelms informing or when conflict is emphasized over consensus. Such drama in news is like spice. A little goes a long way. Too much and the orientational value of the story is spoiled.

Examples of this kind of commercial bias include the tendency to cover the most vociferous parties to a controversy more than the most substantive or those with the greatest public support. Conflict is an essential element of every drama. A protest may feature hours of peaceful speeches, but reporters – particularly those with video cameras – are likely to focus on the moment someone throws a trashcan through a store window. Unless they are very large, peaceful protests may get no coverage at all. This creates a dilemma for protest movements: Become violent and gain coverage but lose sympathy, or emphasize thoughtful debate and be ignored.

A second technique is to treat politics like a sporting event, focusing on who's ahead in polls, strategy, punch and counter-punch, but not on policy or past performance. CNN's president, Jeff Zucker, put it this way: "The idea that politics is sport is undeniable, and we understood that and approached it that way." Not only did CNN provide Mr. Trump enormous amounts of air time based on his penchant for throwing more bombs than Tom Brady, it hired Trump zealots such as his disgraced spokesman Corey Lewandowski and Jeffrey Lord to inject conflict and drama into newscasts.[42] CNN's food-fight "debates" reinforce rather than rationally dissect Mr. Trump's provocative messages, according to Vox's Carlos Maza.[43] CNN's bottom line grows at the expense of public awareness.

Calvin and Hobbes (used with permission)[44]

In all its varied forms, sensationalism contributes to a culture of entertainment that's incapable of confronting the complexity we face as technology accelerates change and as the people of the world become increasingly interdependent.

## A caveat

Sensationalism only characterizes stories where consequence has been *displaced* by emotional appeal. Titillating topics sometimes constitute legitimate news. When a president or another prominent politician sexually harasses women or cheats on a spouse, particularly if that politician emphasizes family values, the public is well-served by knowing it. A leader's private life becomes the public's business to the extent it reveals the person's fitness to conduct the public's business.

## Shaping content to suit advertisers or major investors

Socially responsible journalism is a peculiar business. In most enterprises, owners are free to operate as they and their principal investors wish and earn as much as they possibly can. But professional journalism differs. Owners aren't supposed to use news organizations as vehicles for their own biases. And they are expected to resist pressure from major investors and advertisers to corrupt coverage, even if it means sacrificing some capital or income. Some owners, the Ochs and Sulzbergers at the *New York Times*, Nelson Poynter in Florida, the Knight brothers, the McClatchy family in California, the Meyers and Grahams (and so far Jeff Bezos) at the *Washington Post* have strived to honor this unusual and public-spirited arrangement. But they are increasingly the exceptions.

Would anyone argue that the *Huffington Post* does not reflect the political leaning of its liberal founder Arianna Huffington? Or that Breitbart's coverage is independent of the libertarian-conservative viewpoint of the reclusive hedge fund executive Robert Mercer? Breitbart only became a powerhouse on the far-right after Mr. Mercer invested $10 million in the company.[45] Does anyone believe it's mere coincidence that Rupert Murdoch's conservative perspective matches the bias of the morning and prime time programs on his Fox News Channel or his tabloid newspapers?[46]

News execs often argue that they give the people what they want: The *public* is in control, not owners, major investors, or advertisers. But even though Bill O'Reilly's prime time slot on Fox was the most popular news program *ever* on cable television, he was fired after some 50 advertisers joined a boycott of the O'Reilly Factor.[47] The boycott was sparked by a *New York Times* article revealing that Mr. O'Reilly and Fox News had spent $13 million settling multiple suits against the host for sexual harassment. Those revelations actually *increased* the audience for Mr. O'Reilly.[48]

Complaints of sexual harassment against Mr. O'Reilly went back years, but the Murdoch family renewed his contract – estimated at $25 million per year – the same day the *Times* article appeared.[49] He was dismissed only 18 days later after the departing advertisers sharply reduced Mr. O'Reilly's value to the company. Fifty advertisers counted more than 4 million viewers. Those who paid the piper called off Mr. O'Reilly's tune, *not* the audience.

It wasn't the first time advertisers' preferences trumped those of millions of viewers.

Glenn Beck more than doubled the audience for Fox News' 5 p.m. time slot and dominated his cable rivals. But in 2011 he was eased out after liberal groups organized an ad boycott of his program. "I think his ratings provided us, unfortunately, with empty calories, basically something that we could not monetize," conceded Roger Domal, vice president for eastern ad sales at Fox News.[50] Mr. Beck was replaced by conservatives more compatible with advertisers.

In 2012 Rush Limbaugh called a Georgetown University law student a "slut" and a "prostitute," for testifying before Congress that birth control pills ought to be covered by health insurance. He apologized only after advertisers began fleeing his program.

Advertiser boycotts, recently energized by social media, are still rare. But advertisers need not band together to shape news. Editors know what advertisers desire despite the fire wall journalism's ethical codes erect between advertising and news. The Society of Professional Journalists' Code of Ethics states: "Distinguish news from advertising and shun hybrids that blur the lines between the two."[51]

The idea is to protect consumers from being misled and the news-provider from losing its credibility. But it's often profitable, at least in the short run, for news media to mix the two.

### Pay-for-play

George Habit penned a column reviewing restaurants for the *San Francisco Examiner*, then owned by Philip Anschutz's Clarity Media Group. At Grade the News, the media watchdog website that I directed in the San Francisco Bay Area, we noticed that Mr. Habit's reviews were unfailingly positive and often referred to restaurants that advertised on the same or an adjoining page.

When I called him about this, his candor surprised me. He said his primary job was selling ads. "I use the column as an initiative to get advertisers to run an ad," he explained. Did his editors approve? "The paper gives me a free rein," he responded. So much so that only after we promised to expose the pay-for-play scheme did the *Examiner* agree to halt the scam.[52] We found similar stories-for-ads at the *Palo Alto Daily News*, part of a group of free Bay Area newspapers then owned by the prestigious Knight Ridder chain.[53]

Larger papers ran whole sections written by advertisers, but presented in the form of news. Some had microscopic notices alerting readers that the material was advertising;[54] others no warning.[55] Some ran "featurettes" praising various products and paid for by the product's manufacturer, without labeling them as advertising.[56] For the newspaper it was free content, including press-ready photos and illustrations. Today many run sections labeled "advertising" in small print on the first page, but mix real journalism indistinguishably with promotional articles laid out like news. All of these are instances of what University of Missouri Professor Glen T. Cameron calls "information pollution."[57]

### Hidden advertising on TV news

James Rainey, a media reporter at the *Los Angeles Times*, described a similar covert practice in local television news:

With summer ending, local television news stations recently rolled out their back-to-school features. In 10 big cities, that meant an appearance by a young mother and "toy expert" named Elizabeth Werner.

Werner whipped through pitches for seven toys in just a few minutes. Perky and positive-plus, Werner seemed to wow morning news people in towns like Detroit, Atlanta and Phoenix. They oohed and aahed as they smelled Play-Doh, poked at mechanical bugs and strummed an electronic guitar she brought to the studio.

Though parents might have welcomed the advice, and even bought some of the toys, they probably would have liked to know that Werner serves as a spokeswoman for hire, not an independent consumer advocate. She touted only products from companies that forked over $11,000 (the initial asking price, anyway) to be part of her back-to-school television "tour."

But viewers in several of the cities would have had no way of knowing that Werner's pitches amounted to paid advertising, because their local news stations failed to meet their legal obligation to identify the segments as paid promotions.

The practice goes way beyond Los Angeles and a product or two. Be warned if you are watching a self-proclaimed consumer advocate on local TV news pitching cars, electronics, travel and much more. There's a good chance that your friendly small-screen expert has taken cash to sell, sell, sell.[58]

## Native advertising

More recently even quality online news media such as the *New York Times*, *Wall Street Journal*, and *The Atlantic* are experimenting with "native advertising" – content produced by journalists, but directly sponsored by retailers. The Tow-Knight Center for Entrepreneurial Journalism at the City University of New York recently studied native ads. Among their findings:

[N]ative advertising remains a Wild West. Last December, the FTC [Federal Trade Commission] released guidelines for how publishers should display native advertising. The goal was to help consumers identify these posts as a form of advertising, not news. However, major publishers continue to label and disclose sponsored content in a disparate fashion.

Publishers have adopted dozens of labels for sponsored content, to the point that readers can seemingly find a different disclosure on every site. ("Paid Post" at The New York Times, "Brand Publisher" on BuzzFeed, "Presented By" on The Huffington Post.) Terms like "sponsored" or "advertising" are rarely used. Where and how those labels appear on the page varies just as much. A MediaRadar audit of publishers in 2016 found that 70 percent of websites are not compliant with the FTC's guidelines....

Fifty-four percent of respondents felt deceived by native advertising in the past, and 44 percent were not able to correctly identify the sponsor of the native ad they read. [59]

## Structural advertising influence

By far the most common type of advertiser influence, however, is even more subtle: editors choose story topics and assign "beats"[60] not based on citizens' information needs but in order to attract demographic groups advertisers hope to reach with their messages.[61] The news is structured for the benefit of advertisers.

This subordination of public interest to advertisers' interests leads to two abuses. First, topics that advertisers believe will channel attention to their ads, may get more coverage than they deserve. Think of whole sections of the newspaper devoted to automobiles, real estate, food, entertainment, and travel. But topics that don't sell *products* – foreign affairs, education, religion, science (other than consumer technology), government, transportation, and social issues – get less attention than they merit. The second abuse creates two tiers of citizens: Those members of the community with the best "customer potential" for advertisers will have stories addressed to their interests. But those citizens less able or less inclined to buy will be less likely to have their information needs served. The Maynard Institute for Journalism Education has repeatedly drawn attention to large holes in news coverage corresponding to issues important to the urban poor.[62] Professional sports, on the other hand, is likely to be over-covered because it attracts the eyeballs of young men, a "more valuable" demographic.

## Letting corporate and government publicists supply the news

As repeated layoffs hollow out newsrooms, managers have been demanding that the remaining journalists produce more: more stories per week, more versions of those stories as reporters update newscasts, websites (including audio and video clips), and perhaps write a daily blog or curate an online discussion. Maybe even produce a stream of tweets. *New York Times* Public Editor Arthur S. Brisbane wrote: "For journalists charged with feeding the digital news flow, life is a barely sustainable cycle of reporting, blogging, tweeting, Facebooking and, in some cases, moderating the large volume of readers who comment online. I applaud these journalists for their commitment, but worry that the requirements of the digital age are translating into more errors and eventual burnout."[63]

Public relations agents can ease this overload by suggesting story ideas and supplying some or all of the "reporting." In his book about the British press, journalist Nick Davies calls this "churnalism" – "the rapid repackaging of largely unchecked second-hand material, much if it designed to service the political or commercial interests of those who provide it."[64]

### 'A shift of power from citizens to institutions'

Steven Waldman, author of the FCC's comprehensive two-year study of changes in the media, described a paradox: "One of the characteristics of the modern digital media era is it empowers people. [But] there's this countervailing trend, which basically is a shift of power from citizens to institutions – to government, to companies, because they're in a better position to drive the storyline."[65] They can afford publicists. Most individuals cannot.

According to University of Florida Professor of Public Relations Spiro Kiousis, as much as 70-80 percent of news stories in the U.S. originate either with a press release or contact with a publicist. It varies with the news outlet, he added, but it's "easily the majority" of articles. "The topics and emphasis present in public relations materials will be present in news content, but you're very rarely going to see exact content, copied and pasted. The reality is that it's grabbed and repacked in some kind of news format."[66]

Reliance on public relations will continue to expand, he predicted, due to more news outlets with fewer reporters, a greater ratio of trained public relations professionals to journalists, and the demand to provide news 24/7. The balance of power, he said, has shifted from the journalist to the publicist.

Publicists, Prof. Kiousis explained, strive to shape the public narrative in their client's interest by persuading journalists first, to cover that issue, and second, to adopt the client's perspective as the dominant or most pertinent one, or excluding others from coverage. They also attempt to associate their client's story with topics currently in the news that favor the client's perspective.[67]

In local television news, such "information subsidies," to use University of Pennsylvania Professor Oscar Gandy's apt term, can include video news releases (VNRs) produced by corporations or governments. The video clips look like independent journalism, but promote the products or points of view of their sponsors. VNRs were aired at 69 stations, according to a study conducted by the Center for Media and Democracy's PRWatch.org.[68] Only two of those stations clearly identified the source of the material as public relations rather than independent reporting.

### Outsourcing investigative reporting

Not only are corporations and government publicists programming the journalist-depleted media, political Super PACs (political action committees) have deployed legions of opposition researchers to dig up dirt on rival candidates and feed them to reporters who want scoops but don't have the time to sift through every historical vote and quote of political hopefuls. Joe Hagan, an investigative reporter for *Vanity Fair* and *New York Magazine* described the press' increasing reliance on political operatives in an interview on NPR's Fresh Air:

> What these guys realize is that you can dig up all this
> negative information, but if it's coming from ... a [candidate's]

> press release, it's going to have a lot less gravity with people than if it comes out in a newspaper like the *New York Times*, or it comes out on MSNBC or CNN, or what have you.
>
> There are more of those opposition researchers, and there are maybe less of the reporters. So ... the power ... on the day-to-day reporting in the news cycle is with these opposition researchers.[69]

Politicians have always tried to entice reporters to investigate their opponents, but never on such a scale nor with so much information pre-reported. Why the change? In its 2010 Citizens United decision, the Supreme Court opened the door for Super PACs – organizations loosely affiliated with candidates that are able to solicit unlimited political contributions from wealthy individuals, corporations and unions.[70] "Oppo" researchers have never had more resources.

The obvious problem with public relations' enhanced role in journalism is that those special interests with deep enough pockets to hire publicists have the opportunity not only to set much of the news agenda for the community, but sometimes to write the news for the benefit of their clients. It saves the news organization money in discovering and reporting news, but at a cost to its ethically-mandated independence from those special interests. Groups without such resources become less "newsworthy" and may disappear from coverage. Not least, the public may be blind to the practice because it's usually hidden by news media trying to appear independent and "objective."

Public relations content is socially valuable when it alerts journalists to legitimate stories and when it truthfully represents corporate or government viewpoints. But when strapped newsrooms rely heavily on PR agents to learn what's happening in the community or use press releases for anything more than one clearly-attributed side of the story, they are participating in corporate and official propaganda rather than journalism. The watchdog that depends on the intruder for meals becomes a lapdog.

## The loss of positive externalities

So far, we've been examining negative externalities – ill effects – when journalism is shaped by market forces. The late C. Edwin Baker of the University of Pennsylvania argued that treating news as a market commodity also diminishes at least two broad social benefits of quality journalism.

The basic idea is this: When the market fails to adequately reward news-providers for all the benefits quality journalism brings to democracy, such news is under-produced. It doesn't pay. Here's why.

Citizens too apathetic to keep up with news contribute nothing to the bottom line of media corporations. (They probably don't even contribute to their local public broadcaster!) Yet they reap priceless benefits from good journalism. Professor Baker explained:

> Individuals are tremendously benefitted or harmed if the country makes wise or stupid decisions about welfare, warfare, provision of medical care, the environment, and a myriad of other issues. These harms or benefits depend on the extent and quality of *other* people's political participation. The media significantly influence this participation.[71]

Professor Baker also pointed out that because quality journalism is investigative, it naturally deters corruption among public – and sometimes corporate – officials who act honestly out of fear of being exposed for misbehavior: "Deterrence means, however, that the media has [sic] no 'exposé' – no product – to sell its audience and hence no opportunity to internalize the benefits it produces."[72] Deterrence isn't profitable.

Further, American copyright law allows other media to re-publish the gist of any news report immediately without compensating the news organization that may have spent months digging up and checking the story.

News suffers from a double – maybe even triple – dose of free rider problem. Not only do citizens who don't pay for the news benefit from good government and prevention of corruption, but other news media gain free access to a story they can sell themselves.

Finally, websites such as Google News, which merely aggregate stories reported by others, can attract users without paying for any reporting.

When news media were flush with advertising dollars, it was much easier for news executives to justify stories that didn't carry their weight in the marketplace. But it is much more difficult now.

### 3. Because it's more common and covert than political bias, commercial bias represents the graver threat to democracy

As we navigate news in the 21$^{st}$ century, I would argue that commercialism is the most damaging bias in American journalism. Although most professional news organizations strive to stay above the political fray, favoring neither the left nor the right, some level of commercial bias among them is as common as whiskers on cats. Further, those outlets that do embrace a liberal or conservative slant, are often as commercially as ideologically driven, catering not just to like-minded audiences, but to liberal or conservative investors and funders.

Compared to political bias, commercial bias is covert. News media rarely cover it, much less cop to it. No industry can be counted on to expose its own flaws. Historically, the news business has guarded against the offenses of *individual* journalists. Plagiarism and conflicts of interest are routinely punished, often by firing. But *institutional* malpractice seems immune even from exposure.

In fact, many executives excuse commercial bias, saying it has been part of news since the mid-19th century when businessmen took over newspapering from political parties and small-circulation publisher-printers. But can you imagine the public outcry if doctors dismissed complaints of malpractice or engineers shunned responsibility for collapsed bridges by pointing out that failures have happened before?

Even more common is the argument by some news executives that if entertainment trumps information, the *public* is to blame for reading and watching such content, not the *media* for presenting it:

Junk journalism is the *consumer's* fault. But when news media skimp on expensive ways of attracting attention – investigative and enterprise reporting – and substitute cheap-to-report, entertaining articles to gather a crowd, is it appropriate to blame only the victims? Journalism aspires to be a profession as respected as law or medicine. But who would trust the doctor who tells patients what they want to hear rather than what's healthful? A dentist offering patients candy to ensure repeat business would become a laughingstock if he defended the practice by arguing that he was merely giving people what they want. It's the drug-dealer's defense.

Don't get me wrong: Entertainment is an important part of any news capable of attracting a mass audience. But its task is to *serve* information – to make what's important interesting. Not to make what's merely interesting seem important.

In terms of impact on a society that aims to govern itself, commercial bias corrodes civic engagement far more than a rogue reporter's act of plagiarism or a journalist's off-duty participation in a protest march. Systematically pandering to prejudice, displacing substance with sensation, masking PR and advertising as independent journalism, and pitching the news at potential customers rather than at citizens cause far greater harm.

Because it's hidden, commercial bias creates a public that thinks it knows what's going on – because it pays attention to what news media highlight – but really doesn't. Thinking you know when you don't makes you vulnerable. You drop your guard. The majority in a society more entertained than informed by its news media can be manipulated by the powerful using propaganda, or skillful advertising and public relations. They've been set up.

As Walter Lippmann warned nearly a century ago, the weakest link in democracy has always been the limited willingness of the majority of people to put in the time and effort to become informed, active citizens.[73]

Economist Anthony Downs has argued that ignorance of civic affairs is, in fact, rational.[74] That's because individuals who can't afford lobbyists and major campaign contributions have so little influence over political outcomes – one vote among thousands, or at the national level, 100 million.

Encouraging civic involvement and bracing democracy's weak link is the purpose of socially responsible journalism. Chopping away at it by distracting people from the difficult issues of the day is not just irresponsible, it's antidemocratic. It breeds apathy. Voter turnout in Nov. 2016 was the lowest in 20 years, with 45 percent of those eligible not bothering to cast a ballot.[75]

This chapter has explored a theory of news selection based on a struggle between the "oughts" of socially responsible journalism and market pressures. Next we'll briefly examine three other approaches to understanding why some events and issues dominate the news and others of equal or greater importance get short shrift.

### Exercises and Discussion Topics

1. Imagine you and a friend own and operate a start-up online local news operation. Suppose you heard a tip that Brad Pitt, who was in town to promote a movie, got drunk and was nearly arrested during an altercation at a local bar. And you also know that the city council will meet at noon today to discuss cuts in the city budget. Your friend is finishing two other stories and unavailable. Assuming you can't do both, you must decide whether to spend your day covering the city council meeting or checking out the rumor about Mr. Pitt.

• If you were able to verify Mr. Pitt's misbehavior, which story – that or the city council meeting – do you think would generate more visitors to your site?

• If advertisers paid you based on the number of visitors to your site, which of these two stories would you pursue? Why? Regardless of which story you chose to cover, would you feel any conflict of interest about your decision? Explain why.

2. Search your favorite news source and, if you can, find one or more examples of commercial bias. Describe the manner in

which the commercial bias manifests itself (sensationalism, news shaped by advertiser interests, re-written press releases, etc.). Explain why or why not, this might harm the community.

3. Do you agree with *Los Angeles Times* columnist Bill Dwyre that stories about a celebrity such as Britney Spears' troubles are titillation rather than news? Why or why not?

4. See end note #52 below. What, if anything, is wrong with a local real estate agent writing a news column about looking for or buying houses? Consider debating the issue in class with some taking the position that it's harmful and others that it's informative.

5. Look in any medium claiming to be news for an example of advertising masquerading as news (either unmarked as advertising, or marked ambiguously). What about the content makes you think this is advertising rather than news?

6. Do you think commercialism in news is more the public's fault or the news-provider's fault? Why?

## End Notes

[1] Robert M. Hutchins and the Commission on Freedom of the Press (1947) *A free and responsible press: a general report on mass communication: newspapers, radio, motion pictures, magazines, and books.* (Chicago: University of Chicago Press) p. 57. After World War II, *Time* magazine founder Henry Luce commissioned University of Chicago President Robert M. Hutchins to assemble some of the best thinkers in the nation to consider the role of the press in a democracy. The result was a slim but remarkable book that defined what's come to be known as "socially responsible journalism." By the way, media moguls, including Mr. Luce, loathed the report.

[2] Tommy Tomlinson (5/15/2011) "A team tackles brown lung disease, wins a Pulitzer Prize," the *Charlotte Observer*, online at: http://www.charlotteobserver.com/2011/05/11/2280312/a-team-tackles-brown-lung-disease.html#storylink=cpy.

[3] Project for Excellence in Journalism (1/11/2010) "How news happens–still: A study of the news ecosystem of Baltimore," available online at http://pewresearch.org/pubs/1458/news-changing-media-baltimore.

[4] This is most evident in the codes of ethics of journalism, which most commercial news outlets embrace or use as a model for their own codes. The Society of Professional Journalists' code, for example, begins: "Members of the Society of Professional Journalists believe that public enlightenment is the forerunner of justice and the foundation of democracy. The duty of the journalist is to further those ends by seeking truth and providing a fair and comprehensive account of events and issues." The Radio Television Digital News Association declares: "Professional electronic journalists should operate as trustees of the public, seek the truth, report it fairly and with integrity and independence, and stand accountable for their actions."

[5] On Aug. 18, 1896 Adolph Ochs wrote in a signed editorial after he took over ownership of the paper, "It will be my earnest aim that the New York Times ... give the news impartially, without fear or favor, regardless of party, sect, or interest involved." The entire editorial is available online at: http://www.nytimes.com/1996/08/19/opinion/ without-fear-or-favor.html. "Fair and balanced" is a trademarked slogan of the Fox News Channel. Wikipedia (accessed 8/8/2011) Fox News Channel, online at: http://en.wikipedia.org/wiki/Fox_ News_Channel.

[6] Steve Inskeep (5/13/2011) Morning Edition, National Public Radio. Quote is in introduction to Elizabeth Blair's story, "With billions at stake, firms play name that mop."

[7] Perhaps because it directly calls a news organization's ethics into question, it's the rare news executive who is willing to discuss commercial bias in their product. Even those who pioneered news literacy at the State University of New York at Stony Brook, adamantly refused to acknowledge its existence when I brought it up at their first news literacy conference in 2009.

[8] Julia M. Klein (July/August 2012) "Deconstruction Boom," *Columbia Journalism Review*, online at http://archives.cjr.org/review/ deconstruction_boom.php.

[9] John H. McManus (1997) "Who's responsible for journalism?" *Journal of Mass Media Ethics*, 12, 1 pp. 5-17. Also see Theodore L. Glasser (1986) "Press responsibility and First Amendment values," in Deni Elliott, Ed., *Responsible Journalism*, Thousand Oaks, CA: Sage. In 1947 the Commission on Freedom of the Press wrote: "No public service is more important that the service of communications. But the element of personal responsibility, which is the essence of the organizations of such professions as law and medicine, is missing in communications. Here the writer works for an employer, and the employer, not the writer takes the responsibility." (p. 77).

[10] Conrad C. Fink (1995) *Media Ethics*, Boston: Allyn and Bacon, p. 91.

[11] John H. McManus (1995) "A market-based model of news production," *Communication Theory* 5, 4, pp. 301-338.

[12] I'm relying here on my previous research which culminated in the following book: John H. McManus (1994) *Market-driven journalism: Let the citizen beware?* Thousand Oaks, CA: Sage.

[13] In his book *Newsonomics*, Ken Doctor puts it this way: "Consider the travails of *The New York Times*... One day last April it won five Pulitzer Prizes. The next day, it suffered the indignity of announcing the biggest quarterly loss in its history – $74 million." Ken Doctor (2010) *Newsonomics*, New York: St. Martin's Press.

[14] Steven D. Reese (1991) "Setting the media's agenda: A power balance perspective," in James A. Anderson, Ed., *Communication Yearbook 14*, Newbury Park, CA: Sage, pp. 309-340.

Frank Fitzpatrick, a sports writer for the *Philadelphia Inquirer* provided a case in point in a conversation with Bob Garfield of NPR's On the Media: When asked what would happen if Fitzpatrick had revealed the sleazy side of Phillies' baseball star Lenny Dykstra's life, he responded "Behind everything a baseball beat writer does there's this fear of severing a good relationship [with a source] because without them, in a competitive news environment, you're dead." Had he written candidly about Dykstra's bad behavior, the writer said: "There would have been very few players that would have talked to me. And the manager would have been even more difficult to deal with. You would have been able to do your job, but only in the most routine, uninteresting fashion imaginable. In terms of inside information, you would have been lost." Bob Garfield (7/8/2011) On the Media, WNYC.

[15] Michele McLellan, (2011) "Emerging Economics of Community News," *State of the News Media, 201,* Pew Research Center's Project for Excellence in Journalism, http://www.stateofthemedia.org/ 2011/mobile-survey/economics-of-community-news/.

[16] Nick Davies (2009) *Flat Earth News*, London: Vintage Books, p. 16.

[17] Hutchins Commission cited above, p. 57.

[18] Gene Roberts and Hank Klibanoff (2006) *The Race Beat: The press, the civil rights struggle, and the awakening of a nation,* New York: Vintage Books. This Pulitzer Prize winning book focuses on the few heroic journalists and brave news organizations that stood up to racial prejudice. Their isolation and what they endured, however, documents the resistance of the regional news media to full and fair reports of the struggle for civil rights in the South. Further examples of pandering to racial and ethnic prejudice can be found in Juan

Gonzalez and Joseph Torres (2011) *News for all the people: the epic story of race and the American media*, Brooklyn, NY: Verso Books.

[19] Scott McClellan (2008) *What happened: Inside the Bush White House and Washington's culture of deception*, New York: Public Affairs.

[20] Paul Bond (2/29/2016) "Leslie Moonves on Donald Trump: 'It may not be good for America, but it's damn good for CBS,'" *The Hollywood Reporter*, http://www.hollywoodreporter.com/news/leslie-moonves-donald-trump-may-871464.

[21] Paul Farhi (10/17/2016) "One billion dollars profit? Yes, the campaign has been a gusher for CNN," The *Washington Post*, online at: https://www.washingtonpost.com/lifestyle/style/one-billion-dollars-profit-yes-the-campaign-has-been-a-gusher-for-cnn/2016/10/27/1fc879 e6-9c6f-11e6-9980-50913d68eacb_story.html?utm_term=.aa01a52f23cc.

[22] Farhi, cited above.

[23] Nicholas Confessore and Karen Yourish (3/15/2016) "$2 Billion Worth of Free Media for Donald Trump," The Upshot, *New York Times*, https://www.nytimes.com/2016/03/16/upshot/measuring-donald-trumps-mammoth-advantage-in-free-media.html?_r=0.

[24] Thomas E. Patterson, (6/13/2016) "Pre-primary news coverage of the 2016 presidential race: Trump's rise, Sanders' emergence, Clinton's struggle," Shorenstein Center on Media, Politics, and Public Policy, Harvard University, https://shorensteincenter.org/pre-primary-news-coverage-2016-trump-clinton-sanders/.

[25] Jeremy Diamond (1/24/2016) "Trump: I could shoot somebody and wouldn't lose voters," CNN, http://www.cnn.com/2016/01/23/politics/ donald-trump-shoot-somebody-support/.

[26] Bob Garfield (4/29/2011) "Is HuffPost good for journalism?," On the Media, National Public Radio, segment on the Huffington Post, online at: http://www.onthemedia.org/2011/apr/29/is-huffpost-good-for-journalism/transcript/.

[27] Craig Silverman et al. (10/20/2016) "Hyperpartisan Facebook pages are publishing false information at an alarming rate," *BuzzFeed.*

[28] As we saw in chapter 2, Mr. Cernovich made up stories about Mrs. Clinton's health. Mr. Jones spread, among other fake news, the rumor that Comet Ping Pong pizza parlor was a cover for a child prostitute ring led by Mrs. Clinton (see chapter 2). Hoft's Gateway Pundit carried such fakeries as "Breaking: Creepy new video released of Joe Biden groping little girls." For more on Hoft,

see Andrew Marantz (3/20/2017) "Trolling the press corps," *The New Yorker*, pp. 52-61.

[29] Craig Silverman (11/16/2016) "This analysis shows how viral fake election news stories outperformed real news on Facebook," Buzzfeed News, https://www.buzzfeed.com /craigsilverman/viral-fake-election-news-outperformed-real-news-on-facebook?utm_term=.lkALY39BVm#.hlA2 eNP0vz.

[30] Garfield, "Is HuffPost good for journalism?," cited above.

[31] Angele Christin (8/28/2014) "When it comes to chasing clicks, journalists say one thing, but feel pressured to do another," *Nieman Journalism Lab,* http://www.niemanlab.org/2014/08/when-it-comes-to-chasing-clicks-journalists-say-one-thing-but-feel-pressure-to-do-another/.

[32] Andrew Heyward (3/12/2009) "Do News-providers Live Up to News Literacy Standards?," panel held at Stony Brook University; available online at: http://newsliteracyconference.com /content/?p=498.

[33] Karen Stabiner (March/April 2011) "CJR column mentions The Simpsons: a second look at SEO," *Columbia Journalism Review*, pp. 46-48.

[34] Thomas C. Leonard (2003) *Mark Twain: Press critic.* Berkeley, CA: University of California Friends of the Bancroft Library. The book features Mark Twain's previously unpublished 1870 essay, "Interviewing the interviewer."

[35] McManus, *Market-driven journalism,* previously cited.

[36] Jon Stewart (10/31/2010) Final speech at the Rally to Restore Sanity in Washington, DC, http://www.youtube.com/watch?v=6JzGOiBXeD4.

[37] Deborah Potter (March/April, 2011) "With an edge," *American Journalism Review*, online at: http://www.ajr.org/Article.asp?id=5076. For an update on Bubba, see http://www.bizjournals.com/ tampabay /news/2017/02/08/bubba-the-love-sponge-is-coming-back-to-tampa-bay.html.

[38] Bill Dwyre (1/19/2008) "Media are off their game," *Los Angeles Times*, p. D1, online at: http://www.latimes.com/sports/la-sp-dwyre19 jan19 1,4372597,full.column?coll=la-headlinessports&ctrack=2 &cset=true.

[39] John McManus (5/5/2005) "Giving readers the finger," GradeTheNews.org, online at: http://www.gradethenews.org/ commentaries /finger.htm.

[40] Michael Krasny (11/30/2011) interview with Paula Kerger on Forum, KQED-FM.

[41] Jon Stewart (10/31/2010) "Final speech at the Rally to Restore Sanity in Washington, DC," cited above.

[42] Jonathan Mahler (4/9/2017) "'That is great television': Inside the strange symbiosis between the CNN president Jeff Zucker and Donald Trump," *New York Times Magazine*, pp. 40-69.

[43] Carlos Maza (4/17/2017) "CNN's approach to covering politics prioritizes drama and spectacle over truth telling," Vox, https://twitter.com/voxdotcom/status/854027944947097600.

[44] Calvin and Hobbes cartoons are from Bill Watterson (2005) *The complete Calvin and Hobbes*, Kansas City: Andrews McMeel, volumes 1-4.

[45] Jane Meyer (3/27/2017) "Trump's money man," *The New Yorker*, pp. 34-45.

[46] Although Fox News' line-up for its prime time slots are deeply conservative, and in the case of Sean Hannity essentially pro-Trump propaganda, its less-watched afternoon news programs have hewed closer to the empirical standards of professional journalism. And while the *Wall Street Journal's* editorial page is reliably conservative, its news coverage under Mr. Murdoch has also been middle-of-the-road, unlike his tabloid newspapers. The *Journal's* sophisticated readers would be unlikely to pay its high subscription rates for biased news reports. Murdoch is a businessman first and a conservative second, when the two are in conflict.

[47] Emily Steel and Michal S. Schmidt (4/20/2017) "Fox News ousts O'Reilly, a host central to its rise," *New York Times*, p. A1. Also see Jim Rutenberg (4/20/2017) "Conservative pillar's firing may leave viewers adrift," *New York Times*, p. A1, and Michael M. Grynbaum (4/20/2017) "Murdoch's defiance again gives way to his pragmatism," *New York Times,* p. B1.

[48] Michael O'Connell (4/5/2017) "TV ratings: Bill O'Reilly's audience grows amid scandal, *Hollywood Reporter*, http://www. hollywood reporter.com/news/tv-ratings-bill-oreilly-audience-grows-scandal-991498.

[49] Variety staff (4/1/2017) "Bill O'Reilly sets new contract with Fox News amid sexual harassment controversy," *Variety*, http://variety. com/2017 /tv/news/bill-oreilly-fox-news-contract-harassment-allegations-1202020875/

[50] Brian Stelter (12/25/2011) "In Beck's shadow, rise of 'The Five'," *New York Times*, pg. B1, online at http://www.nytimes.com /2011/12/26/business /media/the-five-rises-on-fox-news-in-glenn-becks-shadow.html?sq=Glenn Beck&st=Search&scp= 3&pagewanted=print.

[51] Code of Ethics, Society of Professional Journalists, online at: http://spj. org/ethicscode.asp.

[52] John McManus (9/13/2005) "SF Examiner and Independent agree to end payola restaurant reviews," Grade the News, http://gradethenews .org/2005/ payola.htm. The *Examiner* made a practice of blurring the distinction between news and ads. In a real estate column on July 22, 2005, realtor Bryan Jacobs advised readers to "hire a realtor." His own ad appeared on an adjoining page. Not only did the *Examiner* write articles to help sell ads, it provided advertisers a chance to write the "news" themselves!

[53] Michael Stoll (7/27/2005) "At free dailies, advertisers sometimes call the shots," Grade the News, online at http://www. gradethenews.org /2005/freepapers1.htm.

[54] Michael Stoll (11/21/2005) "Mercury News renounces microscopic ad label," Grade the News, online at: http://www. gradethenews.org/2005 /microads. htm#microads1. After Grade the News ceased active opera- tion, the *Mercury News* began running similar ads without any advertising label.

[55] Michael Stoll (6/20/2003) "Running ads as news, the Oakland Tribune's real estate section crosses a journalistic line," http://www. gradethenews .org/pages/news percent20as percent20ads.htm.

[56] Michael Stoll (4/15/2004) "Oakland Tribune pledges end to deceptive 'advertorials'," http://www.gradethenews .org/pages2/ advertorial.htm.

[57] John McManus (9/24/2000) "Is it news or is it advertising?" Grade the News, online at: http://www.gradethenews.org/ dreamhost/files/ pagesfolder /Deception.htm. The *Contra Costa Times* grudgingly agreed to label the section after our story. For more examples, see http://www.gradethenews.org/ feat/archives.htm #advertising.

[58] James Rainey (9/15/2010) "The news is, that pitch was paid for; When spokespersons for hire promote products on local TV news shows," *Los Angeles Times*, available online at: latimes.com/ entertainment/news/la-et-onthemedia-20100915,0,370372.column.

[59] Joe Lazauskas (2016) "Fixing native ads: What consumers want from publishers, brands, Facebook, and the FTC," Contently partnered with The Tow-Knight Center for Entrepreneurial Journalism at CUNY and Radius Global Market Research to produce the report. Available at https://the-content-strategist-13.docs.contently.com/v/fixing-sponsored-content-what-consumers-want-from-brands-publishers-and-the-ftc.

[60] Beats are areas of coverage to which reporters are assigned, for example, city hall, health, police, education, courts, etc.

[61] Joseph Turow (1984) *Media industries*, New York: Longman. Also see James T. Hamilton (2006) *All the news that's fit to sell: How the market transforms information into news,* Princeton, NJ: Princeton University Press.

[62] See, for example, Bob Butler (5/7/2011) "Fair and unbalanced: the tale of two trials," Maynard Institute for Journalism Education, online at: http://mije.org/health/fair-and-unbalanced-tale-two-trials#comment-2498; and Jean Marie Browne (Fall, 2011) "Familiar Patterns of Minority Exclusion Follow Mainstream Media Online," Nieman Reports, http://www.nieman.harvard. edu/reports/article/102675/ Familiar-Patterns-of-Minority-Exclusion-Follow-Mainstream-Media-Online.aspx.

[63] Arthur S. Brisbane (1/9/2011) "Hanging on as the boundaries shift," *New York Times* , Week in Review, p. 10; available online at: http://www.nytimes.com/2011/01/09/opinion/09pubed.html?scp=16&sq=Arthur+Brisbane&st=nyt.

[64] Nick Davies (2009) *Flat Earth News* cited above, p. 60.

[65] Steven Waldman (6/17/2011) "FCC report says local reporting in crisis," On the Media, National Public Radio, online at: http://www .onthemedia.org /transcripts/2011/06/17/04. You can read and download the full FCC report here: http://www.fcc.gov/info-needs-communities.

[66] Spiro Kiousis, interviews with the author on 1/20/2011 and updated on 4/7/2017. Professor Kiousis is professor of public relations and the executive associate dean of the School of Journalism and Communication at the University of Florida.

[67] Kiousis, cite above.

[68] Center for Media and Democracy, "Fake TV news, widespread and undisclosed," PRWatch.org, online at: http://www.prwatch. org/fakenews/findings/vnrs. During the presidency of George W. Bush, the federal government also participated in fake news.

[69] Terry Gross (1/21/2012) "How SuperPacs are 'gaming' the 2012 campaign," Fresh Air, National Public Radio, online at: http://www .npr.org /templates/transcript/transcript.php?storyId=146137765.

[70] John Nichols and Robert W. McChesney (2013) *Dollarocracy: How the money and media election complex is destroying America*, New York: Nation

Books. Also see Jane Mayer (2016) *Dark Money: The hidden history of the billionaires behind the rise of the radical right,* New York: Doubleday.

[71] C. Edwin Baker (2002) *Media, markets and democracy,* Cambridge, UK: Cambridge University Press, p. 45.

[72] Baker, p. 49.

[73] Walter Lippmann (1922) *Public Opinion,* reprinted in 1965 by Free Press, New York.

[74] Anthony Downs (1957) *An Economic Theory of Democracy,* New York: Harper and Brothers. Downs wrote: The value of a single vote "is nearly infinitesimal under most circumstances.... The result is an enormously diminished incentive for voters to acquire political information before voting." p. 245.

[75] Gregory Wallace (11/30/2016) "Voter turnout at 20-year low in 2016," CNN, http://www.cnn.com/2016/11/11 /politics/popular-vote-turnout-2016.

# 6

## The Logic of News Selection

*News is what somebody somewhere wants to suppress;
all the rest is advertising.*

*~ Lord Northcliffe*

**K**atie Couric, the first woman to anchor the CBS Evening News, called the reporting during the year preceding the Anglo-American invasion of Iraq in March 2003, "one of the most embarrassing chapters in American journalism." At the time, she was working as host of NBC's "Today Show." Of the case for war, she said she felt pressure from "the corporations who own where we work and from the government itself to really squash any kind of dissent or any kind of questioning of it."[1]

The market-influence theory introduced in the previous chapter would explain such censorship as economically-motivated pandering to a false sense of patriotism among consumers, plus going along with high government officials in order to maintain inexpensive access to scoops and insider information. But professors Edward Herman of the University of Pennsylvania and Noam Chomsky of MIT would argue that even larger forces are at work:

> The mass media serve as a system for communicating messages and symbols to the general populace. It is their function to amuse, entertain, and inform, and to inculcate individuals with the values, beliefs, and codes of behavior that will integrate them into the institutional structures of the larger society. *In a world of concentrated wealth and major*

> *conflicts of class interest, to fulfill this role requires systematic propaganda* [emphasis added].[2]

This chapter will expand our theoretical understanding of news selection by exploring three additional theories – explanations – for which events and issues make headlines and which fall to the margins or are struck from the agenda. The first theory builds on, but goes beyond, the market forces analysis in chapter 5. The second eschews economic motives and portrays news media as passive conduits of official information. The third is the simplest, and earliest – gate-keeping theory. It's particularly applicable to bloggers and very small news operations. We'll explore the central propositions of each:

1. **Accounts of raw events must pass through five ideological filters before they can become news.**

2. **News selection reflects the scope of debate among powerful political and corporate leaders, rather than shining an independent spotlight on the significant issues and events of the day.**

3. **The individual biases of "gate-keeping" journalists govern news selection.**

## The propaganda model of news selection

While market forces buttress more than batter the status of the wealthy, Professors Herman and Chomsky argue that the very purpose of the news media is hegemony – class domination through a set of ideas promulgated by those at the top of society explicitly designed to perpetuate their position and undermine any challenges.

The propaganda model is not a conspiracy theory in which a few powerful political and corporate leaders sit around a table wreathed in cigar smoke and dictate what becomes mainstream and what becomes marginal news. Rather it's a "guided market system." The authors argue:

> Most biased choices in the media arise from the pre-selection of right-thinking people, internalized preconceptions,

and the adaptation of personnel to the constraints of ownership, organization, market, and political power. Censorship is largely self-censorship, by reporters and commentators who adjust to the realities of source and media organizational requirements, and by people at higher levels within media organizations who are chosen to implement, and have usually internalized, the constraints imposed by proprietary and other market and governmental centers of power.[3]

The authors explain that those who own the major media companies and those they choose to run them share a similar mindset with other corporate leaders and with powerful politicians. They are also *inter*dependent: Media firms need access to inexpensive sources of news; elites require a version of reality that legitimizes their power. They can act in concert without discussing it beforehand because their aims and values match. As former *Washington Post* editor Ben Bagdikian has pointed out, the boards of directors of media conglomerates such as Viacom, News Corps, Comcast, and others are drawn from top ranks of major banks and *Fortune* 500 corporations.[4] They are no strangers to each other or to political leaders in Washington, London and elsewhere.

Commercial news media, the authors argue, operate both to maximize profit and to "manufacture consent" for policies that support the status quo or expand the power of wealth. Reports of each day's "raw events" must pass through five filters before they can be published. Their "propaganda model" looks like this:

## Herman and Chomsky's propaganda model of news selection

| World of raw events | Will it sell as news?<br><br>Yes →<br><br>No ☹ | Will advertisers support it?<br><br>Yes →<br><br>No ☹ | Was it provided by inexpensive, establishment sources?<br><br>Yes →<br><br>No ☹ |
|---|---|---|---|

| Will it cost money to defend? | Does it promote Communism or attack private wealth? | |
|---|---|---|
| Yes ☹ | wealth? | *The Public* |
| No → | Yes ☹ | |
| | No → | |

Communism has diminished as a threat since 1988 when their book, *Manufacturing Consent,* was published. But the second part of the final filter, protecting private wealth, remains current. The rise of the Tea Party as well as political activism by the U.S. Chamber of Commerce and wealthy citizens have led to a nationwide cry to shrink the role of government in favor of the private sector. So the final filter screens out stories that seriously question the accumulation of wealth at the top of the income pyramid.

Although the "filter" metaphor suggests that no news or commentary threatening to wealthy elites gets through, professors Herman and Chomsky are really arguing that no challenges to the status quo receive the kind of deep and repeated coverage necessary to engage citizens in a thoughtful debate. The filters block most, but not all, alternative perspectives. This porosity, in fact, is useful. It provides the appearance of an independent press without the substance. Propaganda requires such deception to be effective.

The propaganda model was developed in a period of increasing monopolization of media firms before the World Wide Web made alternative viewpoints so readily available. But the model remains relevant for three reasons:

- Wealthy individuals, such as energy industrialists David and Charles Koch, have banded together to finance think tanks and scores of non-profit organizations to influence public opinion directly and through the media, and to lobby Congress and state legislatures to accept ideas, arguments, laws and regulations that expand or protect their wealth, often at the expense of the public. They bear such common-good names as Americans for Prosperity, American Future Fund, Americans for Responsible Leadership, Americans for Job Security, American Legislative Exchange Council, and Concerned Women for America.[5] All work to manufacture consent for the golden rule – them that's got the gold, make the rules.

- Although the Web enables many new providers of news and commentary to sprout, most of these "digital natives" depend on mainstream news outlets and public relations agents working for government, corporations or special interests such as those mentioned above, to discover what might be newsworthy.[6] Letting others bear the expense of digging up information greatly reduces costs. So publicists, the major cable and broadcast networks, and metro newspapers still set most of the agenda of issues receiving coverage. The Web may enable many voices, but only those backed by deep pockets have a good chance of affecting public discourse.

- As news media have become less profitable, the incentive for owning them is shifting away from economic rewards toward their power to influence public opinion. Wealthy individuals are now able to scoop up what were once crown jewels of journalism for costume jewelry prices. A billionaire bought the *Boston* Globe and the *Worcester Telegram and* Gazette in 2013 for just 5 percent of what their previous owner paid only two decades earlier.[7] While newspapers are no longer able to print money, they can print the news their new owners choose. Or wealthy investors can fund new information sources online such as the Daily Caller and Breitbart to spread their ideology, regardless of whether they earn a profit.

"[There's] an aggressive bid by the very wealthy to control the American news media at a time when it is in a financially weakened state..."[8]

~ Jim Rutenberg, media columnist, *New York Times*

Sheldon Adelson, the casino billionaire, ardent supporter of Republican candidates and Israeli hard-liners, and opponent of labor unions, secretly purchased the *Las Vegas Review-Journal* in 2014. After his identity was revealed, *New York Times* media columnist Jim Rutenberg wrote: "Mr. Adelson is not shy about using his money to influence the politics of his state and country. And the sale was followed by reports of editors suddenly altering articles about Mr. Adelson's business dealings to put them in a more flattering light, or holding from publication articles about him altogether."[9]

Mr. Rutenberg's predecessor, the legendary David Carr, reported on real estate mogul Douglas F. Manchester's 2011 purchase of the *San Diego Union Tribune*, the region's dominant metro daily: "Mr. Manchester has been frank about using the paper to prosecute a pro-development, pro-new-stadium agenda." In 2015 Mr. Manchester flipped the paper, selling it to Tronc, the company that owns the *Los Angeles Times*, but not before stripping it of its valuable real estate. Mr. Carr also wrote about S. Donald Sussman, a hedge fund manager and philanthropist married to Maine Congresswoman Chellie Pingree who bought the *Portland Press Herald*, one of the state's largest papers.[10]

Billionaire investor Warren Buffett bought 63 newspapers in a single month in 2012.[11] While Mr. Buffett has established an admirable "hands off" policy at his flagship *Buffalo News*,[12] he is nearing retirement. His successor at Berkshire Hathaway may exercise less restraint.

To be fair, there are multiple examples of wealthy "white knights" purchasing newspapers. As of 2017, these new owners appear to be investing in quality journalism. John Henry, who purchased the *Boston Globe*, and Jeff Bezos, who bought the *Washington Post* in 2013, come to mind. In 2016, Philadelphia developer H.F. "Gerry" Lenfest donated the city's two dominant newspapers to a new non-profit foundation. He also contributed $20 million to endow it.[13]

Nevertheless, history warns of serious conflicts between honest journalism and promotion of the owner's personal and business interests. Mr. Carr observed:

> If you pull back a few thousand feet, you can see newspapers coming full circle. Before World War II, newspapers were mostly owned by political and business interests who used them to push an agenda. People like William Randolph Hearst and Robert McCormick wielded their newspapers as cudgels to get their way. It was only when newspapers began making all kinds of money in the postwar era that they were professionalized and infused with editorial standards.[14]

As the economic foundation of American journalism crumbles, the propaganda model is regaining relevance. We should be skeptical of news and commentary that passes through all five of the Herman-Chomsky filters. Just as importantly, we should search for news that takes considerable effort to gather, does not rely on official government or corporate sources and tends to challenge rather than confirm the status quo.

## 2. News selection reflects the scope of debate among powerful politicians, rather than shining an independent spotlight on the significant issues and events of the day

In their 2007 book, *When the press fails*, W. Lance Bennett, Regina Lawrence, and Steven Livingston developed the indexing theory to explain why the mainstream media performed so poorly during the run-up to the invasion of Iraq and so well after hurricane Katrina devastated New Orleans. Before the invasion, "the press reported reality during the Iraq years largely as the Bush administration had scripted it, even when that script seemed bizarrely out of line with observable events."[15] Yet just a few years later, the press actively challenged the Bush administration's rosy accounts of its rescue efforts in the wake of Katrina.

Why?

The indexing model of news selection focuses on the relationship between news media and official sources. But in contrast to the propaganda model, Professor Bennett and his colleagues claim the press has no ideology of its own. It's liberal when Democrats are in control and conservative when the Republicans dominate the halls of power. The media are seen simply as followers, almost stenographers, of those in charge of government.

To the extent that debate among political leaders is robust, the authors contend that mainstream U.S. media fulfill their self-professed obligation to empower democracy by informing citizens. But when one viewpoint predominates among officials, the press narrows coverage and citizens are deprived of an adequate range of perspectives:

> In news about most government policy issues, the absence of credible and potentially decisive opposition from inside government itself leaves the mainstream press generally unable to build and sustain counter-stories. This is true even when credible sources outside government can offer evidence to the contrary, and, for the most part, even if opposition exists from domestic public opinion or foreign governments.[16]

This view of the press as a passive follower of the official narrative also explains the press' pack mentality – why different mainstream news outlets cover the same stories in a similar fashion, according to Professor Bennett.

Why such dependence on government officials? "While journalists may know that their sources in government are self-interested, corrupt, even lying, they *need* those same sources to continue producing what their bosses and peers will recognize as legitimate 'news' [emphasis in original]."[17]

Examining news coverage in the period before the invasion of Iraq in 2003, Mr. Bennett and his colleagues found that Republicans in the White House and Congress were making a very public case for war. The response from Democrats was tepid. Without powerful officials to quote in opposition, the press narrowed the range of acceptable viewpoints, conforming to the narrative promulgated by Republican leaders and their appointees in the executive branch of government.

Rather than holding power to account, the authors argue that news media cover politics like sportscasters in a booth above the field. Coverage focuses, play-by-play, on strategy, on who's winning and who's losing, but not on the validity of the claims each side makes or the policy implications of their enactment.

They point to the *Washington Post's* pre-invasion coverage in 2002 and early '03. Reporters who turned up information at odds with the White House narrative had difficulty getting their stories into the paper, much less on the front page, because editors had already decided President Bush was going to war. Their task was to describe when and how it would take place and the government's game plan for mobilizing public opinion – the inside story of how power was being exercised, rather than whether it was being abused.

In the news accounts they analyzed, Bennett and his colleagues found the coverage of hurricane Katrina in 2005 the exception that calls attention to the rule. In that case, the federal government's late and chaotic response to the tragedy allowed political opponents of the Bush administration to dominate the headlines. Further, the administration's early optimistic claims were easily contradicted by reporters navigating the flooded city of New Orleans. The controversy permitted the press the latitude necessary to allow diverse voices to speak through its megaphone.

To the extent that the indexing theory is correct, we should raise our own level of skepticism when political leaders are in substantial agreement – or one side is relatively silent – whether at the national, state or local level.

Given the current political polarization it may seem that the media's index of acceptable viewpoints is currently open wide. But that can change quickly. Recall what happened in 2008, the last time a majority of both Democrats and Republicans came together on Capitol Hill. They bailed out the very Wall Street banks and insurance companies that precipitated the Great Recession. Mainstream media reported the political consensus, but rarely those who challenged it.[18] That's precisely the outcome Edward Herman and Noam Chomsky also would have predicted. Bankers won; struggling homeowners lost.

## 3. The individual biases of "gate-keeping" journalists govern news selection

The final theory of news selection was developed just after World War II, by researchers such as David Manning White and Walter Gieber. Influenced by the notion of gate-keeping pioneered by the sociologists Robert Ezra Park and Kurt Lewin, they hypothesized that news selection reflects the personal interests and biases of individual journalists, especially editors, who control the "gates" through which information passes on its way to the public.[19]

By the late 1950s, these theories began to be seen as too simple, even naive. As early as 1955, sociologist Warren Breed showed how journalists subordinated their personal biases to those of newspaper owners, passed down through executives.[20] But now that the World Wide Web has made it possible for anyone with a computer and an Internet connection to publish news and commentary, such an individualistic theory of news selection again makes sense.

To understand the biases of a particular gate-keeper, it's instructive to see where s/he falls on the social fault lines described in chapter 4. It's also important to profile their self-interest so that you can identify conflicts of interest. An amateur journalist raving about his community just might be the mayor operating under a pseudonym. It happened in Utah.[21] If you know where they're coming from, you'll be in position to anticipate where they're going with their choice of content.

A caveat: Analyzing a gate-keeper's personal biases makes the most sense for one-person blogs and Websites, especially those generating little revenue from advertisers or subscribers. Once a news-provider endeavors to earn money from journalism, s/he encounters the kind of market pressures described in chapter 5. And the more s/he becomes a player in the politics and power relationships of a community, the more s/he will encounter ideological pressure from those currently holding power.

In the next chapter we'll take dead aim on the prime directive of professional journalism – the notion that journalists can and should be objective. We'll find that it is the primary justification for the follow-the-leader kind of coverage that Professor Bennett and his colleagues complain of.

---

### Exercises and Discussion Topics

1. Look over the stories on the front page of the local newspaper, or watch a local newscast or visit a news website and decide whether they support, challenge, or are neutral concerning the way power is exercised in the community. Discuss what "support" or "challenge" might look like, e.g., how would you define each? Which kind of story predominates?

2. Look for a political story and count how many of the named sources quoted are politicians or work for politicians. What proportion of all the named sources in the story do they constitute? Whose voices are missing? Does it seem like the news is too oriented to the viewpoints of officials?

3. Research where a prominent blogger falls on the social fault lines described in chapter 4. Do they help you predict the news selection values of the blogger? If so, how? If not, how do they differ?

4. Build your own theory describing the factors that in-fluence what becomes news. Justify your model.

---

## End Notes

[1] Brian Stelter (5/30/2008) "Was press a war 'enabler'? Two offer a nod from inside," *New York Times*, p. A17, online at http://www.nytimes.com/2008/05/30/washington/30press.html.

[2] Edward S. Herman and Noam Chomsky (1988) *Manufacturing con-sent: The political economy of the mass media*, New York: Pantheon, p. 1

[3] Herman and Chomsky, p. xiii.

[4] Ben H. Bagdikian (2004) *The new media monopoly*, Boston: Beacon.

[5] Jane Mayer (2016) *Dark money: The hidden history of the billionaires behind the rise of the radical right*, New York: Doubleday.

[6] Project for Excellence in Journalism (1/11/2010) "How news happens—still: A study of the news ecosystem of Baltimore," available online at http://pewresearch.org/pubs/1458/news-changing-media-baltimore.

[7] In 1993, the *Boston Globe* was highly profitable with a circulation of just over half a million copies. The *New York Times* paid $1.1 billion for it. Five years later the *Times* paid $295 million for the nearby *Worcester Telegram and Gazette*. But like other American newspapers, their circulation and advertising revenue plummeted in the digital age. In 2013, the *Times* sold both the *Globe* and the *Telegram and Gazette* for just $70 million to the billionaire owner of the Boston Red Sox, John Henry. That's a discount of 95 percent! And the *Times* was still stuck with the *Globe's* pension liabilities. "It's a sweet deal for Henry," observed newspaper economist Rick Edmonds. "The *Globe's* real estate is close in value to the $70 million sales price he paid." See Christine Haughney (8/4/2013) "New York Times Co. sells Boston Globe," , http://www.nytimes.com/2013/08/04/business/media/new-york-times-company-sells-boston-globe.html and Rick Edmonds (8/4/2013) "7 things to know about the Boston Globe's sale to John Henry," Poynter Institute, https://www. poynter.org/2013/seven-quick-thoughts-on-the-boston-globe-sale-to-john-henry/220156/.

[8] Jim Rutenberg (5/27/2016) "Behind the scenes, billionaires growing control of news," *New York Times,* https://www.nytimes. com/2016/05/28/business/media/behind-the-scenes-billionaires-growing-control-of-news.html?_r=0.

[9] Rutenberg, cited above.

[10] David Carr (4/8/2012) "The newspaper barons resurface," *New York Times,* p. B1, online at: http://www.nytimes.com/2012/04/09/business/media/the-return-of-the-newspaper-barons.html?_r=1&pagewanted=2&pagewanted=all&pagewanted=print.

[11] Christine Haughney (6/11/2012) "Investor group buys Orange County Register and other newspapers," Media Decoder, *New York Times*, online at: http://mediadecoder.blogs.nytimes.com/2012 /06/11/investor-group-buys-orange-county-register-and-other-newspapers/.

[12] Christine Haughney (6/17/2012) "Newspaper work with Warren Buffett as boss," *New York Times*, online at: http://www.nytimes. com/2012/06/18/business/media/newspaper-work-with-warren-buffett-as-the-boss.html?_r=1&pagewanted=all.

[12] Andrew Lapin (5/20/2016) "As Philadelphia newspapers turn to nonprofits, who is 'public media'?" *Current*, American University School of Communication.

[14] David Carr, cited above.

[15] W. Lance Bennett, Regina Lawrence, and Steven Livingston (2007) *When the Press Fails: Political Power and the News Media from Iraq to Katrina*, Chicago: University of Chicago Press, p. xi.

[16] Bennett et al, p. 36.

[17] Bennett et al, p. 190.

[18] Dean Baker and Kris Warner (1/1/2009) "Going all out for the bank bailout," *Extra*, Fairness and Accuracy in Reporting, online at http://fair.org/extra/going-all-out-for-bank-bailout/.

[19] Stephen D. Reese and Jane Ballinger (2001) "The roots of a sociology of news: Remembering Mr. Gates and social control in the newsroom," *Journalism and Mass Communication Quarterly*, 78, no. 4, pp. 641-658.

[20] Warren Breed (1955) "Social control in the newsroom: A functional analysis," *Social Forces* 33: p. 179.

[21] Amy Joi O'Donoghue (12/6/2011) "WVC council openly reprimands Winder for actions with the press," *Deseret News*, online at: http://www.deseretnews.com/article/705395438/WVC-Council-openly-reprimands-Winder-for-actions-with-the-press.html?pg=al..

# 7

# Setting Realistic Standards for Judging News and Information

*"Objectivity" placed overwhelming emphasis on established, official voices and tended to leave unreported large areas of genuine relevance that authorities chose not to talk about...*

~ Ben H. Bagdikian, former *Washington Post* editor and ombudsman

**A**merican journalism has long embraced an impossible, and I would argue, undesirable, standard – objectivity.

To see why, consider what a truly objective account of something – say a day in a typical American city – would look like. By definition, an objective view of something is one *unaffected by the viewer*. A biased view is the opposite – one influenced by the viewer, usually through the conscious or unconscious imposition of a set of values.[1] An objective account would capture the occurrences in a locality like a giant video camera on autopilot. It would have to be a magic camera able to see through buildings. And able to capture what's going on below the earth's surface where oil, water, gas or magma is pooling, and the crust may be slipping.

In an objective account of a day's events, the story of each grass blade's growth – or its being cut down in the prime of life by a lawn mower – would be as important as a war or flood. To elevate one over the other would impose the observer's values on the account. Objective reporting would describe *everything* in the enhanced viewfinder of the giant camera, even the things that didn't change. It would be as exciting as watching a bank of surveillance cameras hour after hour. No one would want to consume truly objective news. Way too much information!

American journalism's preoccupation with objectivity has obscured reality as often as it has revealed it. To see why and set out an alternative, this chapter will explore three propositions that apply to all of those purporting to tell us the truth, especially those claiming to provide news:

> 1. **Rather than eliminating bias, objectivity norms tend to hide it.**
>
> 2. **To be useful to society, news *must* be biased, but only in three ways: for the common good; for brevity; and for making what's important interesting.**
>
> 3. **Empiricism, not objectivity, should be the standard for presenting claims of fact.**

Let's begin with the first statement above. As practiced in many newsrooms, objectivity conventions have often obstructed honest reporting and confused both journalists and the public. Let me count the ways:

First, objectivity conveys false assurance that journalists see the world as it is – *without any biases of their own.* That's one reason the media were caught flat-footed when poor blacks rioted in America's inner cities in the 1960s. The commission studying the causes of those fiery disturbances concluded:

> The media report and write from the standpoint of a white man's world. The ills of the ghetto, the difficulties of life there, the Negro's burning sense of grievance, are seldom conveyed. Slights and indignities are part of the Negro's daily life, and many of them come from what he now calls "the white press" – a press that repeatedly, if unconsciously, reflects the biases, the paternalism, the indifference of white America.[2]

The problem of skewed news coverage presented as objective hasn't gone away. After rage about police shootings of unarmed black men led to the Black Lives Matter movement, its leaders learned that national news media presented a more accurate view than local journalists. Nakeema Levy-Pounds, president of the Minneapolis NAACP and a professor at the University of St. Thomas School of Law explained:

> "It's usually a challenge if you're relying only on local media to cover major stories of racial injustice. And the reason is because most of the reporters are white, and their managers are white, and the audiences they're reporting for are mostly white. Therefore, they may think they're being fair, but their reporting reinforces a very mainstream view of protests, for example emphasizing disruption as much if not more than the issues, like chronic police misconduct, something white audiences have almost no personal experience with."[3]

A second problem: Objectivity creates the misperception that news media "reflect" the world like a mirror. In actuality, a few fallible humans assemble a partial description of a tiny percentage of current events with carefully selected words, sounds, and images. Given the time pressures on reporters and the sheer volume of content they are expected to produce, errors and misplaced emphases are inevitable. Even the very best reporting is an incomplete and rough first draft of history.

> "I would like to see us say – over and over until the point has been made – that the newspaper that drops on your doorstep is a partial, hasty, incomplete, somewhat flawed and inaccurate rendering of some of the things we have heard about in the past 24 hours."[4]
>
> ~ The late *Washington Post* political columnist David Broder

Journalism suffers the greatest distortion when the story encompasses multiple simultaneous events that are geographically spread apart, with many conflicting stakeholders, the inability to access all sides, and a turbulent context in which disparate currents of history are colliding. This is most evident during a war, but many of these criteria apply to other newsworthy occurrences. Mainstream media completely failed to reflect the reality that Donald Trump was likely to win the presidency in 2016.

Even when journalists are equipped with cameras, news *represents* rather than *reflects* reality. What becomes news is the result of *when* and *where* journalists pointed their cameras and *what was included*, rather than edited out, during a story's construction. Also bear in mind that people often act differently when they know the camera's red light is on, when they're "on stage."

Nevertheless, news media daily promote their coverage as "complete," "trusted," "All the news that's fit to print." Walter Cronkite, perhaps the most trusted American journalist ever, used to end his 22-minute nightly newscast on CBS with a phrase he privately conceded was ludicrous, "And that's the way it is on..." (and he'd say the date). Off the air, Mr. Cronkite said this: "We fall far short of presenting all, or even a goodly part, of the news each day that a citizen would need to intelligently exercise his franchise in this democracy."[5]

The third problem with objectivity has to do with its *definition*. Even journalists who have sworn allegiance to it can't agree. The late Peter Jennings, the respected anchor of ABC Evening News, once said: "I'm not a slave to objectivity. I'm never quite sure what it means. And it means different things to different people." In a thoughtful essay about the concept, *Columbia Journalism Review* editor Brent Cunningham wrote, "Ask ten journalists what objectivity means and you'll get ten different answers."[6] A standard that nobody agrees on is as useless as a temperance advocate at a fraternity party.

Fourth, objectivity encourages *reliance on official sources*, even when reporters believe they are being spun or deceived. That's because it's much easier to report and defend the accuracy of *quotes* from authorities than to seek and defend the best version of the *truth* a journalist can obtain. A story can be 100 percent accurate – the quotes were perfectly transcribed – but 100 percent wrong. In the run up to the invasion of Iraq, top US officials and the reporters who accurately quoted them were completely wrong about the presence of "weapons of mass destruction."

"The big problem with objectivity is that it has no bias toward truth. You can quote both sides of an issue, and they can both be false. This doesn't bring readers any closer to the truth."[7]

~ Eric Alterman, journalism history professor, City University of New York Graduate School of Journalism

When the official view is considered an objective view, it gives voice mainly to the powerful. The poor and minorities often become invisible in such news, unless they break the law. And then their depiction – in a police mug shot or orange prison jumpsuit – contributes to a divisive stereotype. Objectivity invites journalistic passivity and official manipulation.

W. Lance Bennett, whose analysis of news selection we explored in the previous chapter, places the notion of objectivity at the center of the press' passive acceptance of official versions of truth:

> The hallowed journalistic tradition of 'objectivity' often becomes confused with deference to authority and power.... Setting the news agenda independently, while producing a refreshing diversity of information, would also bring noisy criticisms of bias and crusading – from the very same powerful officials who have come to depend on the current news system as a tool of public relations and governance. This curious confusion of objectivity with power is so profound that journalists who depart from narratives reported by the rest of the press pack are typically challenged by their editors for not getting the story right.[8]

Abandoning objectivity allows journalists to escape the passive observer's role, so that they can *advocate* for the public interest. They are empowered to ask the *public's* questions rather than waiting for officials to act or speak.[9]

Fifth, objectivity pushes journalists toward creating a false balance – equal time or space – when two or more sides do not have equal evidence for their positions. You may personally doubt that human activity is warming the planet. But climate scientists have reached near unanimity that it is.[10] When journalists give the few climate-change deniers equal standing with the legion of scientists warning of serious environmental consequences, they enable obfuscation. They collaborate in confusing the public.

Finally, journalistic objectivity developed historically not so much as a means of pursuing truth as profitability. In the second half of the 19th century, as businessmen took over journalism from small printers, and advertisers became the primary funders of news supplanting political parties, it became more profitable to report from a neutral position and gather as many readers as possible from across the political spectrum. The more readers, the more advertising dollars. Partisan reporting alienated potential customers. A neutral stance also greased access to officials from all parties. And it cut reporting costs, allowing the formation of press associations where a single reporter could cover an event impartially for many newspapers. Standing for nothing was a strategy aimed at getting along with everyone.[11]

Abandoning objectivity does *not* mean that journalists should give up trying to present accurate accounts of events and issues. If journalists don't restrain their individual subjectivity, society won't be able to agree on the nature of its problems or appropriate solutions. Further, accuracy matters *more* when news media investigate on behalf of the public than when they rely on government officials to investigate and merely report what the officials found. When journalists *themselves* uncover corruption or incompetence, they take full legal and moral responsibility. If they want to avoid lawsuits and public condemnation, they'd better get the facts right.

2. To be useful to society, news must be biased, but only in three ways: for the common good; for brevity; and for making what's important interesting

We want – and need – journalists to survey the great buzzing confusion of the world for us and do the laborious job *of picking out and pursuing what's most significant* for us to know. Further, we want them to *package it in interesting ways that invite us to care about the news.* And to *simplify it* so we can get the gist quickly. But each of these three processes introduces bias. Each requires subjective professional judgments.

To my mind, these are necessary biases in a democracy. If we are overloaded with information without a hint as to which is most important, or if the presentation is boring or interminable, most of us shut down. Our impulse to become informed citizens is easily smothered.

The idea that news must be biased to be useful to a mass audience may sound odd. But most of journalism's codes of ethics have stated or implied a public service obligation both in news selection and presentation. They just haven't called it a bias because there's marketing value in the idea that journalists can be – and indeed are – value-free truth-tellers. Claiming to be bias-free allows one to reject any blame when what's reported upsets people. "Don't shoot the messenger!" we journalists plead. "We are neutral, merely reflecting reality."

The most important of these three positive biases is the first. Those events and issues that a community must understand to make wise collective and personal decisions should enjoy a clear preference over others – a bias for what matters. How well public schools are performing ought to – but rarely does – trump how well the nearest professional sports team is faring. What might be done to make the community safer matters more than stories limited to an individual accident, fire or crime. Further, the way these consequential topics are reported ought to reflect a noticeable bias for the common good. Reporting should focus on what the public *needs* to know, rather than on what officials or corporations *want* them to know. In any public controversy, journalists should seek answers to this question: Which approach is most likely to generate the greatest benefit for the largest number, without compromising the basic rights of anyone?

The definition of the common good has expanded in fits and starts over two centuries in the United States. The Constitution promised every citizen "inalienable" rights to life, liberty, and the pursuit of happiness. But until the 20th century, most Americans were denied them. Only after long and painful struggle were African-American slaves, people without property or a certain level of education, and women permitted to vote and provided equal protection of laws. A bias for the common good embraces the well-being of all in the community. And all should be welcome to the public conversation defining it. That ongoing debate about the meaning of the common good in each community should be a central and recurring focus of both news and commentary. Rather than imposing their own views of what the community needs from on high, journalists should ground their daily decision-making in a broad public debate.[12]

The bias for brevity requires journalists to ignore many more issues and events than they cover. Even within a single story, they must prioritize, often leaving out more than they report. The winnowing process is guided by a value system, ensuring bias. But it's necessary because most Americans are too busy to surveil all of the day's relevant developments.

The bias for making what's consequential compelling acknowledges that we are not disembodied intelligences. We're not Vulcans like Mr. Spock. There's a little bit of Homer Simpson in all of us. We sometimes need the immediate reward of human interest, skilled story-telling, and evocative images to attract and hold our attention. Our flickering impulse to become informed citizens is as easily extinguished as a candle in the wind. Apathy is so much easier.

"Three years ago, NPR introduced a new code of ethics that ... dropped an insistence on 'balance,' which had come sometimes to mean that there are at least two equal sides to everything, which simply is not true. The claim of pure "objectivity" was deleted too, as impossible and misleading."[13]

~ Edward Schumacher-Matos, former NPR ombudsman

In addition to objectivity, I'm rejecting two other characteristics commonly held up as journalistic ideals: neutrality and balance.

I think news should always take the *public's* side, rather than taking an aloof, neutral stance. News-providers should be independent, but not impartial. That means asking the public's questions and refusing to bow to pressures brought by special interests from within or without the newsroom. For example, local developers may insist that population growth and new subdivisions signify a prosperous community and media owners may agree, arguing that trees don't buy papers or watch newscasts. But journalists must ask who will benefit and who will be burdened from such development, and what will be the effect on the overall environment and quality of life.

As for balance, giving all sides a chance to make their case is important, but equalizing minutes or paragraphs devoted to competing positions makes sense only when the available evidence for alternative sides is roughly equal. Otherwise it's a false equivalence, a distortion of reality. Here's how *New York Times* Executive Editor Dean Baquet put it:

> I'm not sure I buy the construct of balance. To me, it's fairness... You would never say 'I've done 17.3 stories that the Clinton campaign isn't going to like and I've only done 14.7 stories that the Trump campaign isn't going to like. So let me do 3.6 more that the Trump campaign isn't going to like.' Not only will your head explode, but that's imbalanced coverage.[14]

## 3. Empiricism, not objectivity, should be the standard for presenting claims of fact

In place of objectivity, anyone who provides us with information claiming to be factual should be held to a demanding but reachable standard – *empiricism*. It's a pursuit of truth based on dispassionate observation and logic.

Here is what it requires of *anyone* providing news:

1. The quotes and personal observations are accurate. Someone tagging along with the reporter would see and hear the same things.

2. All fact-claims[15] are presented in context, including the full identification of the source of the claim, except in those circumstances where such identification might realistically put the source at risk of harm. There is no attempt to exaggerate, tell half-truths or mislead, nor to persuade; merely to inform.

3. The process of assembling facts into a narrative is rigorously logical, loyal only to the evidence and the public good, and free from undisclosed conflicts of interest. Good reporters test their generalizations by looking for *contrary* evidence, particularly if their conclusions coincide with their preferences and assumptions.

4. Diverse perspectives from those most affected are included or at least sought.

5. All assertions of fact that are not based on either common knowledge or a reporter's direct observation are attributed to a trustworthy source. Further, claims of fact that are consequential are checked for accuracy, or – second-best – flagged as unconfirmed at the time of publication. When sources disagree, there's an attempt to triangulate toward truth by sources who are neutral and expert or experienced.

6. Finally, news-providers humbly acknowledge that every account of reality is partial and subject to revision. Therefore, they promptly correct errors and omissions.

## What empirical reporting looks like

On December 9, 2011, NPR congressional reporter Tamara Keith provided a textbook example of empirical journalism. Weeks earlier, President Obama had proposed a surtax on millionaires to pay for extending a reduction in payroll taxes on less affluent Americans. Congressional Republicans blocked the tax claiming that it would hit small business owners preventing them from creating jobs in an economy desperate for employment growth.

Rather than merely presenting the contrasting viewpoints of Democrats and Republicans "he said/she said" style and leaving the public confused, Ms. Keith attempted to find millionaire small business owners and ask *them* whether the surtax would affect hiring. She was seeking facts rather than political rhetoric. Practicing unusual transparency, she reported on her own reporting:

> We wanted to talk to business owners who would be affected. So, NPR requested help from numerous Republican congressional offices, including House and Senate leadership. They were unable to produce a single millionaire job creator for us to interview.
>
> So we went to the business groups that have been lobbying against the surtax. Again, three days after putting in a request, none of them was able to find someone for us to talk to.
>
> So next we put a query on Facebook. And several business owners who said they would be affected by the "millionaires surtax" responded.[16]

"NPR's Facebook page has 2.2 million followers," Ms. Keith explained in a subsequent interview with me. "If we're looking for something specific and other efforts have failed, we'll go to the Facebook page and create a query with a link to a Google form. There were hundreds of public comments, some of them from small business owners, but not millionaires." Thirty people filled out the Google form. She read all of the responses but "only found one person who said it would hurt her family business. But she didn't respond to a request for an interview. All of the others said there was no impact." In fact, she explained, most of the small business people said their personal tax rate had little or nothing to do with jobs. Hiring was based almost exclusively on demand for the goods or services their companies offered.[17]

In her NPR report, she quoted several of the millionaire small business people she had contacted, concluding "all of this contradicts the arguments about job creators being made by Republicans in Congress."[18]

Calling the Congressional Republicans' bluff, rather than passively broadcasting what turned out to be a dubious claim, made her nervous, Ms. Keith said. "What gives you pause when you do this kind of story is you feel like you're putting yourself out there. If you do one side vs. the other, you really won't take too much heat. I double and triple and quadruple checked everything. You really are … saying 'I'm the journalist. I did the research and here's what I found.'"[19]

When the story aired, Ms. Keith was prepared to take cover. She feared "outraged millionaires would have called to say 'this really affected me.'" But instead, "the story generated a gigantic response in a way that no story I've ever done has," she exclaimed. More than 30,000 people shared it on Facebook. "The story took on a life of its own."[20]

Such reporting has impact, but doesn't come cheap. Ms. Keith estimated that a conventional "he said/she said" story would have taken just 4-6 hours to create. "The dirty little secret is that you can just record their [Congressional] floor speeches. That's the easiest way" to get each side's position. She calculated that the story she reported required about 30 hours. "I feel lucky that I work at NPR," she added. "They really do just let me play around on something for three to four days and see what happens."[21]

### Emerging from 'he said/she said' to active fact-checking

The ascendance of the shoot-from-the-lip political outsider Donald Trump saw a remarkable transition in mainstream reporting. At the beginning of 2016, most media were reluctant to call out falsehoods. Instead they relied on the traditional passive approach: "Mr. Trump said... but Sen. Cruz denied ...." As 2016 wore on, however, most media switched to a more independent and muscular refereeing of political disagreements. You saw reporting like this: "Mr. Trump claimed .... but the facts are ...." Still later in the year, news organizations went further: "Mr. Trump falsely claimed ..." or "Without offering any evidence, Mr. Trump charged ...." By year's end, the careful NPR Morning Edition host Steve Instep would say:

> Are the media approaching Trump's tweets the wrong way? I mean he's obviously trolling. He obviously doesn't check his facts. He obviously tweets false things. Should we just note he says false things and move on?[22]

Mr. Trump's repeated falsehoods and attacks on respected news outlets appeared to be growing a spine in American journalism.

In the next chapter we'll apply the standards of empiricism using the SMELL test for bias.

## Exercises and Discussion Topics

1. Go online and contrast reports about the same professional sporting event from each team's hometown newspaper. Where do they coincide and where do they differ? Were either of the two media accounts *reflections* of reality or were they *representations* of just part – perhaps what the reporter thought were highlights – of what took place?

2. Do you buy the argument that to be useful to a mass audience journalism ought to have the three biases mentioned in the chapter and only those three? Why or why not? Which would you add or subtract? Why?

3. Find an example in the news of "he said/she said" journalism where the reporter makes no effort to determine which side has the stronger evidence for its view. Find another example where the reporter makes this extra effort.

4. Find an example in the news where you think the reporter should not have granted anonymity to a source. Why not?

5. Find an example in the news where a reporter verified or checked up on information provided by a source.

6. Watch a local TV newscast. Does it give the impression of being comprehensive or in-depth by words or images? How so? Do you think everything significant that happened in the signal area (say a 50-mile radius around the station) was included in the newscast? What, if anything, might have been missing? Were the stories about the significant issues in depth? Which, if any, got short shrift? (Look at the list of news topics in the Appendix for help with this question. Also compare the newscast to the next day's newspaper.)

## End Notes

[1] By values I'm referring to preferences and dispositions of the kind described in chapters 4 and 5, based on personal and institutional self-interest.

[2] Otto Kerner and the National Advisory Commission on Civil Disorders (1968) *Report of the National Advisory Commission on Civil Disorders,* Washington, DC: U.S. Government Printing Office. Excerpt online at: http://historymatters.gmu.edu/d/6553/. Of white bias the Commission concluded: "This may be understandable, but it is not excusable in an institution that has the mission to inform and educate the whole of our society."

[3] Brian Lambert (2/2/2016) "How the Black Lives Matter movement is changing local reporting," *Miniport*, https://www.minnpost .com/media /2016/02/how-black-lives-matter-movement-changing-local-reporting.

[4] Quoted in Nick Davies (2009) *Flat Earth News*, London: Vintage Books, p. 44-45.

[5] Cronkite was addressing the Radio and Television News Directors Convention on Dec. 13, 1976, quoted in Marvin Barrett (1978) *Rich news, poor news: the sixth Alfred J. DuPont-Columbia University survey of broadcast journalism*, New York: Thomas Y. Crowell, p. 24.

[6] Brent Cunningham (July/August 2003) "Re-thinking objectivity," *Columbia Journalism Review* Vol. 42, no. 2, pp. 24-32.

[7] Robert Keener (5/3/2013) "Media Bias: Is slanted reporting replacing objectivity?" CQ Researcher, Congressional Quarterly, http://library.cqpress.com/cqresearcher/document.php?id=cqresrre2013050300.

[7] W. Lance Bennett, Regina G. Lawrence, and Steven Livingston (2007) *When the Press Fails: Political Power and the News Media from Iraq to Katrina*, Chicago: University of Chicago Press, p. 178.

[8] If journalists are to ask the questions of the community they serve, they must meet regularly with members throughout that community to learn their concerns and interests. As the former Knight Ridder news executive and publisher Larry Jinks puts it, "In determining what's important, the journalist needs to have real interaction with the members of the audience rather than simply determining it from on high." (Interview with the author on 6/16/2008).

[9] Union of Concerned Scientists, "The Weight of the Evidence," online at: http://www.ucsusa.org/global_warming/science_and_impacts/ science/weight-of-the-evidence.html. (Disclosure: I'm a contributor to the Union of Concerned Scientists.)

[10] The economic origins of the objectivity standard have been written about by many scholars including Leon Sigal (1973) *Reporters and officials*, Lexington, MA: D.C. Heath; Michael Schudson (1978) *Discovering the news,* New York: Basic Books; Paul Starr (2004) *The creation of the media*, New York: Basic Books.

[11] I confess that it is much easier to say that the selection of topics and the way they are covered should reflect the common good than it is to put it into practice. In hindsight, most would agree that African-Americans and women should have rights equal to those of white males. But what about contemporary controversies over rights: Do trans-gender people have a right to use the bathroom of the sex they identify with, as opposed to their birth gender? How about extending citizenship rights to minors whose parents illegally immigrated? Or offer a path to citizenship for those who have paid taxes and contributed their labor to the economy for many years, but who entered illegally? The common good bias I'm advocating would thrust these topics into the news, reporting on them from multiple perspectives. It would also welcome respectful, fact-based arguments on all sides of such issues.

[12] Edward Schumacher-Matos (2/6/2015) "Last Thoughts: NPR and the balance between ethics and the nation," http://www.npr.org/sections/ombudsman/2015/02/06/382170260/last-thoughts-npr-and-the-balance-between-ethics-and-the-nation.

[13] Dean Baquet (12/8/2016) Interview with Terry Gross, "*New York Times* executive editor on the new terrain of covering Trump," Fresh Air, NPR.

http://www.npr.org/2016/12/08/504806512/new -york-times-executive-editor-on-the-new-terrain-of-covering-trump.

[14] A claim that something is a fact requires that it can be proved true or false. In news, it's usually an assertion specific enough that it can be supported or undermined by evidence. If I say someone is a "terrible" governor, it's hard to know what I mean by "terrible," or how that might be proven true or false. On the other hand if I say the governor is an embezzler, one could check to see if s/he had been convicted of such a crime. Embezzlement has a specific meaning. Personal preferences and beliefs that cannot be shown to be true or false are not fact-claims; they are simply opinions. Opinions should never carry the same weight as fact in a controversy.

[15] Tamara Keith (12/9/2011) "GOP objects to 'millionaires surtax'; Millionaires we found? Not so much," National Public Radio, online at http://www.npr.org/blogs/itsallpolitics/2011/12/09/143398685 /gop-objects-to-millionaires-surtax-millionaires-we-found-not-so-much.

[16] Author interview with Tamara Keith (1/5/2012).

[17] Keith, "GOP objects…" cited above.

[18] Interview with Tamara Keith cited above.

[19] Interview with Tamara Keith cited above.

[20] Keith interview.

[21] Steve Inskeep (11/29/2016) Morning Edition, NPR. The topic was Trump's tweet that he would have won the popular vote if it hadn't been for massive voter fraud in New Hampshire, Virginia, and California.

# 8

## The SMELL Test

*Everybody is sitting around saying, 'Well, jeez, we need somebody to solve this problem of bias.' That somebody is us.*

~ Wilma Mankiller, late Cherokee leader

Some fake news is obviously ridiculous. Take a gander at this image from a website called Worldnewsdailyreport.com.

# SYRIAN REFUGEE RENOUNCES ISLAM AFTER TASTING BACON FOR FIRST TIME

April 5th, 2016 | by Bob Flanagan

"It tastes like heaven!" simply puts [sic] Rakim Shaheed, newly employed at a downtown Toronto butcher shop. "I took one bite of a club sandwich my boss prepared for me and I almost fell off my chair," he told local reporters. "It was like a burst of flavor hit my taste buds and shook me like an earthquake" he recalls, visibly still emotional. "I can't believe no one ever told me it was so good," he adds.[1]

But other fabricated articles have fooled many citizens, been shared widely on social media and perhaps changed the outcome of national elections.[2]

The simplest way to discover if a news article is misleading or fake is to check it out on a legitimate fact-checking website, such as Snopes.com, Poltifact.com, or Factcheck.org. However, these sites only examine the most popular frauds, and rarely as soon as they appear.

A second method is to enter the gist of the story, e.g., "Pope Francis endorses Trump," in a search engine such as Google or Bing. Look for two things: First, whether a reputable news outlet, your nearest big city paper or a national paper such as the *Washington Post* or *New York Times,* or a reliable broadcast network, such as NBC or NPR, has reported it; Second, check whether it's being contested or called out as false, or as advertising. (We'll discuss online ways of vetting news in detail in chapter 11). If professional news organizations aren't reporting it or are describing it very differently, you'll know to doubt the story you are evaluating. Exclamation points, WORDS ALL IN CAPS, inflammatory language, name-calling, and broad generalizations are all characteristics of fake news.

This chapter describes a third way – thinking critically about the content of the article. To reveal hidden bias – commercial or ideological – and distinguish more reliable information from less, use the SMELL test. It can be applied to any statement purporting to be factual in any medium, from face-to-face to Facebook to Fox. Here's how it works:

**S** is for **Source**. Who is providing the information? A traditional news outlet, a special interest group, a neighborhood blogger, the Ku Klux Klan? We'll be asking whether they know what they're talking about. And we'll be looking for conflicts between the source's self-interest and our interest in honest information. The presence of such a conflict doesn't invalidate the information, but it does alert us to a likely slant.

**M** is for **Motive**. Why is the source providing this information? Is it primarily designed to inform, persuade (including sell), or entertain? If persuasion is the goal, we'd be more skeptical, wary of cherry-picked evidence. Entertainers aren't bound by facts at all.

**E** is for **Evidence**. What evidence is provided to support the thesis or gist of the story or message?

**L** is for **Logic**. Does the evidence logically compel the generalizations or conclusions? Are they compatible with what we already know?

**L** is for **Left out**. What is missing either through ignorance or intention? Which relevant facts or stakeholders are absent or marginalized?

Information can be unreliable for three reasons: because it's deliberately distorted, unintentionally biased, or simply inaccurate. Intentional distortion is usually carefully hidden. Like a python draped on a tree in the jungle, propaganda depends for its effectiveness on camouflage. Unintentional biases, in contrast, are so deeply embedded in our way of seeing the world that we don't notice them even though they lie in plain sight. We take them for granted as true or natural, the way that only a hundred years ago federal law considered women unfit to vote. Finally, information can be unreliable due to simple ignorance.

Not long ago, we could rely on the natural enemy of bias and ignorance – robust professional journalism. As it recedes, however, we need to learn how to spot unreliable information ourselves and warn others. We need to take a magnifying glass at least to those messages that most affect our well-being.

## A test case: Global warming

Let's test-drive the SMELL test on a controversy that was at full boil in 2017 – whether or not man-made global warming is real or a hoax. Since it affects the whole planet, the issue is about as consequential as you can get. And with President Trump and his

Environmental Protection Agency director dismantling the Obama administration's efforts to reduce greenhouse gases, no news topic is more contested. Here's the top of an article from the British tabloid *Daily Mail* that my conservative friends sent me:[3]

S: Who is the *Source* of the information?

Analyzing the source of information is the first and most important step in vetting. There are several layers to consider.

The simplest case is when *individuals*, perhaps colleagues at school or at work, provide information about something they have *witnessed*. But usually there are at least two levels of sources: immediate – the person speaking, and secondary – the source(s) of his/er information, e.g., heard it from a friend, read it in a book, saw it on TV, etc. If the latter, we'll need to look carefully at our friend's source material.

Information from *institutions*, e.g., websites or other media, typically has three levels of sources: 1) the organization itself; 2) the author whose name is on the article; and 3) the source or sources the author relied on for raw material. Each layer acts as a filter. Each alters the information for its own purposes and in accord with its own biases. The more links in the information chain, the more opportunity for distortion. (Remember the telephone game where one person whispers a message to another and by the end of the chain, it's unintelligible?) So, whenever possible, it's a good idea to go directly to the source closest to the original event. As a practical matter, that's often a media outlet. The Web makes this easy to do.

To keep things simple, we can usually combine the *author* and *organization* levels when the information-provider is an institution such as a media company. As we saw in chapter 5, most authors work with editors and colleagues and all must comply with standards set by the owner. Those standards are enforced because the institution's reputation and freedom from lawsuits are at risk regardless of which employee authors the information. So unless the article was produced by someone *outside* the organization, such as a guest editorial, we can streamline our analysis to two layers – the institution providing the news or information and the sources quoted within the article.[4]

"As anyone in the business will tell you, the standards and culture of a journalistic institution are set from the top down, by its owner, publisher and top editors."[5]

~ Carl Bernstein, investigative reporter and author

Let's begin our credibility audit with the outermost level – the individual or institution providing the information. It's convenient to judge the reliability of a provider by reputation: "Marcy has never lied to me before," or "The *New York Times* has a reputation for accuracy." That's a valuable shortcut when we know the source well. But there's another way that's less vulnerable to our own blind spots. Whether it's an individual friend or colleague, a website such as The Daily Kos or the Drudge Report, or a national organization, such as NBC News or the *New York Times,* all sources can be judged on three logical criteria, which form the acronym PIE:

1. *Proximity* to the event or whatever information is provided. Was the source an eye- or ear-witnesses with unobstructed access? For information, was the source in a position to know first-hand? Or is the information hearsay passed on from others? When the provider is an institution, such as a news organization, we can ask whether its agent or reporter – or better, multiple reporters – were able to observe events for themselves? How about the sources they quote? The closer the source to the action and the less obstructed the view, the better our chances for reliable information.

2. *Independence*, or freedom from conflict of interest. Does the source stand to gain from telling the story, or describing it in a particular way? Self-interest is such a powerful perception-bender that we're always wise to discount information for any advantage it may generate for the source.

3. *Expertise* or lived *Experience*. Is the source knowledgeable, having studied, supervised or had prolonged experience that would lend confidence to his/er report? For news media and other institutional information-providers, does their agent have specialized knowledge, e.g. a reporter covering courts who has a law degree, or long experience covering the subject?

**The referring source**: The friend who sent me the climate change story is a very successful and wealthy engineer living in South Carolina. His libertarian brand of conservatism goes as deep as orange on carrot. Every link he sends me fits his personal ideology, but that doesn't mean they are inaccurate. However, when I factcheck them, some turn out false. So I begin my analysis with a skeptical, but open, mind.

**The institutional source**: I looked up *The Daily Mail* on Wikipedia. I found that the paper is the second most popular in Britain, that it leans conservative, and is owned by Jonathan Harmsworth, 4th Viscount Rothermere.[6] More conservatives than liberals doubt that humans are warming the planet, at least in harmful ways. So a conservative bias is likely to minimize human-caused global warming.

**Sources within the article**: The first named source is Dr Gavin Schmidt, head of NASA's (National Aeronautics and Space Administration) climate division, but rather than supporting the headline that global warming is due to a natural cause – El Nino (a warming of the Eastern Pacific ocean near the Equator) – the author writes that Dr. Schmidt "claimed that the recent highs were mainly the result of long-term global warming." (The word "claim" is often a give-away that the author doubts the statement.) Dr. Schmidt would seem to have a top PIE score as he heads a deeply resourced scientific effort by a neutral party, the U.S. government, to study climate change. In the following paragraphs Dr. Schmidt is referenced three more times, in each case contradicting the claim in the story's headline that global warming has resulted from the El Nino rather than man-made emissions.

The next source referenced is Bob Walker, Mr. Trump's science advisor. But his comment is pulled from another article, rather than an interview. And he's paraphrased saying NASA's budget for studying the climate, $1.9 billion, was likely to be "axed," not whether the climate is changing. So no need to chart him.

Only after 19 paragraphs does the author report on an interview with a source supporting the headline: "Professor Judith Curry, of the Georgia Institute of Technology, and president of the Climate Forecast Applications Network, said yesterday: 'I disagree with Gavin. The record warm years of 2015 and 2016 were primarily caused by the super El Nino.'" Professor Curry would appear to have a high PIE score. Entering her name in a Google search I learned that she decided to retire early from her professorship and had been criticized for her conclusions about climate change.[7] Nevertheless, she appears to be an accomplished climate scholar, although one of the few on her side of the issue.

The third and final source was David Whitehouse, identified as "a scientist who works with Lord Lawson's skeptic Global Warming Policy Foundation." Whitehouse is quoted saying: "According to the satellites, the late 2016 temperatures are returning to the levels they were at after the 1998 El Nino." And paraphrased: "the massive fall in temperatures following the end of El Nino meant the warming hiatus or slowdown may be coming back."

Wikipedia describes the Global Warming Policy Foundation as "a think tank in the United Kingdom, whose stated aims are to challenge 'extremely damaging and harmful policies' envisaged by governments to mitigate anthropogenic global warming."[8] In other words, the foundation's purpose is to minimize or repudiate the threat of man-made global warming. Mr. Whitehouse is not a climate scientist, but was a science reporter for the respected BBC.[9] Here's how I'd chart the sources, using their initials:

| Assessing Source Credibility with the PIE Chart | | | |
|---|---|---|---|
| | Low | Medium | High |
| Proximity | DW | | GS, JC |
| Independence | DW | | GS, JC |
| Expertise | | DW | GS>JC |

Most journalists who tackle a highly controversial topic interview many more sources. But if it's only three, they will choose the most informed and rational they can find from each side of the issue and then select a neutral expert to guide the reader/viewer beyond "he said/she said" confusion.

Dr. Curry is a good pick for the side disputing global warming. Mr. Whitehouse, however represents a foundation that has already closed its mind on the issue; not a great choice if your purpose is informational. As the head of NASA's climate division, Dr. Schmidt is a great choice for the role of neutral expert. NASA has no vested interest in the issue, but does have resources – far greater than those available to a university professor – to investigate it.

However the author, David Rose, casts Dr. Schmidt, as merely an *advocate* of the position that humans are warming the planet, rather than a *neutral* expert. The *Daily Mail* frames the story as two advocates agreeing with the notion that the planet is warming due to a natural climate cycle versus one advocate for the alternate view, as if all three viewpoints were equally free of conflict of interest and well researched. It's kind of like siding with a former college basketball player and a fan of the Boston Celtics against LeBron James in an argument about how to play the game.

M: What is the source's *Motivation?*

The tone of the story seems mostly informational with both pro and con sources. I found only one hyperbolic sentence, but it was in the headline and thus set the tone of the article: "*Stunning* new data....". Nevertheless, I'll stick with an informative motivation rather than persuasive.

E: What *Evidence* is provided to support the story's thesis?

The thesis or gist can be found in the headline: "Stunning new data indicates El Nino drove record highs in global temperatures suggesting rise may not be down [sic] to man-made emissions." Giving the *Daily Mail*, the benefit of the doubt, I'll assume "down" means "due" in American English.

Beyond the sources quoted, who are contradictory, Mr. Rose provides a graph, an image of the planet showing El Nino, two photos and three video clips. The combination of graphs, images and multiple video clips gives the appearance of a well-researched article. But let's look below the surface.

The graph is key.

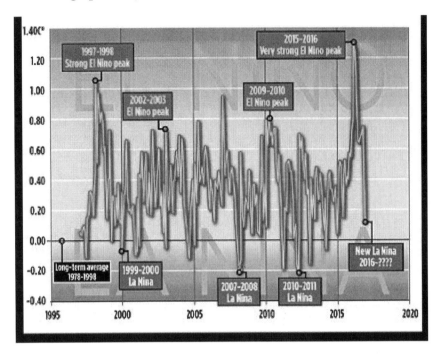

While the source of the graph is unclear, it's labeled as "Temperatures over land." Given that only 29 percent of the earth's surface is covered by land, and because land doesn't absorb heat the way water does, there's a disconnect between claims of *global* temperatures and *land* temperatures. The graph also reveals that the vast majority of these temperature data points between 1998 and 2016 are about half a centigrade *higher* than the graph's baseline, the average between 1978-1998, *whether or not it was an El Niño year*. So even on land, temperatures have risen regardless of El Niño.

The article has a second color-coded image of ocean temperature patterns. You can see the El Niño fading. But no claim of falling temperatures is made. Given the importance of ocean temperatures in measuring climate change, I Googled "ocean temperature changes over time." I found this graph from the Environmental Protection Agency:[10]

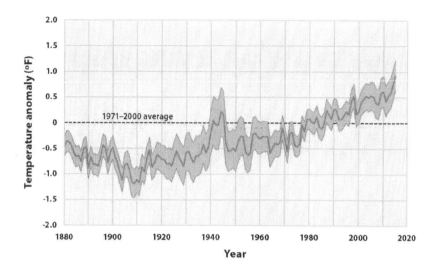

It shows a long-term increase in ocean temperatures that cannot be explained by occasional El Nino events – a second direct contradiction of the story's thesis.

The two photos included in the article also provide no evidence for the story's thesis. One shows a flood in Peru. The other is of President Trump. The first video included actually contradicts the story line and explains how global warming works. The second shows NASA images of the formation of the 2014 El Nino, which no one disputes. The third video shows a flood in California. Flooding is actually a sign of global warming as a warmer atmosphere can hold – and dump – more water.

### L: Does the evidence *Logically* compel the conclusion?

Notice that the headline contains some "weasel" words: "Stunning new data indicates El Nino drove record highs in global temperatures *suggesting* rise *may* not be down to man-made emissions [italics added]."

The evidence presented only shows a 1 degree Celsius drop in *land* temperatures in one year. But land temperatures in the graph fluctuate every year. So it appears the *Daily Mail* is claiming a *single* year's fluctuation in *land* temperatures can be generalized to the entire planet as a *trend*. Climate science, in contrast, is careful to collect data over the *entire globe across many years* before it declares a trend.

### L: What's *Left out* of the story?

A Google search for "global climate change," revealed that 2014, 2015, and 2016 have each set record high temperatures. That's quite an omission in a story about global climate change. The fading El Nino may keep 2017 from setting another record, but a full view of climate data shows El Nino events are bumps on a deeper and longer trend as the planet warms. Here's NASA's graph charting global temperature change since 1880 (with 0 set as the average between 1951 to 1980 and the black line representing 5-year means; the circles show annual means):[11]

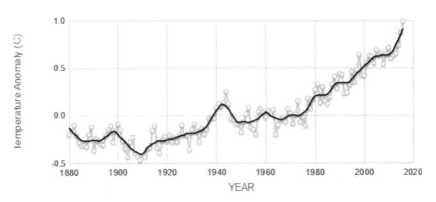

Source: climate.nasa.gov

Conclusion: The *Daily Mail* story is fake news of the most dangerous sort – the kind requiring some analysis to detect. Presenting land temperatures rather than global temperatures appears to be either a deliberate effort to mislead or "stunning" journalistic incompetence. The wonderful news is that with a few clicks you can find all the data needed to unmask a fraud.

### Trouble-shooting the SMELL test

Not every analysis is as straightforward as the *Daily Mail* article allowed. Let's go back through the SMELL test for issues that might arise given the variety of news and information on offer in the digital age.

## What to do when the *Source* is unclear

Legacy news media – the ones that pre-dated the Internet such as newspapers and broadcast stations – are easy to identify as sources. But news providers born on the Web can pose a problem. So how can you apply PIE (Proximity, Independence and Expertise/ Experience) criteria when the source is unfamiliar? Or it has a vague name wrapped in stars and stripes, like "Citizens for American Progress"?

Legitimate Web-only information sources will *always* disclose who they are on their home page or with an "about us" link. If the producer of the content isn't identified, or seems at all coy about describing him/er/itself, believe *nothing* from it. The primary reason an information-provider – whether on a website or online video or in a viral email – chooses not to identify, or to mis-identify, itself is to disarm the audience. *Deception automatically invalidates content.* Treat such sites or email messages like poison ivy. Even if you're itching to, don't enable contagion by forwarding.

To evaluate independence from conflicts of interest – the I in PIE – you'll need to know who sponsors the information-provider – the major donors. Unless it's obvious, websites and other media providing news and information should always state who pays the bills. If the source draws support from advertisers, pay attention to the goods and services in the ads and compare them to the information provided. The greater the similarity between ads and content, the less trust you should repose in the information. Rational advertisers rarely pay to be placed in a critical environment.

If the information source is unfamiliar, investigate it by entering the name in Google or another search engine. Don't trust any sources you haven't vetted to discover their qualifications and sponsorship. Political influence groups, industry trade associations, and some think tanks have been known to adopt misleading names to disguise their self-interest.

Consider the Foundation for Lung Cancer: Early Detection, Prevention & Treatment. Who could wear a whiter hat – or lab coat? But the *New York Times* discovered that the foundation was covertly underwritten almost entirely by the parent company of Liggett, a major cigarette maker.[12] In a story about a massive recall of eggs possibly tainted by salmonella, the *Washington Post* website added what it thought was a helpful link to a site called the Egg Safety Center (www.eggsafety.org). To the *Post's* embarrassment, the site turned out to be run by a PR firm for the United Egg Producers rather than a source of impartial expertise.[13] Even professional journalists need to look beyond that innocent or patriotic name.

In chapter 1, we saw how unreliable the *New York Times* turned out to be in reporting on Iraq's attempts to purchase aluminum tubes as if it were proof of an effort to develop nuclear weapons. So it's useful to apply our PIE criteria to sources quoted *within* a particular message or news account, as we did with the climate change article.

Credible information will *always* include the sources who provided it, identified by position and usually by name. Only sources who would suffer harm from being named should be permitted anonymity, and even these should be identified by position, e.g. "a senior manager who attended the meeting."[14] These identifiers are necessary to help us recognize their biases and decide how much to believe of what the source says. They also get the source on the record, creating accountability. (People speaking with full attribution are normally more careful about their comments than those permitted anonymity. That's why we should always give greater credence to named sources.)

Documentary sources – books, reports, memos, etc. – can be classified by their author(s)' PIE score. The greater the number of sources, the more diverse their backgrounds, and the higher their PIEs, the more trustworthy the story. Also notice diversity because, as we saw in chapter 4, people see the same thing differently depending on their self-interest, and across social "fault lines" of race, class, gender, etc.

How do you discern the information-provider's *Motivation*?

Have you ever engaged in a conversation where you thought the other person was merely informing you and learned too late that it was really a sales pitch? With media, it's often unclear whether the source has gathered our attention primarily to inform, persuade, or entertain.. There's money to be made and influence to be had by cloaking the source's intent.

Governments and corporations often produce content that appears purely *informational*. Oil companies so devoted to environmentalism they portray themselves as jolly green giants; banks lending a helping hand simply to prosper the community; and prospective soldiers promised that they can somehow "be all that [they] can be," if they volunteer for an organization that will train them to kill.

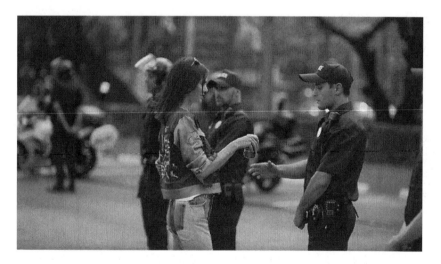

In April 2017, Pepsi launched an ad on YouTube featuring model Kendall Jenner joining an ethnically diverse group of attractive young actors staged as a street protest. In the climactic scene as the faux protesters face a line of actors dressed as police, in slo-mo Ms. Jenner hands a can of Pepsi to a handsome young "cop," who smiles after a long pull. Peace reigns on the street and everyone gets along, thanks to Pepsi.

While probably well-intended, so many people thought the ad trivialized the Black Lives Matter protests and police violence against poor black people that Pepsi pulled the ad after only a day and apologized. If the soft drink maker hoped to show solidarity with young – hopefully thirsty – protesters, they missed the mark. Bernice King, daughter of Martin Luther King Jr., tweeted sarcastically: "If only daddy would have known about the power of #Pepsi."[15]

As we saw in chapter 6, source motivation also can be masked when advertisers seeking the credibility of journalism for thinly disguised commercial messages successfully pressure news organizations. To avoid being fooled, it's useful to learn the characteristics that reveal motivation.

The most obvious tip-off to a source's motivation is the tone established in the content, including images and sound. Trust your instinct. If it *feels* like the real intent is to persuade, or provoke a laugh or sigh, it probably is. Here are the characteristics of content primarily designed to inform, to persuade, and to entertain.

### Content designed to inform

Informers follow the rules of empiricism stated at the close of chapter 7. They stress established facts and careful, specific observation. Every assertion of fact that's not based on common knowledge or the author's direct observation is attributed to a source fully enough for the audience to apply the PIE test.

Informers practice fairness – dispassionately presenting all relevant sides to an issue in a context that aids audience understanding. No cherry-picking of facts to favor one side over another. Informers are careful to include the perspectives of all major parties with something at stake in the issue or event reported.

Informers are faithful to evidence rather than ideology. Informers prefer nuance (shades of gray) over black and white because life rarely demonstrates such sharp contrasts. They employ short, logical inferences to reach their conclusions. They avoid sweeping generalizations. They practice transparency (explaining how they know what they claim to know and warning about what they don't). The format is descriptive rather than argumentative. Except possibly for empathy, the presentation is unemotional. Anger, fear, titillation – all retard reason. No judgment of right or wrong is proffered. No action is called for. Other than being concerned, you get the impression that the source cares little about what conclusion you draw or how you behave in response to the information. Photos and videos are used to document the text. They are neither choreographed nor posed. Natural sound predominates. Music is rare.[16]

These, by the way, are the standards of empirical reporting and what the best news organizations mean by objectivity.

### Content designed to persuade

Because life is complicated and we are busy people, society also gains from principled persuasion that simplifies and explains. Persuasion is principled if it is: 1) true to the relevant facts, rather than manipulating or distorting them; 2) logical in that the evidence provided supports the conclusions drawn; and 3) transparent – content is labeled as opinion or commentary with the author fully identified so we can assess his/er proximity, independence and expertise/experience.

> "[Opinion writers] are not entitled to get the facts wrong or to so mangle them that they present a false picture,"[17]
>
> ~ Clark Hoyt, former public editor of the *New York Times*

During the 2012 Republican presidential primaries *New York Times* op-ed columnist Gail Collins repeatedly stretched Clark Hoyt's standard in describing a 1983 incident in which candidate Mitt Romney put the family's Irish setter, Seamus, in a wind-sheltered portable kennel on the roof of the family station wagon on a summer vacation trip to Canada. Even in a column devoted to Newt Gingrich's legacy, Ms. Collins couldn't resist writing that "Mitt Romney drove to Canada with the family Irish setter strapped on the car roof."[18] This was after fact-finding website PolitiFact cited Ms.

Collins for mentioning the incident in 17 previous columns.[19] By implying that the dog was tied to the roof without protection, the anecdote manipulated the truth to make Mr. Romney seem inhumane.

## Principled persuasion

Principled persuasion usually takes the form of an argument for a particular view of something: Where informers lay out the relevant facts and let readers or viewers decide what they mean, commentators provide a preferred meaning. They often make judgments. Sometimes they call for action. Persuaders often apply an overarching ideology – perhaps pragmatic, liberal, conservative or libertarian – to create a simplified and coherent explanation of events and issues. But there is no attempt to disguise it.

If there is debate, it is civilized and respectful: No name-calling, personal attacks, taunts, shouting, or making fun of opposing persons or positions. There can be disagreement, but all sides listen to the others rather than talking over them. Images and sound are generally similar to those produced when the purpose is to inform.

## Unprincipled persuasion

Unprincipled persuasion involves some type of deceptive manipulation of the information presented or lack of care with fact claims. The tone is often emotional rather than logical. In broadcasts, conflict is common, because as CNN chief Jeffrey Zucker knows, it attracts an audience. In their smart book about intentional bias in messages, *UnSpun*, Brooks Jackson and Kathleen Hall Jamieson warn specifically about efforts to shut off thinking by arousing primal emotions. "If it's scary," they write, "be wary."[20] I'd add: "If they shout, tune it out."

Look for slogans and catch phrases such as "death taxes," "common sense solution," "socialist," "one-percenters," "makers/takers," "snowflakes," or "fat cats," which are often tested in focus groups for how they play on the ears of target audiences. Images are sometimes digitally-altered and always chosen to provoke a specific reaction. They may significantly distort what they purport to describe. Music is sometimes played over words and images to heighten the emotional impact, much as it might be in a motion picture. If you've ever watched a political ad, you know it can be a potent brew.

Calvin and Hobbes (used with permission)

*Content designed to entertain*

An entertainer may, but need not, adhere to facts. Logic, evidence, and fairness matter little. Exaggeration, even absurdity, are common. Emotion, however, is essential. To be successful, entertainment has to move you, even if it's just a smile or cringe. Dramatic images and music are carefully selected and sequenced.

It's tempting to overlook entertainment as a motivation because its primary function is to enthrall us and what it describes is often openly fictitious. But as the English social philosopher/nanny Mary Poppins observed, "a spoonful of sugar makes the medicine go down." Entertainment can leap-frog our rational faculties to exert powerful social effects, including fooling us.

Lauren Feldman, a communication professor at American University explained: "When audiences are exposed to political humor or satire, they are less likely to oppose the information in the message or question whether it is fair or accurate. Ultimately, it can affect the perceptions of a candidate."[21]

Satirists such as Alec Baldwin and Melissa McCarthy on Saturday Night Live, Jon Stewart and Stephen Colbert when they were on Comedy Central, cartoonist Gary Trudeau and Bill Maher of HBO have understood as well as did Aristophanes and Jonathan Swift that humor can be uniquely persuasive. It can disarm our skepticism like a woman panhandling with a baby in her arms.

According to Professor Feldman, Tina Fey's impression of then Republican vice-presidential candidate Sarah Palin on Saturday Night Live hurt the McCain-Palin ticket in 2008. It earned SNL its highest overnight ratings in 14 years. And her impersonations became the most viewed videos on NBC's website during the election year. Millions more watched them on YouTube and Hulu.com. CNN began referring to them as the "Tina Fey effect," and speculated that Ms. Fey's version of Ms. Palin became confused in voters' minds with the real candidate.[22]

"Satirical news matters," wrote Silvia Knobloch-Westerwick, author of a study published in 2017 and professor of communication at Ohio State University. "It is not just entertaining – it has a real-life impact on viewers." She found that viewers tended to select comedy that matched their political views. Even though they knew the programs were not factual, their political views were strengthened by viewing. Satire also generated political interest. "These results suggest that satirical news can engage people who otherwise would avoid political news," she added.[23]

Novels, plays, motion pictures, and cartoons often inform and persuade as well as entertain. Prior to the American Civil War, Harriet Beecher Stowe's widely read account of the brutality of slavery in *Uncle Tom's Cabin* made the practice real – and repugnant – to Northerners. In 1862, Ms. Stowe met President Abraham Lincoln who reportedly quipped, "So you're the little woman who wrote the book that started this great war!"[24] American Studies Professor David S. Reynolds called it "the most influential novel in American history and a catalyst for radical change both at home and abroad."[25]

To avoid being fooled, it's useful to subject satire and fiction to a modified version of the same criteria used for establishing the reliability of news and other information presented as factual. Even if the characters and setting are fictional, do they fairly illustrate the reality they purport to describe? We can ask, for example, how Ms. Stowe learned about plantation life (by looking at her online biography). Was she free of conflicts of interest? Was her primary purpose to entertain or inform, or to persuade? We can also apply the remainder of the SMELL test.

What *Evidence* is provided to support the thesis or gist of the story or message?

Some information-providers possess the confidence of the framers of the Constitution: They believe what they assert as true to be self-evident. They make naked assertions, offered as if there is no need to attribute a claim of fact to an authoritative source, nor to assemble evidence for generalizations.

When providers offer no source or evidence for their claims, we have no choice but to fall back on our assessment of the provider's own credibility and, if mediated, the reputation of the institution on whose pages, airwaves or website the information appears. A distinguished professor writing within his/er expertise for a news outlet that forbids conflicts of interest and checks facts may merit trust, but we should be skeptical of less qualified information-providers, particularly if they are working *outside* of institutions with a reputation for integrity. As a former journalist whose wary editors warned "if your mother says she loves you, check it out," I encourage you to be uncomfortable with the "trust me" school of evidence.

*How do you know that?*

To avoid being fooled whenever we hear an assertion about what's real or true, we should ask: *How do you know that?*

"I heard it on the grapevine" won't do. There are only three adequate answers: 1) I witnessed it; 2) I learned it from one or more sources (documentary or human) who rank high on the PIE source reliability matrix described earlier; 3) It logically follows from information provided in answers 1 or 2.

Trustworthy information-providers should attempt to *confirm* or *verify* at least the most consequential or controversial claims of their sources. Verification means finding at least one other source, independent of the first and with a strong PIE score, who provides a similar description of an event. It's irresponsible to just hand over the megaphone of the media even to prominent sources – *especially* to prominent sources – enabling them to broadcast misinformation. Verification has become even more essential in our present sharply partisan political environment where candidates' spinning is as constant as their grinning and once something is posted on the Web it can metastasize at fiber optic velocity.

### *"Loosening standards of accuracy and verification"*

Partisan pundits and politicians have been emboldened by changes in news media. At the close of 2009 and beginning of 2010, the Project for Excellence in Journalism surveyed mainstream news executives. One key finding: six in ten said the Internet is changing the fundamental values of journalism. "And their biggest concern is loosening standards of accuracy and verification, much if it tied to the immediacy of the Web." One broadcast executive wrote: "I worry that journalistic standards are dropping in that blogging and celebrity gossip and Tweets are being confused with reporting and editing that passes a rigorous standard."[26]

It takes time to find and interview reliable sources; even more time to check their fact-claims. Plus, their responses lengthen and complicate news reports. And all those attributions – "according to Jones," "Smith said," "Adams responded" – slow the reader or listener down. Given the understaffed, constant-deadline, multimedia newsrooms of the early 21st century, it's more important than ever for us to ask: "How do you know that?" of our news and information sources and to map the sources they quote on the PIE chart.

### The nature of photographic and video evidence

Before the era of digital recording of images and software such as Photoshop that allows it to be completely altered so seamlessly that it is difficult to detect, photos and film were seen as the gold standard of evidence. Cameras, we said, don't lie. They capture reality without bias. And they don't forget.

Calvin and Hobbes (used with permission)

The apparent unblinking objectivity of cameras was always an illusion, however. Even in the old days when news photographers wore bandoliers of spooled film cartridges, they often posed their subjects to make the images more dramatic.

But the subjectivity of image creation is even more basic. Anyone who has pointed a camera knows that the images captured show only what's in focus within the lens at a given moment. Left unseen is everything that happened before and after the picture or the video clip was shot and everything that happened in other directions and locations. Editing narrows and manipulates this thin slice of reality even further. "Images are always mediated, and those who choose the angles, shots, et cetera, shape our perceptions," according to Arthur Asa Berger, a professor of visual communication at San Francisco State University.[27] Seeing should *not* lead to believing. (More on this in chapter 9.)

### Does the evidence *Logically* support the conclusions drawn?

The fundamental question here is "Does this make sense?" and we can profitably ask it at two levels: 1) Externally – "Does this make sense in light of everything else I know?" and 2) Internally – "Is the evidence provided *within* the report adequate to support the conclusions reached?"

Obviously, the more you know, the better your answer to the first question will be. (Assuming what you know is correct.) That's why it's important to keep up with news from reliable sources. Information that jars you, that's "too good to be true," or that perfectly fits your biases, is particularly suspect. It requires an especially rigorous approach to question two about its internal logic.

*Dissonant* information puts us on alert. But we are most easily fooled when the answer to question one about whether the new information squares with the old is either "yes" or "I don't know." Because of this vulnerability, we can't stop with question one. For news or information that really matters we have to examine the internal logic.

## Common media logic failures

Whole books are devoted to logic. Here I want to focus on seven related reasoning fallacies and failures of due diligence common to news and information-providers.

**1. Non-sequiturs**: derive from a Latin phrase meaning "it doesn't follow." Politicians frequently promise the sky only to deliver hot air. A frequent theme is that cutting taxes for the wealthy stimulates so much growth, tax revenues will actually rise despite lower rates. As *New York Times* columnist and Nobel-Prize-winning economist Paul Krugman pointed out when the Trump administration floated the idea again in 2017: "history offers not a shred of support for faith in the pro-growth effects of tax cuts. In other words, supply-side economics is a classic example of a zombie doctrine: a view that should have been killed by the evidence long ago, but keeps shambling along, eating politicians' brains."[28]

In March 2017, Secretary of State Rex Tillerson brushed off a 29 percent proposed cut in the State Department budget. He told reporters: "The level of spending that the State Department has been undertaking, particularly in the past year, is simply not sustainable," He explained that current spending reflected the "level of conflicts that the U.S. has been engaged in around the world as well as disaster assistance." The implication was that the level of conflict would decline, making the cuts a reasonable adjustment. He then promised that the department would undergo a review of programs and would "be much more effective, much more efficient, and be able to do a lot with fewer dollars."[29]

The same budget that was "not sustainable" for the State Department, *added* $54 billion for military spending. That's more than the entire State Department budget for 2016. So it doesn't follow that the government could not have afforded to continue present levels of spending for diplomacy (which seeks alternatives to military engagement). There was also no evidence that the "level of conflicts that the U.S. has been engaged in around the world" was lessening. To the contrary, President Trump was escalating military involvement in Syria and Yemen, about to attack a Syrian air base with cruise missiles, and threatening a military strike on nuclear-armed North Korea. Finally, Secretary Tillerson offered no support for the almost certainly counter-factual statement that the department could "be more effective" with almost a third fewer dollars.

Such magical thinking is common not just in government but in the corporate world. Because journalists often fail to point out the illogic of their sources, we have to evaluate them ourselves to avoid being fooled.

**2. Overgeneralizations**: Conclusions should stretch over evidence as tightly as a swimming cap covers an expensive hairdo. There should be little room for doubt to seep in. The evidence presented, plus common knowledge, should compel you to accept the information-provider's conclusion. The broader the conclusion, the more evidence is required.

A frequent type of overgeneralization occurs when anecdotes are presented as proof of something larger. Anecdotes are personal stories – vignettes – that providers properly use to add human interest to their articles. But a series of anecdotes doesn't prove anything, no matter how poignant they may be. They are merely a few data points that might easily be contradicted by other personal accounts the information-provider didn't have – or take – time to gather.

So a news report in which several teachers tell vivid personal stories about students today failing to take school as seriously as young people did 20 years ago doesn't mean that the current generation is less engaged, nor even that teachers agree on this. Had the provider interviewed other teachers, s/he might have reported just the opposite conclusion. Neither would have been logical. *Only a sample where every member of a group has an equal opportunity to be included and the number interviewed represents a majority or a number large enough to allow statistical tests of significance can support generalizations about that group.*[30]

Beware of any generalizations or assertions that are not based on *systematic* evidence-gathering. Otherwise you may fall prey to examples selectively chosen from among contradictory cases to make a point.

Sweeping generalizations go hand-in-hand with imprecise quantifiers like "many," "largely," "a lot," "somewhat" and "up to (some number)." But how many is "many" or "a lot?" "Many" indicates number, not a proportion; it may not come close to a majority. How much is "somewhat?" "Up to" includes every number below it. Such words should alert us to a lack of definite facts or numbers, information that's incomplete if not misleading.

**3. Innuendo**: Innuendo hints that something is true without stating it outright. It's what you read between the lines. When they want to proclaim a conclusion they cannot fully support with facts, information-providers are tempted to rely on innuendo.

On January 10, 2017, the online magazine BuzzFeed published a story titled: "These Reports Allege Trump Has Deep Ties To Russia." The article told about a former British intelligence agent hired as an opposition researcher by Democrats who claimed that Russian agents had compromising information about Donald Trump cavorting with prostitutes on a business trip to Moscow some years earlier. The story suggested that Russian agents were using the threat of exposing the information to blackmail Mr. Trump into favorable policies toward Russian leader Vladimir Putin. News of the dossier had been kicking around official Washington for some months and alluded to previously in other media reports. However, Buzzfeed took a further step. It embedded in its article the raw 35 page intelligence report with all of its salacious details, with this rationale: "Now BuzzFeed News is publishing the full document so that Americans can make up their own minds about allegations about the president-elect that have circulated at the highest levels of the US government."[31]

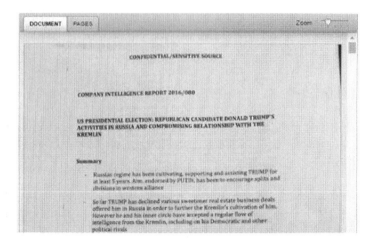

Liberals exulted. Here, they said, was the explanation for Mr. Trump's oft expressed admiration for Mr. Putin and his reluctance to condemn the Russian seizure of the Crimea in Ukraine. It fit their prejudices (and to be honest, mine) perfectly.

A storm of protest followed, led by conservatives, but also joined by some liberals and editors of mainstream news media who called it an irresponsible cheap shot.

To be fair, BuzzFeed's article contained a variety of cautions, calling the information in the dossier "unverified," and pointing out a couple of minor factual errors. But by publishing the raw report, they were, in effect, saying "this is something important for you to know." What they were *not* saying is "this is going to get us millions of new online visitors. It will generate lots of buzz."

The Society of Professional Journalists Code of Ethics states: "Verify information before releasing it," especially information damaging to someone's reputation. And under the section titled "Minimize harm," "Avoid pandering to lurid curiosity, even if others do."[32] BuzzFeed violated these norms. It could have described the existence of the report, as more responsible news outlets did, without detailing any alleged sexual escapades until the federal investigations, which BuzzFeed noted were underway, determined the validity of the report. Instead, BuzzFeed succumbed to commercial bias.

**4. Lack of context**: Civil rights leader Rev. Jesse Jackson once said that "text without context is pretext."[33] In July, 2010, the late founder of Breitbart News, Andrew Breitbart, provided an example. He posted a video on his website that appeared to show Shirley Sherrod, the Georgia rural development director for the U.S. Department of Agriculture, admitting discrimination against whites. The video, however, was maliciously doctored. The unedited version, which surfaced a few days later, showed just the opposite: how Mrs. Sherrod had *overcome* her bitter feelings about whites, who had murdered her father, in order to help a white farmer with a government aid program. But before the truth came out, Ms. Sherrod had been vilified by Fox News' Sean Hannity and Bill O'Reilly (the latter later apologized). She was fired from her job and denounced by the NAACP faster than a knee jerks when struck by a doctor's rubber mallet, only to be reinstated and praised days later by shame-faced officials.[34]

Taking comments out of context is hardly a tactic of conservatives alone. On Jan. 3, 2008, Republican presidential candidate John McCain interrupted a question at a campaign stop. It began, "President Bush has talked about our staying in Iraq for 50 years..." Mr. McCain cut in to say, "Maybe a hundred." Then he added, "We've been in Japan for 60 years. We've been in South Korea for 50 years or so. That'd be fine with me as long as Americans are not being injured or harmed or wounded or killed."[35]

Liberal and Democratic websites, political opponents, even some news programs such as "Democracy Now," reported the "hundred years" quip but not the important qualifier – "as long as Americans are not being injured." It made McCain appear insensitive to the costs of war. At minimum, context requires us to consider the words surrounding those reported, as well as the occasion or location of the words quoted.

It can still be difficult to detect a lack of context, but the Web now offers multiple versions of major stories, particularly at the national and international level. Try to find reports from news organizations operating across bias fault lines, such as nationality or political ideology. Check reports against each other to fill in missing or misleading emphases. Increasingly, online news articles are followed by comment boxes. Sometimes (amid considerable flatulence) you'll find context there. Pay particular attention to reactions from those sources named in the article. More on this in the final chapter.

**5. Flawed comparisons**: These comprise two general types – incomplete comparisons and apples to oranges.

*Incomplete comparisons*

If crime, disease, accidents, test scores, gasoline prices, inflation, or what-have-you is up or down, or if anything is better or worse, always ask, "compared to what?" At minimum, the comparison should include raw numbers and a percentage increase or decrease from a previous or baseline period, e.g., the average price of a gallon of regular gasoline in the U.S. rose 21 cents last year, a 7 percent increase from $3. Both numbers are needed because when the base is small, even a little change can represent a large percentage. Add one to one and you have only one more, but a 100 percent increase. At the other extreme, if the base is very large, even a substantial increase in number may represent only a small percentage change.

Comparisons also ought to include contextual baselines. Saying the average tuition charged by American universities has increased fourfold from 1990 may be misleading without a comparison to the overall inflation rate. Almost everything is more expensive now than it was 30 before. It would be more accurate to compare the increase in tuition in constant dollars, so it's not exaggerated by inflation. Or to compare the proportion of a typical family's income that's consumed by tuition then versus now.

If a trend is claimed there must be at least three data points, preferably more, over a reasonable period of time. That period should be long enough for whatever is being measured to change beyond the range of normal fluctuations. Weekly tallies of new claims for unemployment benefits, for example, bounce around enough that a clear picture of employment trends ought to stretch across at least a month, preferably six months to a year.

*Inappropriate comparisons*

Superficial similarities can mask differences so large the comparison is misleading. In 2002 Saddam Hussein was cast as the new Hitler. It made him seem more threatening and bolstered the case for war. While both were brutal dictators who gassed some of their countrymen, the scale and context of these atrocities and the power of the Iraqi vs. Nazi war machines relative to their neighbors was clearly a peanut to pumpkin comparison. In 2012, another national leader, Israeli Prime Minister Benjamin Netanyahu, invoked comparison with the Nazis, this time with Iraq's neighbor Iran. *New York Times* former Jerusalem Bureau Chief Ethan Bronner wrote: "For Mr. Netanyahu, an Iranian nuclear weapon would be the 21st century equivalent of the Nazi war machine and the Spanish Inquisition – the latest attempt to destroy the Jews."[36] Before you accept a comparison, check for both qualitative and quantitative similarities.

**6. Mistaking correlation for causation**: Brain researchers have a saying about brain cells – neurons: "What fires together, wires together." The architecture of the brain is associational.[37] So it's not surprising that we often think that because two things happen at about the same time, one causes the other. In its eagerness to report diet and medical breakthroughs, the press may jump on studies that associate some risk or benefit with a particular vitamin, herb, diet, or exercise regime. Remember the fascination with vitamin C, beta-carotene, vitamin E, and eight glasses of water a day? None fulfilled early expectations. Recently vitamins E and D have been stripped of their capes and super powers, and coffee is in the telephone booth shedding its mild mannered reputation and emerging as a "wonder drug" protecting against prostate cancer, stroke, breast cancer, diabetes, liver disease and Parkinson's.[38]

"That very issue of correlation and causation is key to anything you have to say about any kind of social science research."[39]

~ Edward Schumacher-Matos, former National Public Radio ombudsman

Scientists require at least three conditions to be met before saying A likely caused B. First, A must precede B. Second, A and B must be correlated or associated in some predictable way. (For example, an increase of A, say proportion of people vaccinated, leads to a decrease of B, perhaps an illness.) Third, the relationship between A and B must not be a mere coincidence. Ice cream sales correlate with drownings. But they don't cause them. The hot summer sun boosts ice cream sales *and* the number of swimmers.

Causality, like truth, is a human construct. Careful observation and logical inferences may build a body of evidence that A causes B, but because humans see reality incompletely and subjectively, we can never be absolutely sure there's no other factor really causing B. Science can never finally *prove* that A causes B, only that it's *probable*.

Complicating matters, the conditions that affect us most have *multiple* causes. An economic recession, for example, may be fathered by the combination of lax government regulation of financial markets, a wave of defaults on house mortgages, and a contraction of money to lend. Furthermore, *different sets of causes* can lead to the same effect. A recession might be caused primarily by the puncture of a speculative "bubble" in stock prices, or by excessive national debt, or by a sharp rise in the cost of oil and other basic commodities.

Nevertheless, the notion of cause and effect helps us condense the confusion of life to a more manageable set of patterns. These

THE SMELL TEST -195-

increase our ability to understand, predict, and sometimes control what's happening around us. Such utility makes claims of cause and effect common components of news and information.

Most leaps from correlation to causation involve more plausible links than between ice cream cone sales and drowning. An example is the idea that watching sexually explicit programs leads to fooling around. Consider how this front-page *Washington Post* story from 2008 begins:

> Teenagers who watch a lot of television featuring flirting, necking, discussion of sex and sex scenes are much more likely than their peers to get pregnant or get a partner pregnant, according to the first study to directly link steamy programming to teen pregnancy.
>
> The study, which tracked more than 700 12-to-17-year-olds for three years, found that those who viewed the most sexual content on TV were about twice as likely to be involved in a pregnancy as those who saw the least.
>
> "Watching this kind of sexual content on television is a powerful factor in increasing the likelihood of a teen pregnancy," said lead researcher Anita Chandra. "We found a strong association." The study is being published today in Pediatrics, the journal of the American Academy of Pediatrics.[40]

"Watching ... is a powerful factor" equates *correlation* (those who watched the most sexual content were more likely to impregnate or become pregnant than those who watched the least) with *causation* (watching those shows was a *cause* of those teen pregnancies). It's certainly possible that watching such programs is a cause of teens becoming sexually active, but this study does not, indeed *cannot*, prove that. By its design, it doesn't establish time order – that the TV watching preceded the sexual activity. What if sexually active teens prefer such programming more than abstinent ones who may find it distasteful? In other words, what if becoming sexually active leads to watching more adult programs?

**7. The fundamental attribution error:** In our individualistic American culture, we tend to over-emphasize personal *character* to explain other people's behavior and underestimate the surrounding *circumstances*. Social psychologists call this reasoning flaw the fundamental attribution error (FAE) because it's so prevalent, so commonsensical.[41]

Ironically, our desire to protect our self-esteem appears to override the FAE in one instance – when *we* misbehave.[42] Then we're only too happy to blame circumstances and absolve our character. Thus the jerk down the street speeds because he disregards others' safety. It's his heedless character. But we speed when we're in a hurry. The circumstances warrant it.

Harvard ethicist Michael J. Sandel provided a real world example: In Congressional hearings Wall Street bankers pointed to difficult circumstances beyond their control to explain the financial collapse of 2008. They were not responsible for the losses at their firms, they maintained. But a year earlier when the economy and their companies were doing well, *voila!* they *were* responsible – and thus deserved their lavish salaries.[43] We're good at looking for situational causes when our own behavior is called into question, but otherwise, we discount it.

Of course, character does count. Those who develop virtuous habits often make better decisions for themselves and others even under adverse circumstances. But the evidence for the situation *also* affecting our actions is overwhelming.[44] People who grow up in desperately poor, crime-ridden neighborhoods that lack successful role models (psychologists say, "you have to see it to be it") and effective schools, are much more likely to be arrested than those who grow up in safe neighborhoods with good schools, positive role models and financially secure parents.[45] Such spirit-sapping social conditions breed crime as surely as stagnant pools are nurseries for mosquitoes. Yet we routinely attribute people's success or failure almost entirely to character.

*It's profitable to exploit the FAE*

The FAE is a logic short circuit that news media exploit with saturated crime coverage. In addition to being cheap to gather, episodic reports of law-breaking – especially violent incidents such as murder, assault and rape – attract a large audience. Fear sells. And fresh cases occur daily. In both text and video, crime has become a news staple, like grains at the bottom of the nutrition pyramid. But relatively few stories explore the social conditions and political decisions that encourage criminal behavior, much less the solutions to such problems.[46] The implication? It's personal. Some people simply choose to break the law. Circumstances are irrelevant, not worth reporting.

Talk shows on TV, and particularly radio, boil over with this unsophisticated way of presenting the world. Many hosts sow resentment to reap ratings. Sometimes big corporations or the wealthy are demonized. But more often these pundits assail liberal defenders of the poor, especially the black and brown poor, who are described as parasites extracting tax dollars from those who work hard and play by the rules.[47]

*Social consequences*

This simplistic way of thinking and reporting has serious consequences. Take the criminal justice system as a case in point. If you think crime is caused by people who are inherently bad, punishing them with lengthy jail terms seems appropriate. As a result, we Americans have the highest documented incarceration rate in the world.[48]

Taxpayers in 18 states now spend more on prisons than universities.[49] And rather than focusing on rehabilitation that might assist inmates returning to society to become productive tax-payers, most states punish them in over-crowded conditions that render them angry and unfit for employment.[50] After serving time, punitive laws deprive felons of rights to vote, eligibility for public housing, food stamps and other forms of assistance. In seeking work they are usually asked to reveal any convictions, further crimping their chances for employment.[51] Seventy-seven percent of those who have served their terms in state prisons return within five years. For federal prisons the recidivism rate is 45 percent. Such churn places additional burdens on police and courts, not to mention the toll on victims of subsequent criminal behavior.[52] Assuming *people* are bad, rather than the *circumstances* of their upbringing, perpetuates the crime problem and creates a drag on the whole of society, not just the target population.

## Finding what is *Left out* or marginalized

It's usually more difficult to notice what's missing or consigned to the margins than what's present and center stage. Consequently, omission and marginalization are among the most powerful and subtle means of introducing bias. They can be either intentional, subconscious or simply an oversight. The effect, however, is the same: an incomplete description of an event or issue renders a warped impression. The degree of distortion corresponds to the extent that what's missing is important to making sense of the news or information.

As we saw in chapter 5, we are all practitioners of manipulation by omission and marginalization. Who among us volunteers our warts to potential employers or romantic interests? And when confronted, who doesn't downplay his/er flaws. Institutions – corporate and governmental – are no different in their relations with news media and the public.

In the spring of 2008, official Chinese news media focused on the violence of Tibetans protesting for greater freedom from China's government while eliminating from the picture any sign of violence on the part of Chinese police. Further, state media described Chinese investment in boosting the standard of living in Tibetan provinces but not suppression of Tibetan culture. It was a carefully managed, one-sided picture. And it was apparently effective across most of China in generating public sympathy for the government and resentment of Tibetans.[53]

Omission is most obvious when a controversy emerges and one side is quoted, but not the other. Or one side is allowed to speak both for themselves and for their opponent. Omission is least perceptible when a small piece of the mosaic of an issue or event is missing. For example, in the run-up to the Anglo-American invasion of Iraq, most Americans were ignorant of bitter disputes within government intelligence agencies over how the Bush administration was using the data about Iraq. "Many journalists knew about this, yet few chose to write about it," wrote Michael Massing in the *New York Review of Books*.[54] It was the failure to include legitimate dissenting voices within the U.S. intelligence community that led the *New York Times* to apologize for its pre-war reporting on May 26, 2004.

*To find missing facts, look for missing stakeholders*

Often missing facts are linked to missing stakeholders. The most likely to be overlooked are the least powerful. To see which individuals or groups affected by the matter at hand should be included, but aren't, try this: After reading the story, list the major stakeholders. Then go through the news or information a second time and note:

1. Which individuals or groups are included and which are not? Do those included have at least one person in a leadership role speaking for the group?

2. Which individuals or groups are mentioned most, particularly in the top half of the article (since readership drops off with length), and which least?

3. Which stakeholder's views are privileged and which are marginalized? Privileged viewpoints are ones that shape the direction of the article, perhaps becoming the angle or frame the reporter chooses for the premise of the story – usually the lead. Marginalized viewpoints are mentioned only in passing or challenged either by the author or another source.

Let me conclude with a humbling caution. The SMELL test can make it more difficult to fool you, but not impossible. A clever information-provider can selectively interview, selectively quote, selectively point the camera, and selectively edit to deceive us. If the topic is unfamiliar, we may strain to know what doesn't make sense and to recognize what has been left out. And if no other news outlet covered the event, we may be at the mercy of the single source. More than once during my doctoral dissertation when I was able to accompany local television journalists in the field, I witnessed them grossly misrepresent reality in a way only those who were present would recognize.

That's why detecting bias should be a *social* enterprise. How it can be will be addressed in the final chapter. But first we must add one more tool to our detective kit – how to "read" video and images.

---

### Exercises and Discussion Topics

1. Apply the SMELL test to any news article you think is primarily designed to inform you.

2. Apply the SMELL test to any news article or commentary you think is primarily designed to persuade you.

3. Find an article beginning on the front page of the local newspaper and analyze the story's sources using the PIE chart.

4. Look in any news medium for examples of any kind of logic problem described in the chapter. Be sure to say which kind of problem you found and explain why.

---

## End Notes

1 "Bob Flanagan" (4/5/2016) "Syrian refugee renounces Islam after tasting bacon for the first time," https://worldnewsdailyreport.com/syrian -refugee-renounces-islam-after-tasting-bacon-for-first-time/. In addition to being ridiculous, Muslims may find it offensive.

If you click on the "About us" tab, and then scroll down to "disclaimer," under an image saying "News you can trust," and read to the last line, you'll see this sentence: "All characters appearing in the articles in this website – even those based on real people – are entirely fictional and any resemblance between them and any persons, living, dead, or undead is purely a miracle."

[2] Craig Silverman and Jeremy Singer-Vine (12/6/2016) "Most Americans who see fake news believe it, new survey shows," BuzzFeed, https:// www.buzzfeed.com/craigsilverman/fake-news-survey?utm _term=.bbjBe 72j6#.jfxp4eLwW.

This poll found that 75 percent of a national sample believed fake news headlines that they had remembered seeing. Other studies have used different methods and reached more conservative conclusions, including the finding that credibility was most influenced not by the name of the news organization associated with the report, but the reputation of whomever forwarded it to the subject. See "'Who shared it?: How Americans decide what news to trust on social media," The Media Insight Project (2017), http://www.mediainsight.org/ PDFs /Trust%20 Social%20Media%20 Experiments%202017/Social_ Media_Experiment _Topline_2017.pdf.

[3] David Rose (11/26/2016) "Stunning new data indicates El Nino drove record highs in global temperatures suggesting rise may not be down to man-made emissions," Daily Mail.com, http://www.dailymail.co.uk/ news/article-3974846/Stunning-new-data-indicates-El-Nino-drove-record-highs-global-temperatures-suggesting-rise-not-man-emissions.html.

This is a good place to warn that Google rankings are based on a proprietary algorithm (a one-size-fits-all set of computer instructions), *not* on any assessment of the trustworthiness of the information provided on sites. When I entered "Is El Nino responsible for global warming?" the *Daily Mail* entry above was the seventh item (of 886,000) and listed on the first page of search results. Placement doesn't guarantee reliability.

[4] The primary exception to this reduction of author and institution into a single blended source is for commentators who are experts themselves. Institutions allow considerable independence to guest experts who write op-ed articles and commentators with advanced degrees, such as a physician writing a medical column or a lawyer interpreting court decisions. In such cases, it's useful to evaluate the credibility of the commentator as well as the institution and the sources cited.

[5] Carl Bernstein (7/18/2011) "Murdoch's Watergate," *Newsweek*, p. 5.

[6] Wikipedia (accessed 4/19/2017) "Daily Mail," https://en. wikipedia.org/wiki/Daily_Mail. You may have been warned against trusting Wikipedia. I use it as a place to begin an investigation, but not usually to end it there.

[7] Wikipedia (accessed 4/19/2017) "Judith Curry," https://en. wikipedia.org/wiki/Judith_Curry.

[8] Wikipedia (accessed 4/19/2017) "Global Warming Policy Foundation," https://en.wikipedia.org/wiki/Global_Warming_Policy_Foundation.

[9] Wikipedia entry on global warming cited above.

[10] United States Environmental Protection Agency (accessed 4/21/2017) "Climate Change Indicators: Sea Surface Temperature," https://www. epa.gov/climate-indicators/climate-change-indicators-sea-surface-temperature.

[11] NASA's Goddard Institute for Space Studies (GISS), (accessed 4/21/2017) "Global climate change: Vital signs of the planet," https://climate.nasa.gov/vital-signs/global-temperature/.

[12] Gardiner Harris (3/26/2008) "Cigarette company paid for lung cancer study," *New York Times*, p. A1, national edition, http://www.nytimes. com/2008/03/26/health/research/26lung.html?_r=1&ref=research&oref=slogin.

[13] Bill Kreuger (9/9/2010) "Egg industry Website gets boost from media during salmonella recall." Making sense of News, PoynterOnline, available at: http://www.poynter.org/latest-news/making-sense-of-news/105509/egg-industry-website-gets-boost-from-media-during-salmonella-recall/.

[14] Some critics of journalism take an absolutist view: no unnamed sources should be allowed, period. But given how secretive – and vindictive – corporations and government agencies have become, I think this is unrealistic. Reporters should always try to get sources to speak with full identification, even if they have to pass over some who wish to go unnamed. However, if a source with uniquely valuable information is both unwilling to go on the record and likely to suffer retribution if named, I think it's permissible to offer that source anonymity. But only if three other conditions are also met: 1) the reporter provides enough information for us to determine the source's proximity to the issue or event, his/er independence, and expertise/experience; 2) any accusations of mis- or malfeasance are independently confirmed by a second source; 3) to avoid being used as a shield for cheap shots, only fact-claims are permitted – no opinions.

[15] Daniel Victor (4/5/2017) "Pepsi Pulls Ad Accused of Trivializing Black Lives Matter", *New York Times*, https://www.nytimes.com/2017 /04/05/business/kendall-jenner-pepsi-ad.html?_r=0.

[16] The most prominent exception I can think of is Ira Glass' This American Life on NPR, which introduces a sound track under the narration. More recently, other news producers have been adding music to add drama and interest, such as the Center for Investigative Reporting's Reveal program.

[17] Clark Hoyt (6/1/2008) "Entitled to their opinions, yes. But their facts?" *New York Times* Week in Review section p. 12.

[18] Gail Collins (1/29/2012) "Newt's real legacy," Sunday Review, *New York Times*, p. 1SR.

[19] Politifact.com (9/13/2011) "Truth-o-meter: Mitt Romney and the dog on the car roof: one columnist's obsession," http://www. politifact. com/truth-o-meter/statements/2011/sep/13/gail-collins/mitt-romney-and-dog-car-roof-one-columnists-obsess/.

[20] Brooks Jackson and Kathleen Hall Jamieson (2007) *Unspun*, New York: Random House, p. 26.

[21] News staff, *Science 2.0* (10/12/2008) "There's An Expert On The Political Effects Of Late-Night Comedy - And She Says Tina Fey Hurts McCain's Campaign," http://www.science20.com/ news_releases /theres_an_expert_on_the_political_effects_of_late _night_comedy _and_she_says_tina_fey_hurts_mccains_campaign.

[22] Heather A. Dean (summer, 2010) "'I can see Russia from my house: Tina Fey's impersonation of Sarah Palin as a template for media coverage in the 2008 presidential election,'" master's thesis, San Diego State University, http://sdsu-dspace.calstate.edu/ xmlui/bitstream/ handle/10211.10/461/Dean_Heather.pdf?sequence=1.

[23] Jeff Grabmeier (1/23/2017) "Not just funny: Satirical news has serious political effects," Ohio State University, published in ScienceDaily, https://www.sciencedaily.com/releases/2017/01/170123115741.htm. Silvia Knobloch-Westerwick, Simon M. Lavis. (2/2017) "Selecting Serious or Satirical, Supporting or Stirring News? Selective Exposure to Partisan versus Mockery News Online Videos." *Journal of Commun- ication*, 2017; Vol. 61, no. 1, pp. 54-81, DOI: 10.1111/jcom.12271.

[24] Ohio History Central (undated) "Uncle Tom's Cabin," Ohio Historical Association's online encyclopedia of Ohio history, http://www. ohiohistorycentral.org/entry.php? rec=1405, accessed 5/23/2011.

[25] David S. Reynolds (6/14/2011) "Rescuing the real Uncle Tom," *New York Times*, p. A21, http://www.nytimes.com/2011/ 06/14/opinion/ 14Reynolds.html?_r=1&hp.

[26] Project for Excellence in Journalism, (4/12//2010) "News leaders and the future," pp. 2-4, http://www. journalism.org/analysis _report/news _leaders_and_future.

[27] Arthur Asa Berger in discussion with the author (6/17/08)

[28] Paul Krugman (4/24/2017) "Zombies of voodoo economics," *New York Times*, p. A21.

[29] Motoko Rich (3/16/2017) "Rex Tillerson, in Japan, says U.S. needs 'different approach' to North Korea," *New York Times*, https://www. nytimes.com/2017/03/16/world/asia/rex-tillerson-asia-trump-us-japan.html.

[30] John McManus (7/1/2000) "How to read political polls like a pro," Grade the News, http://www.gradethenews.org/ dreamhost %20files /pagesfolder/Pollstory3.htm.

[31] Ken Bensinger, Miriam Elder, and Mark Schoofs (1/10/2017) "These reports allege Trump has deep ties to Russia," BuzzFeed, https://www. buzzfeed.com/kenbensinger/these-reports-allege-trump-has-deep-ties-to-russia?utm_term=.kaEl2e6Ee#.mxlAY1PX1.

[32] Society of Professional Journalists (Accessed 4/26/2017) Code of Ethics, https://www.spj.org/ethicscode.asp.

[33] Jesse Jackson (1994) quoted in Sheldon R. Gawiser and G. Evans Witt, *A Journalist's Guide to Public Opinion Polls,* Westport, CT: Praeger, p. 111.

[34] Sheryl Gay Stolberg, Shaila Dewan and Brian Stelter (7/21/2010) "With apology, fired official is offered a new job," *New York Times*, p. A15, http://www.nytimes.com/2010/07/22/us/ politics/ 22sherrod.html.

[35] Kate Phillips (3/27/2008) "McCain said '100': Opponents latch on," *New York Times,* p. A22.

[36] Ethan Bronner (3/28/2012) "2 Israeli leaders make the Iran issue their own," *New York Times* p. A1, national edition.

[37] Dean Buonomano (2011) *Brain bugs: How the brain's flaws shape our lives,* New York: W.W. Norton.

[38] Drucilla Dyess (5/18/2011) "Coffee: New Wonder Drug Found to Cut Prostate Cancer Risk," Healthnews.com, http://www. healthnews.com /Categories/Family-Health/Coffee-New-Wonder-Drug-Found-to-Cut-Prostate-Cancer-Risk.

[39] Neil Conan (10/11/2011) Talk of the Nation, interview with Edward Schumacher-Matos, http://www.npr.org/2011/10/11/141240 659/npr-ombudsman-ponders-journalisms-big-questions.

[40] Rob Stein (11/3/2008) "Study first to link TV sex to real teen pregnancies," *Washington Post*, p. A1, http://www. washingtonpost.com /wp-dyn/content/article/2008/11/02/ AR2008110202592_pf.html.

[41] Lee Ross (1977). "The intuitive psychologist and his shortcomings: Distortions in the attribution process." in L. Berkowitz Ed., *Advances in experimental social psychology* (vol. 10, pp. 173–220). New York: Academic Press.

[42] Dale T. Miller and Michael Ross (1975) "Self-serving biases in the attribution of causality: Fact or fiction?" *Psychological Bulletin* 82 (2): 213–225.)

[43] Michael J. Sandel (2009) *Justice: What's the right thing to do?* New York: Farrar, Straus and Giroux, p. 18. The CEO salary data earlier in the paragraph also came from here.

[44] See Lee Ross, cited above.

[45] See, for example, the social ecology approach pioneered by the Chicago School, e.g., Clifford R. Shaw and Henry D. McKay (1942) *Juvenile Delinquency and Urban Areas*, The University of Chicago Press; Gary Becker, "Crime and Punishment," in *Journal of Political Economy*, vol. 76 (2), March–April 1968, p.196-217; and R. Kornhauser (1978) *Social Sources of Delinquency*, Chicago: University of Chicago Press.

[46] John McManus and Lori Dorfman (2005) "Functional truth or sexist distortion," *Journalism*, 6(1): 43-65.

[47] See Ellen Hume (2003). "Talk show culture," *Encyclopedia of International Media and Communications*, Vol. 4, http://www.ellenhume.com/articles/talkshow1.htm; also John Halpin, James Heidbreder, Mark Lloyd, Paul Woodhull, Ben Scott, Josh Silver, and S. Derek Turner (6/20/2007) "The Structural Imbalance of Political Talk Radio," http://www.americanprogress.org/issues/2007/06/talk _radio.html.

[48] Wikipedia (undated) "Incarceration in the United States," http://en.wikipedia.org/wiki/Incarceration_in_the_ United_States, accessed 7/6/2011.

[49] Christopher Ingraham (7/7/2016) "The states that spend more money on prisons than college students," *Washington Post*, https://www.washingtonpost.com/news/wonk/wp/2016/07/07/the-states-that-spend-more-money-on-prisoners-than-college students/?utm_term=.eee4dd38 cfe8.

[50] Lee Simmons (3/18/2016) "How to fix overcrowded jails," *Insight by Stanford Business*, https://www.gsb.stanford.edu/insights/how-fix-overcrowded-jails.

[51] Michelle Alexander (2012) *The new Jim Crow: mass incarceration in the age of colorblindness*, New York: New Press.

[52] Christopher Zoukis (3/25/2017) "Report Documents U.S. Recidivism Rates for Federal Prisoners," *HuffingtonPost,* http://www.huffingtonpost.com/christopher-zoukis/report-documents-us-recid_b_9542312.html.

[53] David Lague (3/18/2008) "China premier blames Dalai Lama for 'appalling' violence in Tibet," *New York Times*, http://www. nytimes.com /2008/03/18/world/asia/18tibet.html?scp=42&sq=chinese%20suprression%20of %20news%20about%20Tibet&st=cse and (3/18/2008) "China tries to thwart news reports from Tibet," *New York Times*, at: http:// www.nytimes.com /2008/03/18/ world/asia/18access. html?ref=asia.

[54] Michael Massing (1/29/2004) "Now they tell us," *New York Review of Books*, http://www.nybooks.com/ articles/archives /2004/feb/26/now-they-tell-us/?pagination=false

# 9

## Detecting Bias in Images

*Behold these striking pictures. But as you behold them, beware of them, for they are not real. They are fake, the products of media consultants and spin-control artists who are trying to move you or deceive you or persuade you.*

~ Kiku Adatto, author of *Picture Perfect*

**M**an 2.0, also known as Homo Sapiens, evolved some 200,000 years ago, anthropologists estimate. During the last quarter of that period – about 50,000 years ago – humans began to communicate with images. But written language appeared much more recently, just 5,000 to 6,000 years ago. And it began as glyphs, or picture writing – symbols that looked like what they were intended to represent.[1] We have evolved as visual animals. That's why images possess extraordinary persuasive power and can be remembered more easily than words. You can probably recall a face from the past sooner than a name.

Images – moving and still – have never played a greater role in news and information. Text was king in the era of books and newspapers. But videos, photos and data displays are usurping the throne as information moves from paper to pixels. This chapter explores four propositions to help us avoid being fooled by images:

**1. Our brains process images in almost the *opposite* way that they make sense of words.**

**2. Image logic differs radically from text logic.**

**3. Images are easily manipulated.**

**4. We can learn to "read" images, though never as clearly as text.**

In news and information, words and images usually complement each other. But as media ecologist Neil Postman and others have pointed out, they are entirely different ways of communicating. And their effects on us differ greatly.[2]

## 1. Our brains process images in almost the opposite way that they make sense of words

Words are abstract symbols, squiggles or sounds standing for something else. However, the images that appear most often in news and information – photos and videos – almost always directly represent something physical and real. You can't photograph an idea. Photos and videos are concrete and specific. They can't describe abstractions – concepts, theories, hypotheticals, and arguments. While words can generalize, photos and video clips are always anecdotal. They show a part, but not all, of what happened.

Words are consumed in linear fashion, printed left to right in most Western languages, on lines that proceed from top to bottom. It's like eating corn on the cob. Words require structure. To make sense, they must be arranged logically into sentences, paragraphs, and maybe chapters. When we read, the analytical left brain does the heavy lifting. However, images are consumed holistically, all at once like a grape. They don't require context, but convey meaning standing alone. The more intuitive right brain does the processing.

While we may know how to question whether the words of a text constitute a logical argument or truthful representation, we tend to just accept photos and videos as accurate depictions of reality. Typically, we don't apply logic to pictures. We simply react to their aesthetic quality or emotional punch.

A picture, we say, "is worth a thousand words." And "seeing is believing." Some news images seem to capture an event so powerfully that they are burned into our memories. It might be the airliner striking the second World Trade Center tower on Sept. 11, 2001. For baby boomers, it might be a naked Vietnamese girl burned by napalm running down a street shrieking in pain.[3] For people around the globe in August 2015, it might be the image of a Syrian toddler drowned in the Mediterranean fleeing a brutal civil war.

Photo credit: MSNBC

Images are powerful enough that governments work hard to suppress negative ones. In 2008 China blocked images of protesters in Tibet, and particularly the crackdown against them. Zimbabwe expelled foreign reporters who were recording attacks on members of the political opposition. Syria prohibited outside journalists from covering its civil war. In the U.S. during World War II, military censors forbade publication of photos of dead American soldiers to avoid morale problems. In Viet Nam, on the other hand, photographers were free to cover the conflict. Televised images of the fighting – the "living room war" – were thought to have been a major cause of the nation's eventual disenchantment with the struggle.[4] Subsequently, the U.S. military resumed its restrictions. Between 1991 and 2009, photographers were barred from filming even the coffins of American soldiers flown home from Iraq.[5]

## 2. Image logic differs radically from text logic

The Canadian scholars Harold Innis and Marshall McLuhan believed that the medium was *as*, if not *more*, important than the message it conveyed.[6] Professor Postman advanced only a slightly less technologically-determined view of communication. In his delightful book, *Amusing Ourselves to Death*, he argued that the printed word enables ordered, logical, abstract reasoning – just what the public needs to solve complex problems in a democratic fashion. However, visual media – especially photography and videography – are too imprecise and emotionally-arousing for the conversation of democracy. They cannot convey the ideas and abstractions essential to civic debate. His conclusion? Video is more suited to entertain than inform.

As television supplanted print as America's dominant mass medium during the second half of the twentieth century, Prof. Postman predicted that we would come to prefer diversion to rational public decision-making. The proper use for a television, he jested, is to prop up one end of a book shelf or provide light for reading.

Calvin and Hobbes (used with permission)

Television introduces two other differences between images and words. When photos are seen at 30 frames per second, the standard pace of video, they wash over us so quickly that they outpace our ability to critically assess them. We can slow down or re-read a section of text. We can stop and think. But a television broadcast is fleeting, always moving on. We can usually stop and replay a video on the Web, but TV has trained us to watch without interruption. It's also easier to maintain emotional distance in print. Video engages both our eyes and ears in a life-like presentation. We are more likely to cry at a movie than while reading a book.

These characteristics make video the medium of choice for persuasion. Advertisers selling autos, skin creams, and political candidates value its emotional force and too-fast-for-analysis pace. Watching a screen also tends to be a more passive activity than reading. It may catch us with our skepticism shields down. Two University of Chicago researchers reported: "Television viewing was found to be a relatively unchallenging activity requiring little cognitive investment and consistently tied to feelings of relaxation, passivity, and drowsiness."[7]

Calvin and Hobbes (used with permission)

Perhaps the most important difference between words and images is this: The meaning of images arises not from the proposition-then-evidence structure of words organized into sentences and paragraphs, but from mere association. In a photo or video, advertisers put happy, sexy, wealthy, or accomplished people together with a product to imply that the two are related, even that one causes the other. Were someone to put in words the message that drinking Coors Light or driving a BMW will make you hip and irresistible, you'd laugh. Put the same "statement" in a photo or video, however, and advertisers are willing to bet millions that we'll buy it.

Calvin and Hobbes (used with permission)

## 3. Images are easily manipulated

Some think that *faux*tography began in 1989 when *TV Guide* magazine wanted to feature Oprah Winfrey on its cover, but had no photo showing the TV hostess after her successful diet. So they severed dancer Ann-Margaret's head

from her curvaceous body and replaced it with Oprah's beaming countenance. "The truth is, however, that photography lost its innocence many years ago," noted Dartmouth College researcher Hany Farid. "The nearly iconic portrait of the U.S. President Abraham Lincoln (circa 1860), for example, was a fake, and only the beginning of a long history of photographic trickery."[8]

Photo from legendsrevealed.com

Every year, altering images created with cameras becomes easier to accomplish with software such as Photoshop, and harder for consumers to detect. Fashion magazines alter photos routinely to gild Hollywood lilies. Even respected news media occasionally doctor images. *Time* magazine infamously darkened its cover photo of football legend and murder-suspect O.J. Simpson in 1994. The lesson? Seeing such images should never lead directly to believing. Consider the integrity of the source.

Digitally altering photos and videos is a relatively new and powerful technique. But it's far from the only way to manipulate the audience's reception of images. Subjects have long been posed to increase drama. Even minor adjustments in camera placement or the angle of the lens can change our perception. A small demonstration can seem large in a close-up; a substantial group can seem small in a long shot or a panorama. A realtor with a fish-eye lens can make an apartment fit for a mouse look roomy enough for a moose. The camera's height relative to the subject also matters. People shot from above seem smaller and less powerful than those shot from a level plane. Those shot from below seem more powerful.

Consider this photo of Republican presidential hopeful Mitt Romney on the front page of the *New York Times* on January 18, 2012:

Shot from above and at a distance, it conveyed a message that was reinforced by the caption that ran below it: "At a rally for Mitt Romney on Tuesday at the civic center in Florence S.C., the crowd seemed dwarfed by the setting." The Romney campaign certainly couldn't have been happy with the subtly negative impression that Romney could not draw a larger crowd in a conservative Southern state. Possibly as a compensation call, the very next day in the same prominent place above the fold on the front page, the *Times* ran this photo, with the caption: "Leader and target: Mitt Romney drew a crowd in Spartanburg, S.C., but he also drew a barrage of attacks from rivals."

Notice how greatly the camera angle and focal point differed from the previous day's rally photo. Many faces, rapt attention, the American flag centered in the frame – it appears to be an attempt by the *Times* to balance the previous day's most prominent image with a positively-charged photo. (Betcha my daughter's Barbie collection that Romney's aides raised hell with the editor for the previous day's photo!)

As the *Times*' photos demonstrate, focal point powerfully influences interpretation. People or events in the foreground always seem more important than those in the background. Even production values can make a difference, sometimes in surprising ways. Jumpy video shot from a handheld camera often conveys a greater sense of authenticity than video shot from a stable tripod. Cell phone images from bystanders at newsworthy events can generate as great a response as a professional photographer's. Viewed by millions on the Internet, the amateur video of a South

Carolina policeman shooting an unarmed black motorist who fled on foot in April 2015 led to a murder charge against the officer.[9]

Because of time and space limitations in most media – as well as the audience's attention limitations – one or a just a few photos or video clips represent an *entire* event whether or not they typify what happened. Because media images compress meaning into a few frames, they always introduce some level of distortion. They always show just one facet of the event despite the best efforts of photojournalists to honestly record what's taking place.

*Intentional* manipulation can occur through a series of choices. Commercial bias can be conveyed by choosing to cover a raucous street protest rather than more consequential, but visually static, "talking heads" inside a meeting room discussing new laws or policies. Or by going to where demonstrators are confronting police rather than where they are peacefully presenting their views in speeches. In addition to characterizing the entire protest by its most violent component, this has the effect of encouraging violence to gain publicity.

Political slant can arise from pointing the camera at a bleeding demonstrator but not a cop on a stretcher (or vice versa). Or focusing on an outrageous sign by placing it in the foreground while consigning the more reasonable ones to the blurred background.

These choices are usually made back in the newsroom, when editors pick the most dramatic photo from the 100 others the photographer took, or when they cut and paste together a composite minute of the most emotional video clips from an hour of recording. Great television is often poor journalism.

## Manipulating the media by controlling images

So far, we've examined distortions of reality introduced by whomever is operating the camera and selecting which images to exhibit. Now let's look at how those in *front* of the camera manipulate media images. Those with the resources and the authority to design the visual background – the "sets" – for news stories usually understand the power of images very well. They are also familiar with the media's craving for compelling pictures.

"We absolutely thought of ourselves, when we got into the national campaign, as producers. We tried to create the most entertaining, visually attractive scene to fill that box, so that the cameras from the networks would have to use it."[10]

~ Michael Deaver, campaign manager for President Ronald Reagan

In a surprisingly candid interview with PBS host Bill Moyers, Michael Deaver argued that the visuals he orchestrated for network cameras made journalists unwitting instruments of President Reagan's political campaign. Mr. Deaver contended that the messages conveyed by these images overpowered any skeptical words reporters might employ to dim their impact. Words are as effective against images as rocks against tanks.

Karl Rove, President George W. Bush's political advisor, followed Mr. Deaver's playbook. He repeatedly staged presidential speeches with a background of preselected, friendly audiences, often ranks of military personnel. In May, 2003 President Bush could have announced the end of major combat operations in Iraq in May 2003 from the White House. Instead he donned a pilot's green flight suit and was flown across the continent to an aircraft carrier off the coast of San Diego bedecked with a giant "Mission Accomplished" banner. The dramatic flourish made the president look like a war hero.

### Still naive after all these years

Even though we live in the era of easy digital manipulation of images, we still react to pictures as if they convey reality. The doctored video Andrew Breitbart posted on the Web was naively taken as proof that Shirley Sherrod was a racist, not just by casual viewers, but by Agriculture Secretary Tom Vilsack who called her on her cell phone to fire her, and by, of all groups, the NAACP whose mission is to advance the cause of people of color. Both were wiping digital egg from their faces within days.

But less than a year later in the spring of 2011, officials in Washington had still not learned to be skeptical of video from partisan sources. That's when conservative activist James O'Keefe posted secretly recorded video of a luncheon between National Public Radio's chief fund-raiser Ron Schiller and two of Mr. O'Keefe's confederates posing as potential Muslim donors. The video appeared to show Mr. Schiller denigrating Republicans and members of the Tea Party. However an analysis of the original video demonstrated that Mr. Schiller's comments and reactions had been manipulated to make his statements more offensive than they were in reality.[11] By that time, however, NPR's president had been fired and prominent Congressional Republicans had launched a campaign to end government support for NPR.

## 4. We can learn to "read" images, though never as clearly as text

With just a little effort, the visual bias detector on the next page can help to unravel both the choices and the logic of images to reveal underlying patterns. That's useful because most of the time we don't really notice how our attention is being steered.

| Image Bias Detector | | | |
|---|---|---|---|
| Stakeholder Groups | | | |
| Group's name | | | |
| Foreground/ Background | | | |
| Active (aggressor?)/ Passive (victim?) | | | |
| Sympathetic /Neutral/ Un- sympathetic | | | |
| Primary Emotion Elicited | | | |

A. Which stakeholders in the article are *not* included in the image(s)?
_____.

B. What is the "message" of the image(s)?
_____
_____.

C. Is this "message" consistent with the accompanying article? _____.
If not, how does it differ? _____
_____.

D. Which biases, if any, are conveyed by the image(s)?
_____.

Here's how to use it:

Across row one, examine the article accompanying the image(s) and list the principal stakeholders. For each stakeholder group included in the image(s), note whether it is in the foreground – the part of the image that is clearest and usually in the "front" and center of the frame – or in the background.

Next examine whether members of each stakeholder group are portrayed as active (doing something to others or to the environment) or passive (having something done to them). If the image shows a conflict, note whether members are shown as aggressors or victims.

In row four, indicate whether the image represents each stakeholder group as worthy of our sympathy, our antipathy, or neither. In the final row, name the emotion each image arouses in you toward each group's members.

What's not included in a photo is as important as what is.

In question A, the detector directs your attention at those stakeholder groups affected by the news, but left out of the image(s) accompanying the story. If a major group is ignored both in the story and the image(s), we should wonder whether the omission expresses bias against that group, perhaps that they "don't count."[11]

Question B asks for your impression of what the image "says." Consider what emotion it pulls from you and to whom it directs sympathy. Also keep in mind the meaning of camera placement and focal point.

In question C, you'll compare the main premise of the article to the message of the photo. In traditional news media, photos and text are gathered by different people. Editors generally select the photo that best illustrates the story. If a story about a person is negative, they'll find a photo of that person looking downcast, even if it's not recent.

But if the image and story are contradictory, it may suggest a bias – that either the photographer or the author got it wrong. Question D asks you to put all of the information from the matrix and the preceding questions together. Is there a partisan bias in the image(s)?

Many news articles include one or more photos, drawings, or video clips. If there are more than one, you may need to analyze each with the detector. However, if they are similar, you may be able to group them together as if they were parts of one larger collage.

In print and the Web, a caption (or cutline) briefly describes or identifies an image and is usually placed under or next to it. Use it as an aide to interpreting the image, but focus mostly on the image itself.

*Applying the detector*

Notice your reaction to the photo on the next page, which ran on the front page of the *New York Times* on Aug. 10, 2008. It describes an incident in the brief war between Georgia and Russia.

The caption reads: "A Georgian man wept over the body of a relative on Saturday after Russian airstrikes in Gori hit two apartment buildings." Two Georgian soldiers are also in the photo.

## RUSSIA BROADENS MILITARY CAMPAIGN AS ALL-OUT WAR THREATENS GEORGIA

A Georgian man wept over the body of a relative on Saturday after Russian airstrikes in Gori hit two apartment buildings.

Do the photo and its accompanying caption move you with pity? For whom? Who look like the aggressors and who are the victims, according to this photo? Editors typically choose from scores or hundreds of photos those that support their news reports. In

August, coverage in the *Times* emphasized Russian attacks and Georgian suffering. Editors chose photos like this one.

But three months later, the *Times* editors chose different photos taken at the same time as the first, as the story line began to reflect Georgian aggression in the contested South Ossetia region on the Russo-Georgian border.

On Nov. 6, the *Times* ran the photo above with the caption: "Georgian forces fired rockets at South Ossetia in August." The headline read, "Georgia fired more cluster bombs than thought, killing civilians, report finds." One day later, a story headlined "Georgia claims on Russia war called into question" reported that "newly available accounts by independent military observers of the beginning of the war between Georgia and Russia this summer call into question the longstanding Georgian assertion that it was acting defensively against separatist and Russian aggression."[13]

In the first photo, the Russians are attacking and killing civilians. In the second, the Georgians may be doing the same. Notice that in both cases the photographers were shooting from the Georgian side of the battlefield. As we discussed in chapter 3, what you see depends on where you stand. During the conflict, the *Times'* coverage reflected a Georgian perspective and so did the first photo. Months later, when the other side of the story was told, *Times* editors chose an opposite photo. It's another reminder that even newspapers with standards as lofty as the *New York Times'* are writing the first draft of history. Real-time accounts of events, particularly large ones taking place over a geographic region, are always subject to revision.

If we ran the first photo above through the image bias detector, it would look like this:

| Image Bias Detector | | | |
|---|---|---|---|
| **Stakeholder Groups** | | | |
| **Group's name** | Georgians | South Os-setians | Russians | |
| **Foreground/ Background** | Fore-ground | | | |
| **Active (aggressor?)/ Passive (victim?)** | Passive/ victims | | | |
| **Sympathetic /Neutral/ Un-sympathetic** | Sympa-thetic | | | |
| **Primary Emotion Elicited** | Pity | | | |

A. Which stakeholders in the article are *not* included in the image(s)? _South Ossetians,___Russians_____.

B. What is the "message" of the image(s)? _Pity the Georgian civilians killed by the Russian Air Force_____.

C. Is this "message" consistent with the accompanying article? Yes. If not, how does it differ?_____.

D. Which biases, if any, are conveyed by the image(s)? _Pro-Georgian; anti-Russian._____.

## Two caveats

Researchers such as John Fiske have shown that television content is "read" differently by different audiences.[14] Because the "message" of images is not spelled out in words, viewers' interpretations will differ even more than in an analysis of text. These interpretations are likely to divide along the social fault lines described in chapter 3. So collecting the impressions of a diverse group of evaluators will bolster the validity of any conclusion you might reach.

A second caution arises from the aforementioned tendency of media to rely on one or just a few visuals per story. No photo or video clip can tell the whole story of even a simple event, much less a complex issue. Nor can we reasonably expect all stakeholders to appear in the photos selected for publication. Therefore, *every* image reflects a bias, a subjective reduction of reality.

It's useful to note such bias. But be careful. The case for a partisan bias – as opposed to a bias for the common good – should be based on a *pattern of choices*. Take the photos of the 2012 Romney campaign shown above. Neither was doctored. Both were reflections of reality. But the first had a negative cast and the second positive for Mr. Romney. There was no *pattern* of bias. In contrast, most of the early photos of the Russian-Georgian war reinforced a bias in the coverage that was pro-Georgian and anti-Russian. Only months later, in hindsight, did the *Times'* reporting and photo selection correct that early bias. To establish bias in images or video clips you have to ask: Of all possible images of any event, is there a pattern among those chosen that distorts reality?

Now that we've learned to detect bias in videos and photos, we're ready to consider how spinmeisters artfully combine words and images to climb inside our heads. We'll examine the most common tricks of the misinformation trade in the next chapter.

## Exercises and Discussion Topics

1. Think quickly of your third grade teacher. Did his/er image come to mind before the name? How much time elapsed before you could recall the name?

2. Find an example of where you felt manipulated by either the camera's angle or distance from the subject. What did the photographer do to influence your interpretation? Why did you feel it was a manipulation?

3. Find an example of a digitally manipulated image or video and share it with the class. What impact do you think it had on viewers?

4. Find an example of a powerful social actor manipulating a news photo by controlling the background image. How did the manipulation work? How effective do you think it was?

5. Find a news photo and analyze it using the image bias detector. Explain your conclusions.

## End Notes

[1] In this paragraph I'm relying on the following three Wikipedia sources: 1) "Anatomically modern humans," online at: http://en.wikipedia.org/wiki/ Anatomically_modern_humans# Modern_human_behavior; 2) "Rock art," at: http://en.wikipedia .org/wiki/Rock_art#Age; and 3) "Earliest writing," at http://en. wikipedia.org/wiki/Earliest_writing. All were accessed on 8/22/2011.

[2] Here I'm relying on Neil Postman (1985) *Amusing ourselves to death*, New York: Penguin; Arthur Asa Berger (2008) *Seeing is believing*, New York: McGraw-Hill ; D. A. Dondis (2000) *A primer of visual literacy*, Cambridge, MA: MIT Press; Joshua Meyrowitz (1998) "Multiple media literacies," *Journal of Communication*, vol. 48, no. 1, pp. 96-108; Herbert Zettl (1998) "Contextual media aesthetics as the basis for media literacy," *Journal of*

*Communication,* vol. 48, no. 1, pp. 81-95; and Paul Messaris (1998) "Visual aspects of media literacy," *Journal of Communication,* vol. 48, no. 1, pp. 70-80.

[3] Nick Ut, an *Associated Press* photographer, won a Pulitzer Prize for his June 1972 picture of a screaming girl burned with napalm. He also helped get the girl to a hospital, where she spent the next 14 months and, against odds, survived.

[4] The Museum of Broadcast Communications (undated) "Vietnam on television," online at: http://www.museum.tv/eotvsection.php? entrycode=vietnamonte. Accessed 6/3/2011.

[5] Julian E. Barnes (2/27/2009) "Pentagon lifts media ban on photos of war dead," *Los Angeles Times,* online at: http://articles.latimes.com /2009/feb/27/nation/na-war-dead-photos27.

[6] Harold A. Innis (1991; original 1951) *The bias of communication,* Toronto: University of Toronto Press. Marshall McLuhan (1994; original 1964) *Understanding media: the extensions of man,* Cambridge, MA: MIT Press.

[7] Mihaly Csikszentmihalyi and Robert Kubey (1981) "Television and the rest of life: a systematic comparison of subjective experience," *Public Opinion Quarterly,* 45 (3): 317-328.

[8] Hany Farid (undated) "Digital doctoring: Can we trust photographs?" Dartmouth College Library, pdf version available at: http://www.ists.dartmouth.edu/library/327.pdf. Accessed on 1/18/2012.

[9] Mark Berman (2/5/2015) "Mistrial declared in case of South Carolina officer who shot Walter Scott after traffic stop," *Washington Post,* https://www.washingtonpost.com/news/post-nation/wp/ 2016/12/05/mistrial-declared-in-case-of-south-carolina-officer-who-shot-walter-scott-after-traffic-stop/?utm_term=.603a0029df26.

[10] Bill Moyers (11/22/1989) "Illusions of news," second part of the series "The public mind," interview with Michael Deaver, Public Broadcasting Service, Washington, DC.

[11] Scott Baker (3/10/2011) "Does raw video of NPR expose' reveal questionable editing & tactics?" TheBlaze.com, http://www. theblaze.com/stories/does-raw-video-of-npr-expose-reveal-questionable-editing-tactics/.

[12] San Francisco State Professor Arthur Asa Berger suggests compiling a broader list of opposite roles played by principal stakeholders in the photo: for example, who is portrayed as honest/devious, powerful/weak, or wealthy/poor.

[13] Michael Schwirtz (11/6/2008) "Georgia fired more cluster bombs than thought, killing civilians, report finds," *New York Times*, p. A18, online at: http://www.nytimes.com/2008/11/ 06/world/europe /06cluster.html?ref=europe] and C.J. Chivers and Ellen Barry (11/6/2008) "Georgia claims on Russia war called into question," *New York* Times, p. A1, online at: :http://www.nytimes. com/2008/11/07/world/europe/07georgia.html?_r=1&scp=1&sq=Geor gia%20Claims%20on%20Russia%20War%20Called%20Into%20Question &st=cse.

[14] John Fiske (1987) *Television culture: Popular pleasures and politics*, New York, Methuen.

# 10

## The Spinmeister's Art: Tricks of the Misinformation Trade

*The customized manufacture of public discourse ... has become epidemic.*

~ Stuart Ewen, author of *PR! A Social History of Spin*

As we enter the 21st century, America employs a record number of public relations agents – people with a talent for making a case to the public for the benefit of their *clients*. At the same time, we are laying off a record number of journalists – people skilled at breaking those cases open for the benefit of the *public*. In 1980 the ratio of public relations practitioners to journalists was nearly equal. By 2014, PR operatives outnumbered journalists by almost six to one and climbing.[1] The late *New York Times* media columnist David Carr described the result:

> There is a chance that historians will examine this period in American history and wonder if journalism left the field. In part, it is the triumph of the spinners, top to bottom. Since the media reached the height of its powers in the 1970s, there has been a pervasive effort to gain custody of public information in both the public and private sector. A working reporter cannot walk into a Gap store in a mall, let alone a police station, and ask a question without being swarmed by bureaucracy.[2]

Lest you think Mr. Carr exaggerates, when his *Times* colleague David Barstow attended hearings on whom to blame for the massive Gulf of Mexico oil spill of 2010, he found "... there would be more

PR people representing these big players than there were reporters, sometimes by a factor of two or three."[3]

This chapter explores three propositions:

1. **As professional journalism atrophies, public relations practitioners are growing bolder and more sophisticated.**

2. **We can predict when deception is most likely, thus know when to raise our level of skepticism.**

3. **The publicists' technique of choice is framing information to lead audiences in a particular direction without their noticing.**

Spinning facts to gain advantage or deflect responsibility is as old as Adam blaming Eve, who in turn blamed the serpent, for the consumption of forbidden fruit. But public relations as an occupation came into its own only in the 20th century.

In 1900, news was carried on a single mass medium – the newspaper. In a scant hundred years, radio, then broadcast television, then hundreds of cable and satellite channels, and finally the Internet have made media as common as air and its use as habitual as breathing. Because news conveys the power to define the reality upon which people act, corporate and government officials began to deploy publicists to bend media accounts to their own purposes.

"If you put a U.S. congressman in front of a microphone and ask what the weather is ... you're going to get spin. They're just constantly processing political consequences of every single word they utter."[6]

~ Bob Garfield, co-host of NPR's On the Media

The White House did not name an official press secretary until Franklin Roosevelt became president in 1932.[4] Today even First Ladies have press secretaries and just about every corporation and government agency employs platoons of them. All because perception is power.[5]

## 1. As professional journalism atrophies, public relations practitioners are growing bolder and more sophisticated

By 2017 heels-over-head spin had replaced facts in many White House press briefings. Only a day after President Trump's inauguration, his press secretary, Sean Spicer, told reporters: "That was the largest audience to witness an inauguration, period." Aerial photographs showed the claim to be so preposterous, PolitiFact gave it its [liar, liar] "pants on fire" rating.[7]

Mr. Spicer's fabrication was part of a spin cycle begun by Mr. Trump himself. Candidate Trump, who often handled his own PR with Twitter, repeatedly asserted that NATO was "obsolete." Months later President Trump declared it a "great alliance," and said "It's no longer obsolete." What made it suddenly relevant, he claimed, was that, at his urging, it had begun to fight terrorism. That startled NATO officials whose soldiers had been fighting terrorists alongside the U.S. since 2001.[8] In the first weeks of his presidency, Mr. Trump stated that he would have won the popular vote if millions of fraudulent votes were not cast for Mrs. Clinton. Soon after, he tweeted that President Obama had wiretapped his campaign's phones. As of May 2017, Mr. Trump was unable to provide any evidence for either claim. And, of course, for years Mr. Trump maintained that President Obama had been born in Kenya and thus was not eligible to be president. But in September 2016, he acknowledged the obvious: "President Barack Obama was born in the United States. Period."[9]

Because Mr. Trump's spin has so often been demonstrably erroneous, the press has become comfortable calling it out. This happened infrequently in the past.

Whether you loved it or loathed it, the administration of Dick Cheney and George W. Bush was unusually successful at manipulating a compliant news media during its first term. Just about every politician spins like a top, but the first administration of the new century spun on the scale of a planet. To spread its message, the government secretly paid journalists like Armstrong Williams, a commentator on education issues, to shill for its policies.[10] The government even created and distributed fake news with private contractors pretending to be reporters.[11]

During the long and bitter war with forces opposing the Anglo-American occupation of Iraq, the administration developed another brilliant, if exploitive, strategy – to provide private Pentagon briefings and contracting business opportunities to retired military officers who acted as expert sources for mainstream news media. They enjoyed these benefits so long as they parroted administration talking points in their role as purportedly neutral military analysts. As the *New York Times* reported in 2008, "the Bush administration has used its control over access and information in an effort to transform the analysts into a kind of media Trojan horse – an instrument intended to shape terrorism coverage from inside the major TV and radio networks."[12]

"The muscles of journalism are weakening and the muscles of public relations are bulking up – as if they were on steroids."[13]

~ David Barstow, *New York Times* investigative reporter

For an up-to-date list of political deceptions, visit FactCheck.org, Snopes.com, or PolitiFact.com.

Conservatives don't own spin. PolitiFact "awarded" Democrats the 2011 "Lie of the Year" for saying Republican Congressman Paul Ryan's plans for Medicare would kill the program.[14] In 2013, President Obama "won" for saying "If you like your health care plan you can keep it."[15] Of the seven "Lies of the Year," so far six have involved political actors. Republicans have "won" four, Democrats two. At Fact-check.org at the University of Pennsylvania, both Democrats and Republicans have been found guilty of distorting the factual record and smearing the other in campaign advertising and PR efforts.

Political and governmental spin may get the most attention, but for sheer volume, the prize for making the public dizzy goes to special interests *outside* of government. In her 2010 book, *Merchants of Death*, University of California - San Diego historian of science Naomi Oreskes addressed the growing gap between the scientific community's near-certainty and the public's then rising doubt that human activity was warming the planet. In an NPR interview, she explained:

> There has been a systematic effort organized by people outside the scientific community to undermine the scientific data and to convince all of us that the scientific jury is still out in order to delay government, business and community action on taking steps to prevent further man-made climate change.[16]

A similarly self-serving effort at muddying public opinion about the health risks of smoking was executed by the tobacco industry during the last half of the 20th century.[17] Polluting the infosphere pays.

## 2. We can predict when deception is most likely, thus know when to raise our level of skepticism

See if this rings true:

$$\text{The probability of deception} = \frac{\text{The benefit to be gained or loss avoided}}{[\text{The cost of being exposed}] \times [\text{The likelihood of being exposed}]}$$

Are you more likely to shade – or hide – the truth if doing so gives you a substantial advantage or avoids harm? And if the chance of your deception being discovered is low, will that encourage you? How about if it matters little or a lot if you are caught?

This benefit/cost relationship occurred to me on a fine autumn afternoon during a two-hand-touch football game when the miscreant I was supposed to cover caught a pass and scampered for a touchdown. I dove at the artful dodger, but only one hand made contact with the tail of his t-shirt. To cover my shame, I claimed to have tagged him with two. Had a teammate caught him short of a touchdown, I would have copped to missing him. But the touchdown raised the value of the loss my deception avoided. Even though my credibility was on the line, I knew my lie could not be convincingly refuted. The Palo Alto Saturday Football and Ice Cream Society lacked instant replay capability. (Sigh ... and my mom used to call me "honest John"!)

Of course the costs and benefits of deception are calculated by the deceiver. As those trying to avoid deception, we would have to *infer* their values – high, moderate or low – because we can't read their minds. But our estimates are likely to be useful in deciding when to take a fact-claim with a grain – or sack – of salt.

We should be most wary of fact claims when deception offers great benefit or avoidance of significant loss to the deceiver and there is either little cost to the deceiver if caught or only a slight chance that the misinformation will be exposed in time to negate the benefit. Before the First Gulf War, for example, the U.S. military led the press to believe that Kuwait would be invaded by sea.[18] The actual attack came through the desert. The benefit of misleading the press – and through them, the Iraqis – was for the Allies an almost casualty-free victory over Saddam Hussein's occupation forces. When the deception became obvious after the invasion, there was little cost. In war, it's almost assumed that the press will be used to gain strategic advantage. As Aeschylus noted 2500 years ago, "In war, truth is the first casualty." It's as true today during the "war on terror."

Knowing the track record of the information-provider also helps. During the Vietnam conflict, American reporters became so used to inflated accounts of the harm inflicted on the enemy, they called the military's evening briefings "the five o'clock follies."[19]

The likelihood that a deception will be discovered varies with the number of people who are aware of it, their personal stake in it, and the power of the deceiver to identify and punish anyone who would expose it. The fewer who know of the falsehood and the greater their stake in it, the less possibility one of them will disclose it intentionally or by accident. The Ponzi maestro Bernie Madoff, for example, shared the truth about his investor swindle with just a few associates who had as much to lose as he did were it to be revealed. The most secure conspiracies are small and the conspirators are like-minded. Additionally, the more certain it is that a whistleblower will be punished and the more severe the sanction, the less likely that it will be disclosed.

These conditions for successful deception are met most completely at the command levels of military and paramilitary forces, such as the CIA, FBI and police forces. Their employees are trained to obey leaders unquestioningly. They can face severe penalties for disclosing government secrets. Even being suspected of disclosure can bring punishment.[20] Although all of these agencies are branches of government, public access laws, such as the Freedom of Information Act, rarely succeed in forcing disclosure in time to head off adverse consequences. Finally, their opponents – nations or groups at war with us and those suspected of treason or crime – are unlikely to be considered credible disclosers should they be allowed to give their side of the story.

When leaders of such hierarchical government agencies speak, we are most vulnerable to being misled. When Secretary of Defense Robert McNamara assured Americans in the mid-1960s that the U.S. was winning in Viet Nam and when CIA Chief George Tenet confirmed White House claims of weapons of mass destruction in Iraq almost four decades later, we didn't learn that neither was true until hundreds of thousands of deaths later. The poet John Milton may have been correct when he famously wrote "Let [Truth] and Falsehood grapple; who ever knew Truth put to the worse in a free and open encounter?" But as Mark Twain observed, "A lie can travel halfway around the world while truth is putting on its shoes."[21] In the digital age, lies can run global laps around their refutation. Falsehood can inflict irreversible damage before truth prevails.

Corporations cannot imprison those who would disclose deception, but they can fire them and jeopardize their careers by stigmatizing them as disloyal employees – not "team players."

Corporations may also acquire the right to sue whistleblowers who have signed away their free speech rights in order to gain employment or separation benefits. Additionally, corporations operate beyond the reach of "sunshine" laws that open government meetings and documents to public inspection. Unlike legislative bodies elected by voters, candidates for corporate boards of directors are hand-picked by executives to ensure ideological consonance. Consequently, it is difficult to uncover corporate deception. The collapse of Enron in 2001 and the implosion of huge Wall Street investment firms that plunged much of the world into recession in 2007 were not foreseen even by the elite business press. To the contrary, *Fortune* Magazine named Enron as "America's Most Innovative Company" for six straight years prior to its bankruptcy.[22]

## 3. The publicists' technique of choice is framing information to lead audiences in a particular direction without their noticing

Outright lies are more likely to be exposed than half truths. And once exposed, they can lead mainstream journalists to become more skeptical of the source. So skillful PR agents operate in the twilight zone between truth and falsehood. Eric Alterman, a columnist at *The Nation*, described it this way: "They are able to provide data that for journalistic purposes is entirely credible. The information is true enough. It is slanted. It is propagandistic. But it is not false."[23] Recall again the story of Adam and Eve. The serpent offered an alluring half-truth to tempt Eve: humans would become like God in knowing good from evil. True enough, but he conveniently omitted the parts about multiplying the pain of childbirth, and a life of toil and sweat culminating in death.

The most common and successful means of influencing news coverage is through framing messages so they reflect well – or at least better than they might otherwise – on the agent's client. Framing covers a collection of techniques that subtly lead the audience in a particular direction. Frames lay down tracks for the audience's train of thought. They are effective to the extent that they trigger or activate a set of understandings in our heads about how the world works, or ought to work. They exert their greatest influence when we are least aware of them.[24]

What's common to all frames is that they exclude significant parts of the story, much as a picture frame encloses one part of a wider panorama and leaves everything else out. Because our senses engage with what's in the frame – including whatever prior knowledge it triggers in our brains – it's hard to notice what's *not* there. Frames grease the skids for consonant ideas and marginalize those outside their boundaries.

After Al Qaeda was revealed as the perpetrator of the murderous attacks of 9/11/2001, some liberals, such as University of California cognitive scientist George Lakoff, argued for a criminal justice frame: Find those responsible for the crime and bring them to justice. The administration of George W. Bush, however, chose a much broader frame – a "war on terror." Instead of an effort limited to finding and punishing Osama bin Laden and others associated with the 9/11 attack, the U.S. began what was to become America's longest war committing tens of thousands of U.S. soldiers and hundreds of billions of U.S. dollars to a war with an indigenous Afghan Islamist group calling themselves the Taliban ("students" in Arabic).

Once the "war on terror" frame was adopted, it appeared to make sense to support one side in an Afghan civil war (the Northern Alliance), to install a government and attempt to impose a pro-American democracy by force on a tribal society deeply suspicious of outsiders and non-Muslims. The pursuit of Bin Laden, which would have been front and center in a criminal justice frame, became a secondary concern. It became almost irrelevant when the "war on terror" frame was used as justification for the subsequent invasion of Iraq. Regardless of which frame you think was most appropriate, the consequences of choosing one over the other brought the nation more than a decade of war and incurred more than a trillion dollars of national debt.

Inserting frames into text and images can be subconscious, due to the blinders of our national culture, class, race, gender, etc. Or it can be carefully crafted – propaganda. For example, when Massey

Energy's Upper Big Branch mine exploded on an April afternoon in 2010 killing 29 workers, the company framed the worst coal mining disaster in 40 years as "an act of god," a natural occurrence in an inherently dangerous occupation. After months of investigation, however, the federal government decided that failure to prevent the tragedy was an act of Massey and cited massive and routine neglect of safety procedures.[25]

Sources that journalists quote can be expected to spin, but the task of journalism is to expose such manipulation. And, of course, journalists should avoid spinning themselves.

> "I've often joked that if I ever write an autobiography, I'm going to title it, 'Waiting for people to lie to me.'"[26]
>
> ~ Veteran *Washington Post* reporter Glenn Kessler

The best journalists expose spin by challenging or contradicting it. They can either find a source to voice the challenge, or make their own statements, usually by way of adding context. If, for example, a source framed violence against a woman by saying "the way she dressed invited sexual assault," the journalist could quote an expert, who might say "violence against women is never justified by their appearance." Or add context, such as "Domestic violence laws in the state do not take the victim's appearance into consideration." But as journalism lapses into harried "churnalism," the task of noticing frames and avoiding the trap they spring on our thinking falls more and more to us as critical consumers.

### Priming

A common framing device is priming. Polling prior to the March 2000 primary election in California demonstrated its power. Pollsters read accounts of a political ballot initiative to likely voters. In certain counties, a short summary of the proposition was read: "Proposition 21 provides changes for juvenile felonies – increasing penalties, changing trial procedures and required reporting." In those counties, likely voters said they opposed Prop. 21 by a 17-percentage-point margin over those who approved. But in other, similar counties, when pollsters added the following sentence – "The Juvenile Crime Initiative increases punishment for gang-related felonies, home invasion robbery, car-jacking and drive-by shootings, and creates a crime of gang-recruitment activities" – likely voters favored it by a 23-point margin. A one-sentence expansion of wording contributed to a 40-point difference in public opinion.[27] That's because phrases like "car-jacking," "gang," and "drive-by-shootings" conjure images in our mind's eye. These prime us to respond in a certain way by provoking emotions that we may act on without even noticing. Our brains are organized to automatically bring to mind associated memory traces.[28] Although the pollsters intended no manipulation, pundits and political and commercial message-makers frequently do.

### Framing with value-laden words and phrases

One of the most common framing devices consists of choosing a *particular word or phrase* that is subtly loaded. Linguists have shown that words and phrases carry baggage, or "entailments." Professor Lakoff begins his framing classes at U.C. Berkeley by telling students: "Don't think of an elephant!" as an example of how impossible it is to encounter the word "elephant" and not think of one.

Examples of value-laden words and phrases in public discourse are as common as teeth in sharks. Take the word "progressive." That's what many political liberals now like to call themselves. It suggests that they favor progress. And it erroneously implies that non-progressives do not. Or the phrase, "free market." Almost every market is regulated – and therefore to some degree un-free. (Even the black market is regulated – by gangsters.) But those who favor market solutions have succeeded in joining the two words at the hip, giving the term a positive twist. Calling a tax cut, "tax relief," similarly implies something positive, a cessation of suffering or perhaps injustice. It suggests that taxes, which are necessary for any society to provide protection and build infrastructure, are inherently oppressive. Calling the federal inheritance tax a "death tax," makes it seem absurd and applicable to everyone who passes away rather than to the heirs of a tiny percentage of the population.

Another type of loaded term is the code word, or "dog whistle." It is designed to spark particular interpretations – usually negative – among some listeners without alarming others. Anti-Semitic, anti-Muslim, anti-immigrant code words were common during the 2016 political campaigns. In July, Mr. Trump re-tweeted the image below, which originated, whether he knew it or not, from a white supremacist website:[29]

**Donald J. Trump** ✓
@realDonaldTrump

## Crooked Hillary - - Makes History!

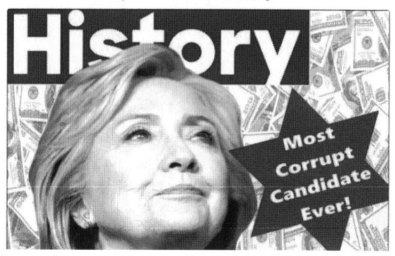

Many people may not have noticed the imposition of a six-pointed star, similar to the Jewish Star of David, on a pile of $100 bills as symbols used by anti-Semites to arouse hatred among those who believe the old trope of Jewish control of the world's money. Although he vigorously defended the ad as innocent, in November his campaign ran a final video ad portraying Ms. Clinton as a pawn of global power brokers that featured pictures of financier George Soros, Goldman Sachs CEO Lloyd Blankfein and Federal Reserve Chair Janet Yellen, all of whom are Jews.

Josh Marshall of TalkingPointsMemo deconstructed the ad:

> The Trump narration immediately preceding Soros and Yellin proceeds as follows: "The establishment has trillions of

dollars at stake in this election. For those who control the levers of power in Washington [**start Soros**] and for the global [**start Yellen**] special interests [**stop Yellen**]. They partner with these people [**start Clinton**] who don't have your good in mind."

For Blankfein: "It's a global power structure that is responsible for the economic decisions that have robbed our working class, stripped our country of its wealth and put that money into the [**start Blankein**] pockets of a handful of large corporations [**stop Blankfein**] and political entities."

"This is an anti-Semitic ad every bit as much as the infamous Jesse Helms 'white hands' ad or the Willie Horton ad were anti-African-American racist ads," Mr. Marshall concluded. "Which is to say, really anti-Semitic."[30]

### Framing by naming

In the book of Genesis, Adam gets to name all the animals of the earth. This symbolizes dominion over them. The same happens in news. Every partisan group tries to get the media to use its labels. Naming something can steer public interpretation and thus advance the namer's cause. Unless the name meets early and strong opposition, it's likely to be accepted, along with its ideological structuring of the situation.

For example, the administration of George W. Bush named its plan for a military attack on Iraq "Operation Iraqi Freedom." From that perspective the actions of U.S. and British military forces in March and April of 2003 could be called "liberation." That term elicits a more favorable response than a more neutral word like "invasion." Likewise, labeling Iraqis fighting U.S. forces as "terrorists" rather than "resistance fighters" stacks the deck in favor of the Americans. Some people may associate the term "resistance" with the French underground and others who heroically fought Nazi occupation.[31]

Similarly, calling the people under arms on one side "militants," "extremists," or "gunmen," and those on the other "the army," "police," or "soldiers" delegitimizes the first group in favor of the second. After all, isn't almost everyone in the police or army a "gunman" (or gunwoman)? And who is more militant than the military? Across the sweep of time, have soldiers always held the high moral ground versus less organized fighters? How about our own history? Were the Minutemen who fired on British Redcoats from behind trees less justified than their uniformed opponents?

### Framing with stereotypes

Stereotypes are often used to frame people, places, and events. A stereotype is a generalization about all members of a group based on the characteristics of a few. They can be positive (Asians are good at math) or negative (men are insensitive and combative).

Stereotypes can be subtle. Have you noticed a tendency in the press to call well-spoken black people "articulate" but rarely apply the same term to white people? Under the surface, might the author be indicating surprise to find articulate African-Americans? And an assumption that most black people are inarticulate?

Similarly, the physical attributes of women may be commented upon much more often than those of men. Women may be called "matronly," for example. But we have no similar word for men. (Patronly?) The implied stereotype is that a woman's value lies in her appearance. Candidate Hillary Clinton's pantsuits and ankles drew comment in political reporting, as did Florida Republican Katherine Harris' use of makeup back in 2004. What have these to do with their ability as political or government leaders?

### Framing with themes

A fifth framing device is a *theme* running through a story. Consider how reporters at the *San Jose Mercury News* framed the death of a man who had fractured his wife's skull before dying in a hail of police bullets when he pulled a gun on officers investigating the beating:

> This is the story of Dan McGovern, who friends and family say loved cars, cops, guns and most of all, the woman he met after paying $3,000 to a professional matchmaking service.[32]

The article barely mentioned domestic violence. Instead it described a simple but good man, driven to apparent "blue suicide" by his consuming love for a manipulative foreign bride who done him wrong. A female colleague of the reporters who wrote the story complained: "It's not a love story when a man beats a woman so seriously that she goes to the hospital with severe head injuries." Recognizing the bias, the *Mercury News* ran an article the following day that quoted several domestic violence experts contradicting the victim blame frame.[33]

### Framing with metaphor and simile

Similes and metaphors constitute especially powerful framing devices. Both compare different things whose similarities help convey a point. What makes them so potent is the ability to transform something complex and perhaps not well understood into something simple and familiar that suggests a commonsense interpretation.

Metaphors and similes are wonderful instructional and story-telling tools, and thus they are of great value to journalists, particularly opinion writers. The danger is that we may overlook considerable differences in reality between the two things that are compared and be captivated by eloquence rather than convinced by evidence.

Major public policy debates are a good place to find these framing devices. Before the 2003 invasion of Iraq, Secretary of State Colin Powell used a simile for Iraq that came to be called the Pottery Barn rule: "If you break it, you own it."[34] At the time, Secretary Powell was cautioning the administration to think twice about going to war because it would incur a moral obligation to repair the damage to Iraq.

Notice the simplicity of the Pottery Barn rule – only seven words. And its familiarity. Who hasn't seen a sign like that in a store? Furthermore, the audience can see some similarity between the things being compared, as with all successful similes. A shattered country seems at least a little like broken pottery. Finally, the moral obligation in either case to offer restitution for the damage fits our cultural values so well we take it as common sense.

But what metaphors and similes *obscure* is as important as what they reveal. For starters, the Pottery Barn is made whole, indeed happy, by the purchase of the broken pot. But the dead in a war cannot be brought back. No restitution can compensate the thousands of Americans who lost their lives or limbs or the many-times-larger number of Iraqis killed or injured.

Further, unlike pottery, a nation is not up for sale. And the simile distracts us from a more central moral question: whether a nation may violate the United Nations charter to invade another country without first having been attacked. Breaking pottery doesn't violate international law; unprovoked invasion does.

Good journalists help the audience see through ideologically-loaded similes and metaphors employed by sources, and avoid creating them. But as journalism shrivels, the task falls to us. Whenever you hear a persuasive simile or metaphor, consider all the ways the two situations *differ*.

In the final chapter we turn to the growing number of ways the Internet allows us to break frames open to check the validity of news and information.

## Exercises and Discussion Topics

1. Look through the news to find a situation where an institutional spokesperson or political figure appears to be spinning the facts. Describe what s/he said and why you think it's misleading. Did the reporter find a way to counter the spin? If so, how. If not, how might the journalist have alerted readers to the spin?

2. Think about the last time you thought of misleading someone – perhaps a teacher about why you missed class or failed to turn in an assignment on time. Did you follow the

same logic I did in deceiving my fellow football players?

3. Again thinking about your own experience, how have others used framing to get you to see things their way? Describe their strategy.

4. Look for partisan framing in value-laden words or phrases in the news. They should be common in source statements, but absent in reporter statements and opinion-writing. Find an example in both kinds of statements. Explain what the partisan value is and why you think it's indicated by the word or phrase. (Note: they don't have to be in the same article.)

## End Notes

[1] Robert W. McChesney and John Nichols (2010) *The death and life of American journalism*, Philadelphia: Nation Books. The authors use data from the U.S. Bureau of Labor Statistics to estimate that the ratio of public relations practitioners to journalists has changed from approximately 1 to 1 in 1980 to more than three to one in 2008. The 2014 estimate using BLS data was 5.7 to one. See Colin Jordan (12/18/2015) "The PR industry has a big problem," Adweek, http://www.adweek.com/digital/the-pr-industry-has-a-big-problem/.

[2] David Carr (12/10/2007) "Muckraking pays, just not in profit," *New York Times*, p. C1, online at: http://www.nytimes.com /2007/12/10/ business/media/10carr.html?_r=1&oref=slogin.

[3] John Sullivan (May/June 2011) "True enough: the second age of PR," *Columbia Journalism Review*, pp. 34-39, available online at: http://www.cjr.org/feature/true_enough.php.

[4] W. Dale Nelson (1998) *Who speaks for the president? The White House press secretary from Cleveland to Clinton*. Syracuse, NY: Syracuse University Press.

[5] As their ability to shape public discourse has grown, publicists have sought to justify and gain respect for their craft by comparing themselves to lawyers. Attorneys advocate for their clients in courts of law and public relations "counsels" advocate for theirs in the "court" of public opinion. But it's like comparing an apple to a road apple. Unlike a court of justice, in the court of public opinion there are no rules of evidence, nothing to prevent hearsay or rumor. No counsel is appointed to ensure a fair hearing for those unable to afford representation. There are no hand-on-bible oaths to speak truth under

penalty of perjury. In fact, there is no law against lying to the public. In the court of public opinion there is no judge to referee the matter and insist each side have its full say. There is no power to compel testimony or the production of documents, or to protect vulnerable witnesses from reprisal. And there is no jury of peers listening intently, only a distracted public paying occasional attention. None of the protections against half-truths and deception, nor the enhancements for seeking truth that characterize courts of law exist in the wild and wooly infosphere that shapes public opinion.

[6] Bob Garfield (10/28/2011) "Is transparency always a good thing?" On the Media, National Public Radio.

[7] Linda Qiu (1/21/2017) "Donald Trump had biggest inaugural crowd ever? Metrics don't show it," Politifact, http://www.politifact.com/truth-o-meter/statements/2017/jan/21/sean-spicer/trump-had-biggest-inaugural-crowd-ever-metrics-don/.

[8] Lauren Carroll (4/12/2017) "Donald Trump changes NATO position: 'It's no longer obsolete'" Politifact.com, http://www.politifact.com/ truth-o-meter/statements/2017/apr/12/ donald-trump/donald-trump-nato-i-said-it-was-obsolete-its-no-lo/.

[9] Aaron Sharockman (9/16/2016) "Full flop: Donald Trump abandons Barack Obama birther conspiracy," Politifact.com, http://www.politifact. com/truth-o-meter/statements/2016/sep/16/donald-trump/full-flop-donald-trump-abandons-barack-obama-birth/.

[10] Paul Mcleary (4/18/2005) "Money for nothing, and the news ain't free," Columbia Journalism Review, available online at: http://www. cjr.org/politics/money_for_nothing_and_the_news.php.

[11] Zachary Roth (10/13/2004) "Video news releases – they're everywhere," Columbia Journalism Review, available online at: http://www.cjr.org/behind_the_news/video_news_releases_theyre_eve.php.

[12] David Barstow (4/20/2008) "Message machine; Behind TV analysts, Pentagon's hidden hand," New York Times, p. A1; available online at: http://query.nytimes.com/gst/fullpage .html?res=9501E7DF103CF933 A1575 7C0A96E9C8B63&scp=1&sq=Pentagon+and+news+consultants&st=nyt.

[13] John Sullivan, referenced above, p. 34.

[14] Glenn Kessler (3/4/2011) "Democrats keep misleading on claimed budget 'cuts'," Washington Post, available online at: http://voices. washington post. com /fact-checker/2011/03/ democrats_keep_ misleading_on_c.html.

[15] Angie Drobnic Holan (12/12/2013) "Lie of the Year: 'If you like your health care plan, you can keep it'," PolitiFact, http://www.politifact.com/ truth-o-meter/article/2013/dec/12/lie-year-if-you-like-your-health-care-plan-keep-it/.

[16] Naomi Oreskes (1/24/2012) "Op-ed: The verdict is in on climate change," Talk of the Nation with Neal Conan, National Public Radio. Also see Jane Mayer (8/30/2010), "Covert operations," *The New Yorker*, pp. 60-63; and Juliet Schor (3/20/2011) "Who's really upset?" *New York Times* online feature, Room for Debate at: http://www.nytimes.com/ roomfordebate /2011 /03/17/the-politicized-light-bulb/whos-really-upset-with-energy-efficient-products?scp=1&sq=climate%20change%20 deniers%20and%20tobacco&st=cse.

[17] Stanton A. Glantz, John Slade, Lisa A. Bero, Peter Hanauer, and Deborah E. Barnes, Eds. (1996) *The cigarette papers.* Berkeley: University of California Press; available online at: http://ark.cdlib.org/ark:/13030/ft8489p25j/.

[18] Philip M. Taylor (1995) "War and the media," address at the British Royal Military Academy at Sandhurst. Mr. Taylor is a professor at the Institute of Communications Studies at the University of Leeds, UK, available online at: http://ics.leeds.ac. uk/papers/vp01.cfm? outfit=pmt&folder=34&paper=39.

[19] *Time Magazine* (2/12/1973) "The press: Farewell to the follies," available online at: http://www.time.com/time/magazine/article /0,9171,903831,00.html#ixzz1dEbsaCEH.

[20] Before trial, the soldier suspected of giving classified documents to Wikileaks, Pvt. Bradley (later Chelsea) Manning, was kept in solitary confinement and subjected to harsh imprisonment. See David Leigh (3/16/2011) "You can hear Bradley Manning coming because of the chains," *The Guardian*, available online at: http://www. guardian .co.uk/media/2011/mar/16/hear-bradley-manning-because-chains.

[21] Twainquotes.com (accessed on 8/11/2011) online at: http://www.twainquotes.com/Lies.html.

[22] Wikipedia (accessed on 6/3/2011) "Enron," online at: http://en.wikipedia.org/wiki/Enron.

[23] John Sullivan, referenced above, p. 36.

[24] My thinking has been most shaped by George Lakoff (1996) *Moral politics,* Chicago: University of Chicago Press; Vincent Price and David Tewksbury (1997) "News values and public opinion: A theoretical account of media priming and framing," in *Progress in Communication Sciences*, Eds. George Barnett and Franklin J. Boster, Greenwich, CT: Ablex, pp. 173-212; and

Stephen D. Reese (2001) "Prologue: Framing public life: A bridging model for media research," in Stephen D. Reese, Oscar H. Gandy Jr. and August E. Grant, Eds. *Framing public life,* Mahwah, NJ: Lawrence Erlbaum.

[25] Wikipedia (accessed 6/6/2011) "Upper Big Branch mine disaster," on line at: http://en.wikipedia.org/wiki/Upper_Big_Branch_Mine_disaster.

[26] Glenn Kessler (1/10/2012) "Political Fact-checking under fire," Talk of the Nation, NPR, available online at: http://www.npr.org/2012/01/10/144974110/political-fact-checking-under-fire.

[27] The Field Institute (2/29/2000) "Prop. 22 still running ahead," Berkeley, CA: University of California Data Archive.

[28] Dean Buonomano (2011) *Brain bugs: How the brain's flaws shape our lives,* New York: W.W. Norton.

[29] Jose A. DelReal and Julie Zauzmer (7/8/2016) " Trump's vigorous defense of anti-Semitic image a 'turning point' for many Jews," *Washington Post,* https://www.washingtonpost.com/politics/trumps-vigorous-defense-of-anti-semitic-image-a-turning-point-for-many-jews/2016/07/08/720858e2-4450-11e6-bc99-7d269f8719b1_story.html?utm_term=.36429bcdd31f.

[30] Josh Marshall (11/5/2016) "Trump Rolls Out Anti-Semitic Closing Ad," http://talkingpointsmemo.com/edblog/trump-rolls-out-anti-semitic-closing-ad.

[31] Terrorism is a tactic – trying to achieve a political goal by instilling fear in a population through violence against civilians – rather than a side in a conflict. Both states and insurgent groups can employ terror to gain their ends.

[32] Sean Webby and Roxanne Stites (2/28/2001) "Man's failed marriage to Russian bride was prelude to fatal shooting," *San Jose Mercury News,* p. A1.

[33] John McManus (3/10/2001) "Is wife-beating ever a love story?," Grade the News, online at: http://gradethenews.org/dreamhost%20files/pagesfolder/Mcgovern1.htm. Notice the value of having women in the newsroom who were able to catch the gender bias, which took the men by surprise. It's another reason why diverse newsrooms are superior to those that don't reflect society's fault lines.

[34] *Frontline (*March 2008) "Bush's War" Part 1, Public Broadcasting System, online at: http://www.pbs.org/wgbh/pages/frontline/bushswar/.

# 11

## Online Tools for Sniffing Out Bias, Including Our Own

*Know thyself.*

~ Ancient Greek proverb

$B$y this point I hope that bias in news and information has become more visible. But sometimes slant can be so subtle that we need help to detect it. Fortunately, the Web makes it possible, and sometimes easy, to accomplish this.

This chapter will explore five propositions:

1. **We can – and ought to – become aware of our own biases (even though it may be as appealing as a colonoscopy).**

2. **Professional fact-checking organizations are popping up like mushrooms after a spring rain.**

3. **The Internet puts vetting tools and a virtual reference library at our fingertips 24/7, enabling us to conduct our own fact-checks.**

4. **Social media allow us to collaborate in vetting content with others who may be more knowledgeable.**

5. **The Web can even help us discover people and perspectives that are ignored or marginalized in mainstream U.S. media.**

Socrates, the fifth century BCE father of western philosophy (and first suicide philosopher), left no writings, but his words deeply impressed his student Plato who quotes him saying, "The unexamined life is not worth living."[1] It's worth noting, however, that when Socrates examined the lives of jaded Athenians, they decided *his* was not worth continuing. As you may recall, they insisted he drink a fatal draught of hemlock. Examining our biases may not kill us, but it's likely to entail discomfort. As with a colonoscopy, it's not just the pain of ascending the down staircase; we're also afraid of what we might discover about ourselves.

## 1. We can – and ought to – become aware of our own biases

Our partisan biases distort how we perceive the world around us. When shared, they can create a culture of injustice, allowing us to rationalize discrimination and repression. When bias is incorporated into political agendas and then into law, catastrophe follows. Across history and in too many places today, prejudices based on religion, race, ethnicity, gender and sexual orientation have led to oppression, war, slavery, murderous pogroms and genocide. Unscrupulous leaders always play on popular biases and couple them with fear to catapult themselves to power. Our unexamined biases make us their pawns. Partisan biases divide 21st century American society, preventing us from seeing and embracing our common humanity, breeding indifference to others' suffering, resentment, even hatred.

### Three obstacles to overcoming bias

While we may agree that we ought to identify and diminish our core biases – particularly those that build our identity at others' expense – doing so is difficult for at least three interlocking reasons:

1. *Cultural blindness* – biases we share with those around us, and with those we admire and with whom we choose to associate in life and online – are difficult to notice because they seem normal or natural rather than distortions of reality.

2. *Motivated blindness* – our biases often buttress our selfish interests, and even more importantly, our self-esteem. Thus

acknowledging them can create uncomfortable cognitive dissonance between what we have done or want to do and what we *ought* to do. If nothing else, it's painful to admit we're wrong. More painful still to accept guilt for actions the bias justified. We don't see what we don't want to see.

3. *Social pressure* – failure to share the biases of colleagues, friends and family can alienate us from them. As social animals, we fear isolation and dread being ostracized.

Triply reinforced, our core biases are devilishly difficult to dislodge.

The Web was intended to overcome bias, to unite humanity in mutual understanding. But it can also empower division. It is so vast and varied we can always find people online who share our mindset, no matter how warped. And once found, their reflection of our own biases assure us that we are not crazy, not alone. In fact, we may be the elect who know better than others.

> "So much of how people view the world has nothing to do with facts. That doesn't mean truth is doomed, or even that people can't change their minds. But what all this does seem to suggest is that, no matter how strong the evidence is, there's little chance of it changing someone's mind if they really don't want to believe what it says."[2]
>
> ~ Julie Beck, senior associate editor at *The Atlantic*

Have you ever been amazed that a nation of people as intelligent, educated, civilized, as *Christian*, as Germany's population was before World War II could have systematically murdered six million fellow citizens – people who lived next door and fought side by side in the trenches during World War I – simply because they were Jewish? Or wondered how slave owners in the ante-bellum South could have thought buying, selling and enslaving other humans was moral? Or that some families in Asia and the Middle

East still consider the murder of their daughters "honor killings" because they were seen with a man from the "wrong" religion or caste? Or that inner city gangs can shoot people almost exactly like themselves, but wearing a different color or inhabiting a different block? Or that some people who prostrate themselves in prayer five times a day can behead others who worship the same God?

The fundamental attribution error (*over*estimating the influence of personal character on behavior and *under*estimating social circumstances) prompts us to think of these people as moral reprobates, perhaps even monsters. We like to think we would never act as they did, that our character or conscience is superior to theirs. But most of the people in pre-war Germany and the Confederate South were average humans going along to get along with the biases of their culture and time. That doesn't exonerate them, but it does emphasize the importance of recognizing how bias undermines our sense of humanity. And how much misery it causes.

### Cultural blindness

Consider the case of the American South before the Civil War – and a century after it when you include the legal chains of Jim Crow legislation. If you happened to be born white, you grew up in a society where slavery, and later discrimination against blacks, was accepted as normal, even natural. It was based on the notion among whites that black people were childish, lazy, and mentally inferior. From that perspective, blacks needed the supervision of whites for their own good. A white Southerner once told me that blacks were "the highest form of animal, lowest form of man."

These racialist ideas were not confined to the Southern states. In 1859 the Supreme Court of the United States held that blacks were simply the property of their owners with no independent human rights. For centuries, following the voyages of Columbus, the assumption of white superiority made European domination of other peoples around the globe seem appropriate, the natural order of things.

### Motivated blindness, motivated reasoning

Racial bias provided a ready rationalization for economic exploitation. European nations tortured reason to cloak the *benefits* of their domination of South America, Africa and South Asia as "the white man's *burden*."

In a cotton-farming economy dependent on slave labor, Southern plantation owners profited from "the peculiar institution." The money generated from the cotton trade also supported churches, local merchants and artisans. Arguments against slavery threatened the system that put bread on their tables. Even poor whites, though sometimes disdained as "trash" by wealthier classes and disadvantaged by competition from unpaid labor,[3] received a boost to their self-esteem; they could console themselves with being "better" than blacks. There was ample motivation to turn blind eyes to injustice.

Imagine the anguish of even *considering* the humanity of black people: the brutality of slavery directly contradicted the fundamental demand of the dominant religion of the South – to love others as one's self. Those troubled by the cruelty of slavery, as was Thomas Jefferson, experienced a painful clash between their moral beliefs and actions. He wrote of slavery, "I tremble for my country when I consider that God is just." But he didn't liberate his slaves, nor refrain from taking sexual liberties with a slave woman.[4] Like other slave-holders, his racial bias supported his selfish interest. Even for this most brilliant and morally sensitive man, self-interest conquered conscience. Most of his countrymen simply put it out of mind.

### Social pressure

Failure to share racial bias, or to oppose it, led to dire consequences. Blacks who resisted slavery were whipped or killed. Their assailants faced neither legal consequences nor social disapproval. Quite the opposite, as photos and descriptions of lynchings demonstrate. Abraham Lincoln declared an end to slavery in the deep South in 1863 and it was outlawed after the Confederacy surrendered. But for decades afterwards vigilantes such as the Ku Klux Klan terrorized blacks who would assert equal rights. The few whites who stood up for blacks were humiliated and ostracized as "nigger lovers." As historian Joel Williamson wrote: "White people could not prescribe and enforce a precise role upon black people without prescribing and enforcing a precise role upon themselves."[5] As late as the 1960s, freedom-seeking blacks, and whites who traveled to the South to promote the equal rights of African-Americans, were jailed, beaten and sometimes murdered.[6]

For blacks – and whites as well – racial bias was a heavily fortified, deeply entrenched prison that degraded both the inmates and the jailors. The Civil War that first breached that prison cost a greater number of American lives – the vast majority of them young *white* men – than World War I, World War II, Korea and Viet Nam combined.[7]

Racial bias, of course, was never confined to the South. Mob lynchings occurred as far north as Duluth, Minnesota (in 1920) and some of the worst rampages targeting blacks occurred outside the former Confederate states. While racism is no longer as virulent and discrimination is now prohibited by law, subtle racial bias remains as American as apple pie.[8]

Biases play an enormous role in American politics. Campaign ads fasten on prejudices like ticks on deer, generating fear and loathing of immigrants, homosexuals, transgender people, religious minorities, the poor, people of color, unions, big government, "elites," and even big corporations. Unfortunately, playing to such biases appears to work. Logic? Not so much. "When it comes to political views, actual logic does not really change many people's views at least in the short term," argued James Fallows, national correspondent for *The Atlantic*. "If you look at the way political elections are carried out, and the way people make up their minds on large issues, it's partly logic, but it's also what you could think of as tribalism. It's loyalties to what the people you like think."[9] Note that Fallows was writing years before the political rise of Donald Trump whose campaign rallies pumped up prejudice and resentment.

## How to uncover your biases

Surfacing your biases is a bit like the "examination of conscience" that Catholics are urged to undertake before confession. It demands ruthless honesty. Fortunately there are tools to help. Visit www.implicit.harvard.edu. There you can evaluate some of your own biases.

Project Implicit is based on the idea that we are often biased without knowing it, or at least without being willing to admit it. It has a bank of diagnostic quizzes you can give yourself to reveal deep predispositions for or against people based on race, disability, religion, sexual preference, size, etc.

The Implicit Association Test asks you to make snap associations between sets of positive and negative words and photos of people with different characteristics, such as skin color, ethnicity, or weight. For example, if you take longer to associate positive words with blacks than with whites and less time to connect negative words with blacks than whites, the researchers believe you may have a bias. Journalist Sally Lehrman wrote of Project Implicit:

> The team has studied automatic reactions through more than 5 million Web-based tests so far. About 80% of users have shown a preference for young over old. Nearly the same proportion of self-identified white people and Asians have a more favorable impression of white faces relative to black ones. Users also prefer able-bodied people over those with limited physical abilities, straight people over gay and thin people over heavy ones.

> Even more disturbing was that these biases operated below the level of conscious thought.

> Our automatic reactions often don't match the conscious attitudes we hold, the researchers have found, and yet we act on them every day. Even though a majority of people explicitly expressed the opposite view, for instance, most test takers implicitly considered Native Americans less "American" than white citizens. Native Americans themselves, however, strongly disagreed. Asian Americans also fell short of belonging, according to users – even those who were Asian American themselves. The team discovered

> it was easiest for test-takers to associate harmless objects with white people. And what about black people? With them, users of all races found it easier to associate weapons.[10]

See how you do on these common prejudices: skin tone, religion, gender, race (blacks and whites), Asians, Arabs, age, disability, sexual preference, and weight. Make a note of the results. Consider that they might just indicate a set of biases that you carry. (Yes, I was embarrassed too! But don't feel bad. Making them visible is the first step toward easing their grip.)

## 2. Professional fact-checking organizations are popping up like mushrooms after a spring rain

The sheer volume and persuasive power of fake news and outright partisan propaganda before the 2016 elections spurred efforts by Facebook, Google, and others to find some means of labeling false and misleading news reports. But as of mid-2017 no algorithm or artificial intelligence program has been developed that's equal to the task.[11] Given the exorbitant cost of hiring human evaluators to monitor the millions of messages and videos posted online every minute, it's unlikely the Web will be purged of information pollution anytime soon. Our best defense is to build our own habits of systematic skepticism.

As demonstrated in chapter 8, we can find fact-checking help online for at least some of the misleading information being pumped into the infosphere. The first of these, **Snopes.com** was founded to debunk urban legends in 1994. **FactCheck.org**, was launched at the University of Pennsylvania in 2003. Others followed in response to the 2004 "Swift Boat" political ads targeting Sen. John Kerry during his run for president. In a sign of their growing importance, **PolitiFact.com**, operated by the *Tampa Bay Times*, won the Pulitzer Prize for its "Truth-O-Meter" ratings of politicians' claims in 2009. Glenn Kessler's **Fact Checker** (www.washingtonpost.com/blogs /fact-checker) column at the *Washington Post* grades the seriousness of falsehoods by awarding from one to four "Pinocchios." The Associated Press has fact-checked politician's claims since 1993, as part of the coverage it offers affiliated news media (https://

www.apnews. com/tag/APFactCheck). In 2017, the *New York Times* launched its first full-time fact-check team.

Over the last five years fact-checking operations have begun at the state and metropolitan level.[12] PolitiFact has entered partnerships with local news media in Florida, Georgia, Texas, Virginia, New Hampshire, Pennsylvania, North Carolina, New York, Missouri, Illinois, California, Colorado, Iowa, Nevada, Rhode Island and Wisconsin. (To find PolitiFact's state fact-checking sites visit PolitiFact.com, then the "editions" tab, then "states.") Focusing on Arizona is **AZ Fact Check**, a partnership among the *Arizona Republic*, Phoenix 12 News, and the Cronkite School of Journalism and Mass Communication at Arizona State University. The Duke Reporters' Lab lists 115 active fact-checking sites worldwide, with 45 located in the U.S. (https://reporterslab.org/fact-checking/).

Most fact-check sites are themselves searchable by entering the title or gist of a political claim you want to check. They also vet political speeches, ads and quotes in news media in an ongoing attempt to hold politicians accountable. And some will allow you to submit new claims you'd like them to check. Collectively they represent an antidote to some of the poison in the infosphere. To find out if one of these sites can verify a claim, simply enter the gist followed by "and factcheck" in a search engine such as Bing, or Google, e.g. "Hillary Clinton earned six-figure fees for Wall Street speeches and factcheck." This allows you to check a claim made by her opponents on multiple fact-checking sites simultaneously. (Turns out, she did.)

In addition to websites dedicated to checking facts, there are various groups across the political spectrum that monitor news media performance, including bias. Here are a few: On the left, there's Media Matters for America (www. mediamatters.org) and FAIR (Fairness and Accuracy in Reporting at www.fair.org); toward the center lie *Columbia Journalism Review* (www.cjr.org ), and WNYC's On the Media (www. onthemedia.org); and to the right you'll find AIM (Accuracy in Media, at www.aim.org), and the Media Research Center (www.mrc.org). (Disclosure: I subscribe to *Columbia Journalism Review* and contribute to On the Media.)

### 3. The Internet puts vetting tools and a virtual reference library at our fingertips 24/7, enabling us to conduct our own fact-checks

Fact-checking sites sift only a small fraction of the chaff appearing online. So we need to develop our own skills for vetting news and information.

#### Online tools for information detectives

As we saw in chapter 8, the place to begin is with the *Source* of news or information. Fraudsters can mimic real news sites with fakes that look like and have similar domain names as authentic news outlets. (A domain name is what comes just before .com, .org, .edu, .gov, .net, .info.)

#### Fake News sites

You may have received an email or social media post with a link to this domain name, "abcnews.com.co." Here's what it might have looked like:

Seems legit. But it's not really ABC News. It's a fake news site. The real ABC News site's domain name is similar: "abcnews.go.com." So how do you avoid being fooled?

Mike Caulfield has written a short, smart Web book called "Web literacy for student fact-checkers" (https://webliteracy .pressbooks.com/). As with the SMELL test, he begins with the *source* of the information. Enter the domain name of any unfamiliar source in a new Google search with this search term: [website to be checked] - [website to be checked]. In this case, "abcnews.com.co - abcnews.com.co." This tells Google to find any articles about this website, but exclude the website itself. Here's the result:

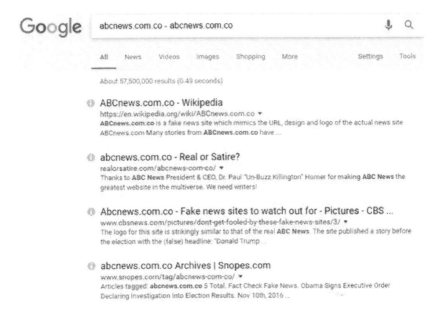

All results on the first page, all from reputable sources such as Wikipedia and Snopes, label the site as fake. It's wise to perform such an easy check on any site that is new to you.

One tip on Web hygiene: Sometimes a link on a website or email will look authentic, but actually direct you to a different site than what appears on your screen. Always hover your mouse or touch over a link that seems in any way suspicious. You will see the true domain name preceded by the phrase "Go to" at the bottom of your email program or browser. If it differs from what's printed, don't click. It's a "phishing" scam.

*Checking for fake images*

Suppose you're sent a link with a photo you suspect may have been mislabeled or doctored. Google's Chrome browser has a nifty feature called "reverse image," that tells you the origin of the picture. Let's say you received a tweet or link to a website about Hillary Clinton fainting at a memorial for 9/11 – an actual event – and it contains a photo suggesting that Mrs. Clinton is lying at death's door:

You can right-click any image you see on a website or in search results. Choose: "Search Google for this image," and a new tab will open. In this case you'll see that the photo is not of Mrs. Clinton at all. It was used by fake news sites to back up the "sick Hillary" meme discussed back in chapter 2.

*Checking for fake video*

Suppose someone sends you a link to a YouTube video "proving" something that you are skeptical about. You can cut and paste the URL (Internet address) of the video into Amnesty International's **YouTube DataViewer** (http://www. amnestyusa. org/sites/default/customscripts/citizenevidence/) and it will reveal the metadata accompanying the video, telling you when it was uploaded to YouTube. If it were uploaded before the event it's supposed to document, you know it's fraudulent. The DataViewer will also break the video into thumbnail images and allow you to use

Google's reverse image function to find when they or similar images first appeared online and where they appeared. Fake news sites will often grab online video from elsewhere and present it as if it documents the event they are reporting on.

*Going upstream to find the original source*

Often content on social media or a website originated elsewhere. To evaluate the source, go *upstream* to its first appearance on the Web. Responsible sites will always indicate the source of content from elsewhere. And we can go there to evaluate it. But in an era of fake news and viral content, the originating source may not be disclosed. In such a case we can highlight the headline and copy it into Google or other search engine. We can do the same *within* the story if there is a particular claim we want to check, perhaps a source, a poll, or an organization. We can highlight the text in question and right-click with Chrome, then select "Search Google for "[highlighted text]" and find articles on the same topic. We'd choose the one with the earliest date to find the original source.

Here's an example from a site my conservative friends often cite, Zerohedge.com:[13]

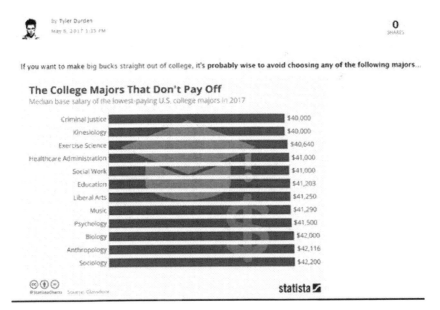

by Tyler Durden
May 8, 2017 3:35 PM

0
SHARES

If you want to make big bucks straight out of college, it's probably wise to avoid choosing any of the following majors...

**The College Majors That Don't Pay Off**
Median base salary of the lowest-paying U.S. college majors in 2017

| Major | Salary |
| --- | --- |
| Criminal Justice | $40,000 |
| Kinesiology | $40,000 |
| Exercise Science | $40,640 |
| Healthcare Administration | $41,000 |
| Social Work | $41,000 |
| Education | $41,203 |
| Liberal Arts | $41,250 |
| Music | $41,290 |
| Psychology | $41,500 |
| Biology | $42,000 |
| Anthropology | $42,116 |
| Sociology | $42,200 |

statista

Suppose you wanted to know which majors "don't pay off." The creative graph is sourced to "statista." Move your cursor over it, and you'll notice it's linked to Statista.com, a site that aggregates various statistical information. There you'll find the same story Zerohedge put under Tyler Durden's byline, headline and all, *lifted almost word-for-word* from a story published three days earlier by Niall McCarthy of Statistica, as well as the same graph.[14] (It would have been nice if Mr. Durden indicated the story was cut and pasted from Statista, rather than presenting it as his own on Zerohedge. But he did at least attribute the graph to Statista and referenced Mr. McCarthy as if he had interviewed him.)

The Statista story, however, cites another source, Glassdoor.com, as the provider of the figures in the graph. They provide a link, so it's easy to find the study on Glassdoor (a website that allows employees to anonymously rate their employers). But if there were no link, you could highlight and search Google for "Glassdoor.com and lowest salaries by college major." On page 21 of the study, you will see that the salary numbers Statista used to create its graph were accurately transcribed.

But how did Glassdoor come up with its salary figures? For that, look at the "methodology" section that reputable researchers provide. There you'll find that the salaries are based on an analysis of 46,900 resumes filed with Glassdoor, between 2010 and 2017. And the salaries are not averages, but *estimates*. The authors appropriately listed the limitations of their research near the end of the article:

> REPRESENTATIVENESS: Our study is based on anonymized resumes from Glassdoor for which users reported having earned a college degree between 2010 and 2017. We do not examine those with less than a college degree, and we examine both workers who went on to grad school during the first five years after college, as well as those who did not. *Our sample may not be representative of all college graduates during this time period, or of the broader U.S. workforce.* [Emphasis added][15]

So the graph is *not* based on a scientific sample of American college graduates, but rather from seven years of resumes filed with one website, and it mixes graduate degrees with college majors.

While it's possible that college graduates of the majors listed earn the least, the Glassdoor study does not – and cannot – prove either that U.S. graduates with these majors earn the least, nor even that the salaries accurately reflect the U.S. workforce. In fact, the Glassdoor study concerns something else: "The pipeline problem: How college majors contribute to the gender pay gap."

There's a second problem beyond the lack of *evidence* in the Zerohedge and Statista articles. Their identical headlines are inflammatory and *illogical*. The very lowest salary reported, for criminal justice majors, was $40,000 per year. To say such a major "doesn't pay off" would require evidence that students spent more in tuition than their lifetime earnings in the field (assuming "pay off" is simply a measure of salary rather than job satisfaction). The stories do not even attempt such a comparison. An accurate headline would have read: "Employees using a rate-your-employer website who majored in liberal arts reported earning lower salaries than those with science majors." Not exactly click bait!

*Vetting individual fact-claims*

Often, rather than vetting an article online, you'll just want to verify a fact-claim you heard in the news, or from a friend. You no longer need to spend a day in a research library.

Browsers such as Bing, Google and DuckDuckGo are edging closer to natural language searches, where you just type in a question. If that fails you can always enter *key word phrases* to get answers. Suppose you wanted to check a claim by a politician that the American Health Care Act passed by the U.S. House of Representatives in early 2017 fulfills Mr. Trump's campaign promise not to take away anyone's Medicaid coverage. Enter the simple question: "Will the American Health Care Act reduce Medicaid coverage?" in Google News and here's what you'd see:

In the second paragraph of the *New York Times* article you'd find: "It will change the rules and subsidies for people who buy their own insurance coverage, and make major cuts to the Medicaid program, which funds care for the poor and disabled."[16] But suppose you mistrust the *Times* as too liberal. You could sample any of the other choices above and find the same answer. One, the respected independent website, FiveThirtyEight.com, quantified the expected impact on Medicaid: "The Congressional Budget Office, the nonpartisan agency that calculates the economic effects of legislation, estimates that the net effect of the changes would be 14 million fewer people on Medicaid."[17] Although this health care plan had yet to clear the Senate, President Trump pushed for, and then celebrated, its passage in the House, despite his campaign promise. Checking this fact took fewer than five minutes.

*Not all search results are equal*

When looking through search results, bear in mind that Google and Bing rankings are based on an algorithm that includes no human monitoring of the *trustworthiness* of the information presented. So be sure to choose sources with the highest PIE score: .edu websites often belong to universities, usually excellent sources of independent expertise. Same for .gov sources, particularly at the federal level. (This may be changing, however. In May 2017, Scott Pruitt, Mr. Trump's choice as administrator of the Environmental Protection Agency began purging independent academic scientists on the EPA's science advisory board and replacing them with employees of the fossil fuel industries, as well as taking down some scientific appraisals of climate change from the EPA website that do not agree with his position of denial.)[18]

Professional news media with their own reporter on scene, particularly one who specializes in covering the topic at issue, are usually good picks. They score high in proximity, as well as independence, sometimes even in expertise. National broadcast networks, especially PBS and NPR, have strong reputations. Cable news channels less so. Although surveys consistently show the public trusts local TV news outlets the most,[19] those who study their content often find them superficial and sensationalistic.[20] Further, the company owning the largest number of local stations, Sinclair, has used them to advance a conservative political agenda.[21] For depth on breaking news, magazines such as *The Atlantic*, *The Economist*, *The National Review*, *The New Yorker*, *The Weekly Standard*, *Mother Jones* and *Harpers* are worth perusing. On radio and podcasts on the web, Fresh Air with Terry Gross and Forum with Michael Krasny are reliable choices. Although still shrinking, most major metropolitan papers remain useful, factual sources for local news.

Calvin and Hobbes (used with permission)

## Other Web tools

Another resource worth mentioning is **Google Scholar** (https://scholar.google.com/intl/en-US/scholar/about). It provides access to abstracts and sometimes full texts of studies conducted by university researchers in many fields. Two advantages are the depth of an academic study and the enhanced credibility of peer-reviewed research. There are also two drawbacks. The writing is often as stiff as an octogenarian at daybreak. And because of the review process, the data lag current events by at least a year.

**Google Advanced Search** (https://www.google.com/advanced_search) is a powerful tool allowing you to specify additional terms of your search, such as language, dates and regions, to find pins in the Internet haystack.

**Google Public Data Explorer** (https://www.google.com/publicdata/directory) "makes large, public-interest datasets easy to explore, visualize and communicate. As the charts and maps animate over time, the changes in the world become easier to understand. You don't have to be a data expert to navigate between different views, make your own comparisons, and share your findings," according to the company.

Another national resource is **Times Topics** at the *New York Times* (http://www.nytimes.com/pages/topics/) In its own words, "Each topic page collects all the news, reference and archival information, photos, graphics, audio and video files published on topics ranging from Madonna to Myanmar. This treasure trove is available on articles going back to 1981." Most metro papers' websites can also be searched for local issues. These files are invaluable for discovering what public figures said in the past and compare it with present positions and actions. You need not rely on John Oliver or Seth Meyers to expose contradiction and hypocrisy.

Want to see how a particular meme or news article is spreading on social media? **Storyful Multisearch** is a free app you can add to the Chrome browser. With the Multisearch extension you can quickly query keywords across Twitter, YouTube, Tumblr, Instagram and Spokeo. Click on the extension, enter your search term and it will open up new tabs for each social network showing the search results in each.

### Trustworthy sites for general facts

By applying the SMELL test, you can assemble a collection of news and information providers that you trust. Here are a few suggestions compiled by Christopher Callahan and Leslie-Jean Thornton of the Walter Cronkite School of Journalism and Mass Communication at Arizona State University,[22] along with a few of my own nominations:

**Wikipedia.org** is a great place to start a background search on almost any topic. Lately, it also covers breaking news. It has been widely criticized for inaccuracy since anyone can write or edit its entries. But since 2005, it has taken precautions against false content by requiring citations to other published materials. It's not an ironclad defense against manipulation or falsehood, but has improved its reputation. While it's not a definitive source, Wikipedia can provide a capsule view that can later be checked against more authoritative sources.

**InfoPlease.com** combines an almanac, dictionary and the Columbia Encyclopedia.

**Publicagenda.org** provides non-partisan background on key public issues from crime to education to environment to health care to social security.

**USAFacts.org** is an ambitious effort that went online in 2017. Funded by former Microsoft CEO Steve Ballmer, it tracks money as it passes from tax-payers, through the U.S. government and out into agencies and projects.

**American Fact Finder,** (https://factfinder.census.gov /faces/nav/jsf/pages/index.xhtml) provides a wealth of statistics about the U.S. population from agriculture to wholesale and retail trade compiled by the U.S. Census Bureau.

**The World Factbook** (https://www.cia.gov/library/ publications/the-world-factbook/) describes itself this way: "provides information on the history, people, government, economy, geography, communications, transportation, military, and transnational issues for 267 world entities."

**The New York Times Newsroom Navigator** (http: //www.nytimes.com/interactive/technology/navigator.html?_r=0) provides an extraordinary list of hundreds of reference websites used by reporters at the *Times*.

*Politics*

**Project Vote Smart** (www.votesmart.org) advertises itself as "The voter's self-defense system." It reports on the voting records and positions of both national and state candidates for office, campaign finances, "political courage," and the ratings of candidates by special interest groups from abortion rights to environment issues to gun rights to women's issues. (Disclosure: I contribute to this project.) The project's nifty Vote Easy Website won the 2011 Webvisionary Award. It allows you to compare your stance on major public questions with every candidate running for national office that you are entitled to vote for based on where you live. The candidates who agree with you come forward on the page and those who disagree remain in the background. It looks like this:

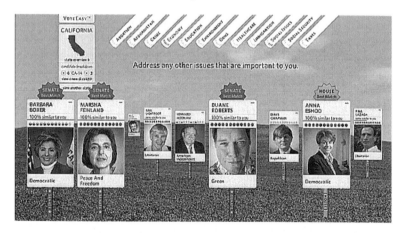

**Congress.gov** (https://www.congress.gov//). Originally named Thomas.gov for Thomas Jefferson, it is maintained by the Library of Congress. It contains vast amounts of well-organized information about all U.S. House and Senate legislation, the *Congressional Record*, email and postal addresses for legislators, founding documents like the Constitution and much more. It's searchable by bill text, topic and number. You can also browse bills sponsored by any legislator.

**FedStats** (https://fedstats.sites.usa.gov/) provides links to statistics from more than 100 federal agencies.

**General Accounting Office** (www.gao.gov) is the investigative arm of Congress and makes its reports public online within days of providing the information to legislators.

*Opinion Polls*

Because polling is as much art as science, it's always wise to aggregate several polls asking similar questions and take the mean, or average, of their results. It's risky to rely on a single poll's numbers. Also recognize that pollsters routinely push people to offer opinions about things they know little about. Such opinions are unstable and likely to change. Unscrupulous pollsters craft questions in such a way as to bias responses, e.g. "Do you approve of the barbaric practice of abortion?"

**Gallup** (www.gallup.com) is one of the oldest national polling organizations and one of the more trusted. You can search its archive of polls.

**Roper** (https://ropercenter.cornell.edu/) also does reputable polling on public issues, and is searchable.

**Pew Research Center** (www.people-press.org) provides quality polls on politics and press issues with excellent graphic displays.

*Health*

**National Center for Health Statistics** (https://www.cdc.gov/nchs/) provides information about public health and various diseases.

**U.S. Food and Drug Administration** (www.fda.gov) provides useful alerts and information about the safety of the food supply and medicine.

**U.S. Consumer Product Safety Commission** (www.cpsc.gov) evaluates a variety of consumer goods for threats to health or safety.

*Science*

The **National Academy of Sciences** (http://www. nationalacademies.org/) bills itself as "where the nation turns for Independent, expert advice." You can access and search thousands of scientific reports on a wide variety of scientific issues from earthquake preparedness to adverse effects of vaccines, all for free.

The **American Society for the Advancement of Science** (www.aaas.org/) publishes the magazine *Science* and provides free policy statements on most of the controversial public issues of the day.

*Crime*

**FBI Uniform Crime Reports** (https://ucr.fbi.gov/) provides a wealth of national and state data on numbers and trends of various types of crime.

**National Criminal Justice Reference Service** (www. ncjrs.gov) provides in-depth information about corrections, juvenile justice, courts, crime prevention, victims, etc.

*Environment*

**U.S. Environmental Protection Agency** (www.epa. gov) provides information on topics from acid rain to drinking water to pesticides to UV index to waste. (See earlier warning that this site may no longer reflect scientific consensus.)

**Environmental Defense Fund** (https://www.edf.org/) is a non-profit organization seeking to protect the environment.

*Consumer information*

**ConsumerReports.org** is the source with a perfect PIE chart. It's proximate – testing products in its own labs and reporting first-hand on the results. It's independent, accepting nothing from companies whose goods it evaluates, declining even advertising to avoid any conflict of interest. And its expertise is unparalleled. Unfortunately, you have to pay a small annual fee to subscribe. Of course, you can look up products for free in *Consumer Reports* magazine, which is carried by almost every public library. (Disclosure: I subscribe to this magazine.)

**Consumer Financial Protection Bureau** (https://www .consumerfinance.gov/?gclid=CNiR9ffo5dMCFRBEfgodr3sMtw) describes itself this way: "We are ... a U.S. government agency that makes sure banks, lenders, and other financial companies treat you fairly." There are also trustworthy answers to many personal finance and money questions.

**Amazon.com** doesn't conduct any of its own evaluations, but allows customers to review products, giving them from one to five stars. Since Amazon sells a wide variety of appliances and consumer goods, you can get some idea of how pleased customers have been for many purchases. And the service is free. **AngiesList.com** carries ratings of local service providers – painters, roofers, plumbers, contractors and the like, even doctors and dentists. These are submitted by customers and monitored by AngiesList to avoid companies stuffing the ballot box for their own services or to "dis" competitors. **Cnet.com** provides free evaluations of high tech consumer goods like laptops, TVs, cameras and smart phones. **Yelp.com** carries free customer evaluations of local restaurants and other retailers and provides a map that makes it easy to find what you're looking for.

Be careful. All ratings systems that rely on consumer evaluations are susceptible to false reviews.[23] Yelp has been criticized for this vulnerability. David Segal, author of the *New York Times* blog, The Haggler, wrote: "As a consumer review Website, Yelp is so big and influential that it has given rise to a small, semi-underground group of entrepreneurs who, for a fee, will post a rave about your company. Others will post a negative review about your rivals."[24] According to Mr. Segal, Yelp has been refining its automated filtering system in an attempt to thwart such fraudulent reviews with mixed results. By the way, Mr. Segal does *not* endorse consumer evaluations conducted by the Chamber of Commerce's Better Business Bureau.[25] They are not independent.

## 4. Social media allow us to collaborate in vetting content with others who may be more knowledgeable

"The ecology of knowledge has filled out. The ability of people to engage in discussions and to get additive knowledge and perspectives is orders ... of magnitude better than it was."[26]

~ David Weinberger, senior researcher at Harvard's Berkman Center for Internet and Society

One of the newest ways to avoid being fooled is to ask your friends and colleagues on a social network like **Facebook, Linked-In** or **Twitter** to respond to a fact-claim or whole article. Collectively our professional and friendship networks have vastly greater knowledge than we do as individuals. Fact-checking is naturally a social activity.

## 5. The Web can even help us discover people and perspectives that are ignored or marginalized in mainstream U.S. media

One of the greatest blessings of the Internet has been the ability of previously voiceless people to put their viewpoints before the public, to emerge from the silence. But the Web doesn't merely give voice to the voiceless, it allows us a multiperspectival view of news that would have been impossible even for someone with access to the world's greatest library in 1990. With a few keystrokes you can find alternate reports about the same events and issues. Look for information sources that differ from each other along the fault lines – race, geography, gender, political orientation, etc. – detailed in chapter 4.

Here's an example. Absent the Internet, the average American citizen would have had to settle for a handful of news reports about Emmanuel Macron's historic election to lead France in May 2017. And all would have reflected an American point of view.

A search of Google News returned 789,000 articles from around the world. They ranged from an editorial in India's *The Hindu* expressing relief that right-wing nationalist candidate Marine Le Pen had lost, to a headline in the British newspaper, *Express*, with the headline, "Five more years of FAILURE" quoting Brexit advocate Nigel Farage's disappointment with the election, to Haaretz in Israel reporting on the reaction of French Jews, to Al Jazeera quoting people of color in mostly Muslim areas in and around Paris. Had I stopped by the world's best newsstand I couldn't have accessed nearly as many different perspectives as Google provided in one second.

The fact that many of the articles are written in languages other than English presents only a small problem. Both Google (translate.google.com) and Microsoft (www.bing.com /translator) can translate a block of text or an entire Web page almost instantly for free, even if you don't know which language you are looking at. If you open a foreign language site in Chrome, Google will ask if you'd like it translated. Such computerized translations don't measure up to a professional's work, but do allow the reader to capture the gist of an article.

Travel abroad provides a wider and wiser perspective on the U.S. and life in general, but airfare and hotels are expensive. You can gain a global point-of-view reading the news on foreign websites at little or no cost. I've placed a list of international news sources reporting in English in the notes at the end of this chapter.

## A final word

We are living through as profound a period of change in our information environment as humans have ever experienced. And it's happening at warp speed. The ability to identify reliable news and information in the digital age is essential not just for individuals, but for the whole society. Governments can require corporations to reduce pollution of the atmosphere, but the First Amendment renders the government powerless against most pollution in the infosphere. It's up to us. The eminent newspaper columnist Walter Lippmann's warning is as relevant today as when he wrote it in 1920:

> All that the sharpest critics of democracy have alleged is true if there is no steady supply of trustworthy and relevant news. Incompetence and aimlessness, corruption and disloyalty, panic and ultimate disaster must come to any people which is denied assured access to the facts. No one can manage anything on pap. Neither can a people.[27]

## Exercises and Discussion Questions

1. Visit Project Implicit at www.implicit.harvard.edu, and explore some of the bias tests. If you feel comfortable about it, say what you found. Do you think the test is valid? Why or why not?

2. Find a claim that seems dubious to you in a news or commentary article – or viral email or political ad – and check it out on Snopes.com, Politifact.com, or Factcheck.org. to see if it's factual.

3. Conduct your own fact-check online on a fact-claim that has NOT been vetted on any professional fact-checking service.

4. Find a photo or video on the Web and use Google's reverse image function or Amnesty's DataViewer to track down where it came from and when.

5. If you have a Facebook, Twitter, or Linked-in account, try to engage your friends in fact-checking a claim you've heard. Were they helpful? Describe the process and result?

6. Take an issue that's prominent in U.S. news media and explore how it's reported on the Website of a foreign news service. What similarities did you discover? What were the major differences?

7. Repeat the exercise in #6 with a local issue of interest. Did you find an alternate view of the issue? If so, how many and how did at least one differ in their approach?

## End Notes

[1] Wikipedia (accessed on 6/13/2011) "Socrates," online at: http://en.wikiquote.org/wiki/Socrates. Socrates agreed to take his own life rather than give up his philosophical inquiries about the wisdom of prominent Athenians.

[2] Julie Beck (3/13/2017) "This article won't change your mind," *The Atlantic*, https://www.theatlantic.com/science/archive/2017 /03/this-article-wont-change-your-mind/519093/.

[3] Nancy Isenberg, (2016) *White Trash: The 400-year untold history of class in America*, New York: Penguin Random House.

[4] Joyce Oldham Appleby (2003) *Thomas Jefferson* , New York: Times Books, p. 140.

[5] Joel Williamson (1984) *The crucible of race: black/white relations in the American South since emancipation*, New York: Oxford University Press, p. 24.

[6] Stanley Nelson, Director (5/16/2011) "Freedom Riders," The American Experience, Public Broadcasting System, available online at: http://www.pbs.org/wgbh/americanexperience/freedomriders/.

[7] The editors of Time-Life Books (1991) *The Enterprise of War*, Alexandria, VA: Time-Life Books.

[8] Jeffrey M. Jones (8/ 4/ 2008) "Majority of Americans Say Racism Against Blacks Widespread," Gallup Poll, Princeton, NJ, online at: http://www.gallup.com/poll/109258/majority-americans-say-racism-against-blacks-widespread.aspx.

9 Bob Garfield (4/29/2011) interview with James Fallows, "The birth certificate and legacy of presidential rumors," On the Media, NPR, online at: http://www.onthemedia.org/transcripts/ 2011/04/29/07.

10 Sally Lehrman (2007) "Believing is seeing: Optical illusions and social stereotypes," Poynter Online: http://www.poynter.org/ column.asp?id=101&aid=130118.

11 Mark Scott (5/1/2017) "In Europe's Election Season, Tech Vies to Fight Fake News," *New York Times*, https://www.nytimes.com /2017/05/01/business/europe-election-fake-news.html?_r=0.

Several algorithm-based systems show promise. **Project Fib** will label some Facebook articles as "verified." And **B.S. Detector** provides a fake news alert for some fake news Websites. Both are available at the Google Chrome webstore.

12 Cary Spivak (December/January 2011) "The fact-checking explosion," *American Journalism Review*, available online at: http://www.ajr.org/ article_printable.asp?id=4980.

13 Tyler Durden (5/6/2017) "The College Majors That Don't Pay Off," Zerohedge.com, http://www.zerohedge.com/news/2017-05-06/college-majors-dont-pay.

14 Niall McCarthy (5/3/2017) "The College Majors That Don't Pay Off," Statista, https://www.statista.com/chart/9216/the-college-majors-that-dont-pay-off/.

15 Andrew Chamberlain and Jyotsna Jayaraman (April, 2017) "The Pipeline Problem: How College Majors Contribute to the Gender Pay Gap," Glassdoor.com, p. 26, online at: https://research-content. glassdoor.com/app/uploads/sites/2/2017/04/FULL-STUDY-PDF-Gender-Pay-Gap2FCollege-Major.pdf.

16 Margot Sanger-Katz (5/4/2017) "Who Wins and Who Loses in the Latest G.O.P. Health Care Bill," *New York Times*, https://www. nytimes.com/2017/05/04/upshot/who-wins-and-who-loses-in-the-latest-gop-health-care-bill.html?_r=0.

17 Anna Maria Barry-Jester (5/2/2017) "The 4 Big Changes To Health Care In The Latest GOP Bill," FiveThirtyEight.com, https:// fivethirtyeight.com/features/the-4-big-changes-to-health-care-in-the-latest-gop-bill/.

[18] Coral Davenport (5/8/2017) "E.P.A. reduces scientists' role on a key panel," *New York Times*, p. A1.

[19] Pew Research Center for the People and the Press (9/12/2010) "Ideological News Sources: Who Watches and Why," online at: http://people-press.org/files/legacy-pdf/652.pdf. Other surveys with differently phrased questions shuffle the order. For example, an organization called Public Policy Polling conducted a survey in January 2010 resulting in much lower trust figures, but led by Fox with 49 percent, 10 points ahead of second place CNN. See Andy Barr (1/27/10) "Poll: Fox most trusted name in news," Politico.com, online at: http://www.politico.com/news/stories /0110/32039.html.

[20] Stephen Waldman (2011) "The information needs of communities," Federal Communications Commission; chapter 3 on television is available online at: http://transition.fcc.gov/osp/inc-report/INoC-3-TV.pdf. The entire report is available as a download at: http://transition .fcc.gov/osp/inc-report/The_Information_Needs_of_Communities.pdf. Also D.J. Cavanaugh (7/20/2016) "Why 'If It Bleeds, It Leads' Is Actually Good for Local Advertisers," *MediaShift,* http://mediashift.org /2016 /07/bleeds-leads-actually-good-local-advertisers/.

[21] Michael J. de la Merced (5/8/2017) "Sinclair said to be near deal for Tribune Media," *New York Times*, p. B2.

[22] Christopher Callahan and Leslie-Jean Thornton (2007) *A Journalist's guide to the Internet*, Boston: Pearson.

[23] David Streitfeld (8/19/2011) "In a race to out-rave, 5-star Web reviews go for $5," *New York Times,* p. A1, available online at: http://www.ny times.com/2011/08/20/technology/finding-fake-reviews-online.html.

[24] David Segal (5/21/2011) "A rave or pan or just a fake," The Haggler, NewYorkTimes.com, online at: http://www.nytimes. com /2011/05/22/yourmoney/22haggler.html?_r=1&ref=thehaggler.

[25] David Segal (2/26/2011) "But who will grade the grader?" The Haggler, NewYorkTimes.com, online at: http://www.nytimes .com/2011/02/27/your-money/27haggler.html?scp=1&sq= fraudulent+consumer+reviews&st=nyt.

[26] Brooke Gladstone (2/17/2012) "The changing nature of knowledge in the Internet age," interview with David Weinberger, author of *Too big to know*, On the Media, WNYC, online at: http://www.onthemedia.org/ 2012/feb/17/changing-nature-knowledge-Internet-age/transcript/.

[27] Walter Lippmann (1920) *Liberty and the News*, New York: Harcourt, Brace and Howe, p. 11 in Kindle version.

**International news sources in English**

– Agence France-Presse https://www.afp.com/fr

– Al Jazeera (Qatar) http://www.aljazeera.com/

– *Asahi Shimbun* (Japan) http://www.asahi.com/ajw/

– BBC (United Kingdom) http://www.bbc.com/

– *Buenos Aires Herald* (Argentina) http://www.buenosairesherald.com/

– CBC (Canada) http://www.cbc.ca/news

– *China Daily* http://www.chinadaily.com.cn/

– *Copenhagen Post* (Denmark) http://cphpost.dk/

– *Corriere della Sera* (Italy) www.corriere.it/english/

– *Daily Star* (Lebanon) http://www.dailystar.com.lb/

– Der Spiegel (Germany) http://www.spiegel.de/international/

– *The Guardian* (Nigeria) https://guardian.ng/

– *The Guardian* (U.K.) https://www.theguardian.com/us. The Guardian has a U.S. version that visitors from the U.S. are automatically directed to.

– *Haaretz* (Israel) http://www.haaretz.com/

– Japan Today https://japantoday.com/

– *Le Monde Diplomatique* (France) http://mondediplo.com/

– Mexico News Daily (Mexico City, Mexico) http://mexiconewsdaily. com/

– *The Nation* (Pakistan) http://nation.com.pk/

– *Novaya Gazeta* (Russia) https://www.novayagazeta.ru/. One of the very few newspapers in Russia free of government control, you'll need to use Chrome's translation service to read the paper in English.

– *The Standard* (Kenya) http://www.eastandard.net/

– *Hurriyet Daily News* (Turkey) http://www.hurriyetdailynews.com/

– *Toronto Star* (Canada) https://www.thestar.com/

– *Tehran Times* (Iran) http://www.tehrantimes.com/

– *The Times of India* http://timesofindia.indiatimes.com/

– *The Times of London* (U.K.) https://www.thetimes.co.uk

# Appendix

## How to Evaluate the Quality of News

*You can't improve what you can't measure.*

~ Business proverb

**N**ews articles can be free of partisan bias but still not very good – not useful in helping the community orient itself to reality or in encouraging empathy. As recently as 2001, you could count on reasonable news quality in most metropolitan newspapers, the four broadcast TV networks – PBS, ABC, CBS, and NBC – NPR radio stations, and some local TV stations. But that was then. Now, even Pulitzer Prize-winning newspapers require scrutiny.

The flight of advertisers has drained away reporting and editing resources from all mainstream media. And as formerly competing newspapers are clustered under one owner in a region, executives are choosing to lower standards in order to cut costs. With the monopolies created by these clusters, they know consumers have nowhere else to go for comprehensive local news. This chapter will demonstrate how to measure news quality so you can demand better. But perhaps an even better reason to assess news quality is to discover which new providers of news on the Web can be relied upon.

## Guiding principles

Over the past 200 years, news has been defined as broadly as anything that's new to its audience. But during the last half century, almost every American newspaper and the majority of broadcast stations – commercial and nonprofit – have adopted a narrower definition, something called *socially responsible journalism*.

Throughout this book I've argued that the primary purpose of socially responsible journalism is to help as many people as possible *make sense* of issues and events that affect their lives. News makes informed choices possible: how to improve the quality of life through the environment, schools, jobs, transportation, health, or government. A secondary purpose is to create empathy – to generate concern for other people, especially people in need.

In journalism, entertainment (elements that make a story more interesting) plays an important role, because it can enlarge the audience. But entertainment cannot be the primary purpose of news. Entertainment must *serve* information and empathy. As I argued earlier, making what's important engaging and building a sense of community – with great writing, photos, video, and graphics – is the journalist's challenge. Making what's merely interesting *seem* important by placing it at the top of newspapers, newscasts, or websites is deceptive. It signals the most common and destructive type of bias in news produced by profit-seeking corporations – commercial bias.

Many of us have been conditioned to accept a commercial definition of newsworthiness rather than a public service version. Most of our news media operate as businesses. Some have trained us to value how *interesting* news is more than how *informative* it is or how much concern for others it invites. So some of the yardsticks below may seem unfamiliar. But give them a chance.

**A report card for local journalism**

Grade the News used scientific sampling techniques to evaluate the quality of the most popular newspapers and local TV newscasts in the San Francisco Bay Area. With help from students and interns at Stanford University, we evaluated several thousand stories over a year on seven measures of journalism quality, then weighted each story's score based on its length - to come up with a set of grades. You can see a Flash animation of the analysis at: www.gradethenews.org/feat /recentgrades/ flash.htm.

## How to grade the news

The news scorecard I propose here is simpler than the evaluation system we used at Grade the News. And it can be applied to a single story or to an entire newscast, website, newspaper, or magazine. It's not comprehensive; it says nothing about the article's accuracy, for example, or the quality of the writing or videography, or whether the news organization got the story first.

But it does measure whether the article (or articles) addressed a consequential news topic, the informational richness of the report, the amount of empathy it built for fellow humans, the number and expertise of sources, whether basic standards of fairness were met, and whether the sources reflected diversity given the community and the topic.

### Underlying assumptions

Assumptions are always risky. But they are necessary to create a relatively simple way of evaluating news. They are based on my experience directing Grade the News (www.gradethenews.org).

First, I assume that if a news-provider is consistently choosing less newsworthy topics or reporting with little compassion or knowledge gain on the part of citizens, quoting few sources, or neglecting fairness or diversity, then not even the flashiest writing and camera work can salvage the journalism. It's like spraying cologne on a skunk.

I also assume that the *purposes* of journalism influence its content more powerfully than the *technology* that brings it to our attention. The medium is *not* the message, though it does affect it. Good reporting on television and radio may legitimately be briefer than on the Web or on paper, but the goal and ethics are the same, regardless of the medium. As you'll see, the news scorecard levels the playing field among the technologies delivering news.

Finally, I acknowledge that creating a one-size-fits-all scorecard for content as varied as news, which is conveyed through technologies as different as the newspaper, radio, television, cell phone, and Web, for reviewers with diverse levels of education and interest, requires compromises. This news scorecard will measure no story perfectly, but I hope it will aid your evaluation of every story.

### Ground rules

*How many articles should I analyze?* That depends on how broadly you want to generalize your finding. Every story of at least average length is fair game. Most newsrooms have minimum standards of quality that are applied before any story meets the public.

But the larger your sample of stories, the more credible any conclusion you draw about a blogger, reporter, or news-provider will be. If your aim is to evaluate a particular news-provider, you'll want to look at multiple stories – preferably over several days. (If you evaluate a mainstream news organization, don't buy "slow news day" excuses for poor performance. Only passive newsrooms depend on breaking events to fill their time or space.)

If you want to see which news-provider is the best, rate them on the same news cycle (evening newscasts and online postings, and the next morning's newspaper). That way they have the same "raw material" of events to cover.

*Should I save the story?* As a practical matter, record radio and TV newscasts so you can pause to evaluate after each story, or look at them more than once. Archive the newspaper and save Web stories to a file on your computer. The individual story is our unit of analysis.[1]

*Which stories should I evaluate?* To simplify the task and apply it evenly across print, broadcast, and Web, I suggest you only evaluate stories editors signal as important. Editors flag the importance of an article in three ways:

1) Placing the story at the top of the newscast, newspaper, or main Web page (Because most people have little time for news, editors make it easy to find the most significant stories.)

2) Devoting more time or space on a story (Brevity is always a virtue in journalism, primarily because of the scarce attention of the audience. If a story goes long it should be unusually consequential.)

3) Using large, bold headlines, photos, and graphics. (For layout editors, size matters.)

Journalism's importance conventions provide a powerful hint of any news-provider's priorities. If these signals are used to promote stories designed more to turn heads than to fill them – aimed more at audience wants than needs – it's a sign that profit trumps public service. What they are doing may be news, but it's not socially responsible journalism. By their placement, length, and headlines, you shall know them.

In *newspapers*, the most significant articles begin on the front page and other section fronts. Readership studies say these are the most-read pages. The stories on them are the ones to analyze.

Because TV has so much less time than newspapers and websites have space, television journalists only have room for top stories. So I suggest examining their entire premiere evening newscast (the longest one within the most popular viewing period, 6–11 p.m.), or at least the first half-hour.

The most important stories on a news website are those on the home page. Scrolling down, choose the first 10 to 20 stories with the largest and boldest headlines.

### Judge media on their most influential stories

There is simply too much happening on any given day for any news medium to do it all justice. They must impose a hierarchy on events and issues. Evaluating the stories they put toward the top of that value order carries three benefits:

> 1. It rates news-providers on their most influential stories – those the largest number of consumers will see.
> 2. It's fair to apply professional standards of quality, because this represents their best work.
> 3. It makes it easier on you, the evaluator, by reducing the total number of articles you have to assess to rate a provider.

Skip stories in print or on the Web that are shorter than five paragraphs, and skip radio and TV stories that are shorter than 20 seconds. Treating a story as a "brief" indicates the news-provider's belief that it matters little. Ignoring the briefs also avoids dragging down a news-provider's score on stories it doesn't consider important. (Don't worry! If it consistently shortchanges important stories, that will show up in your analysis as under-covered topics.)

Finally, call any ties in your judgment of news quality in favor of the news-provider. Doing this and paying more attention to its best articles will win credibility for your analysis – and maybe even grudging respect within the newsroom. Most journalists are sincerely trying to do the best that executives allow.

### *Evaluating opinion articles*

The news scorecard is designed primarily to help you judge reporting quality rather than opinion articles. It can be used for hybrid opinion-reporting articles, such as advocacy journalism, articles by columnists appearing on news pages, as well as videos and blogs in which the author reports on something in addition to his/er commentary. But the scorecard is not well suited to editorials and op-eds. Such articles usually contain few sources and need not give all sides in a controversy a chance to make their best argument (although the best do). Nor is the scorecard intended for specialty publications covering only Hollywood, sports, or other entertainment.

*Ignore the ads*

Analyze only what's presented as news. Skip advertisements and advertorials – material laid out in columns, like news, but labeled as advertising, including so-called native advertising or sponsored news.

## Introducing the news scorecard

One scorecard is good for rating a single story or an entire "edition" of news – newspaper, newscast, or website on a particular day. Begin by identifying the date, then the station's call letters ( e.g., WMAL) or the paper's or website's name, and then the time of broadcast or edition (e.g., "Valley"), if the paper zones editions. Note the time you accessed a news web- site.

If you are evaluating an edition, stop after each story and go through the questionnaire, placing a hatch mark (|) in the appropriate space for each question. After evaluating the final story, tally the number of stories in each category and place that number in the parentheses. Then add the points for each question and enter them at the right margin in the space marked "total points."

# News Scorecard

**Date** presented_____ News-provider_____

Newscast/Web **time or edition**_____

**1. Story topic?** Put a mark next to the single topic that best matches the primary subject of the story:

**Core Topics**

| | |
|---|---|
| Politics/Government*: | ( ) |
| Natural disaster: | ( ) |
| Education: | ( ) |
| Economics/Business: | ( ) |
| Crime/Justice: | ( ) |
| Health: | ( ) |
| Environment: | ( ) |
| Major fires/Accidents: | ( ) |
| Weather: | ( ) |
| Transportation/Housing: | ( ) |
| Consumer reporting: | ( ) |
| Military: | ( ) |
| Science/Technology: | ( ) |

*Add 1 bonus point for each story in this category.*

*Total core topic stories _____*

*Total points (2 points each + bonus points) _____*

**Peripheral Topics**

| | |
|---|---|
| Celebrities: | ( ) |
| Minor fires/Accidents: | ( ) |
| Lifestyle/Pop Culture: | ( ) |
| Sports: | ( ) |
| Novelties: | ( ) |
| Other: | ( ) |

*Total peripheral topic stories =* _____

*Total points (1 point each)* _____

**2. Social impact?** (*Apply only to stories about core topics*) Rate the story on two dimensions: (1) whether the story provides information at least 10percent of the community can use to make sense of an issue or event of consequence (orientation) and 2) whether the story made you care about the people in it (empathy). Put a mark next to the appropriate quadrant for the story.

1:_____( ) 2:_____( )
Low on both          Low orientation, high empathy

3:_____( ) 4:_____( )
High orientation, low empathy    High on both

*Total points* _____

**3. Number of named sources?** Give ½ point for each named source, up to a total of 3 points per story. But if a source is an independent expert, give 1 point for each. Points per story:_____

_____

_____.

*Total points* _____

**4. Fair?** Does the story involve a *controversy or accusation?* If no, skip ahead to the next question. If yes, are two or more sides presented? Put a hatch mark in the appropriate space.

Yes:_____( ) No:_____( )
Subtract 2 points for each "No."    *Total points subtracted -____*


**5. Gender diversity of named sources?** Are 40percent or more of named sources in the story female? Put a hatch mark in the appropriate space.

Yes: _____( )
No:_____ _____( )

1 point for each "Yes" in print, ½ point for video, 0 points for each "No."                              *Total points _____*


**6. (Video only) Apparent racial or ethnic diversity?** Place a mark for each named on-camera source in the story.

| | |
|---|---|
| African-American: | ( ) |
| Asian-American: | ( ) |
| Euro-American: | ( ) |
| Hispanic-American: | ( ) |
| Native-American: | ( ) |
| Other/Couldn't tell: | ( ) |

Are 40percent or more of named sources in story *non*-Euro?
Yes: _____( )
No:_____( )
Give ½ point for each "Yes," 0 points for each "No."
                              *Total points _____*

**7. Extra credit questions:** *(Stories about <u>core topics</u> only)*

a) *Depth?* Put a hatch mark for text stories 40 paragraphs or longer or for video stories 4 minutes or longer. Number of in-depth reports:_____( )

Multiply each by 2 for *total points* _____

b) *Investigative report?* Put a mark for each original investigation. (For text stories, must be 40 paragraphs or more; for video stories, must be 4 minutes or longer.) Number of investigative reports: _____( )

Multiply each by 3 for *total points* _____

c) *Presentation?* Put a mark for each story with on-site audio, video, or informational graphic: _____

_____( )

1 point for each; *Total points* _____

**Overall quality score:** Add point totals for questions 1–7 _____ ÷ number of stories _____ = _____

At the bottom of the scorecard add your point totals and divide by the number of stories for an average grade. A+ = 9.5–10; A = 9.0–9.4; B+ = 8.5–8.9; B = 8.0–8.4; C+ = 7.5–7.9; C – 7.0–7.4; D+ = 6.5–6.9; D = 6.0–6.4; F = less than 6.0. Round decimals of .05 and greater up to the next tenth.

Most stories will earn between 1 and 10 points. The lowest grade a story can earn is -1 (an unfair peripheral story with no sources). With extra credit, the maximum amount a story can earn is 17. Thus a few in-depth or investigative reports on core topics can compensate for a larger number of mediocre stories. The grading system recognizes that few news opera-tions have the resources to give every story the investigation or depth it deserves.

You will notice that it's difficult to get a high score or any bonus points if the topic of the story is peripheral to the primary purpose of journalism. This penalizes commercial bias, which may direct significant reporting resources to less significant stories.

Specific instructions for each question

*Question #1 – The primary topic of the story:* For each story, place a hatch mark in the space following the appropriate topic, among the core or the peripheral group. Give core stories two points and peripheral stories one. Because information about politics and government usually affects our lives more than other news, each story in this category gets one bonus point.

If you are evaluating multiple stories, add up the hatch marks in each category and write the total between the ( ). For question 1, write the total in the space below the topic boxes.

*Explanation*

A core story is usually about something of greater, more lasting importance than a peripheral story. It's typically more newsworthy. Place the story in the *single* most appropriate category. Many will overlap. Use your best judgment about the primary topic. Don't split hairs over one topic versus another as long as both lie within the same category – core or peripheral; the point values will be the same.

*Core stories* are about the following topics:

POLITICS/GOVERNMENT – candidates, campaigns, government actions, deliberations or hearings, victims of government action or inaction; includes U.S. and foreign governments. (Many government stories overlap with more specific categories below; for example, a school board action overlaps with education. If most of the story describes a meeting, keep it in this category; otherwise record it in the more specific category below.)

NATURAL DISASTER – floods, earthquakes, tornadoes; must involve at least the potential for great human or physical damage. (Quakes causing less than $1 million in damage go in "minor fires/accidents.")

EDUCATION – all education levels, from kindergarten (even preschool) to university; includes school readiness, testing, teachers, and facilities.

ECONOMICS/BUSINESS – anything about the economy, including stocks, labor, wealth, poverty, employment, and private companies.

CRIME/JUSTICE – crimes (including domestic terrorism), trials, investigations, prevention efforts such as gun control, other parts of the justice system including bail, parole, and prisons.

HEALTH – medical care, insurance (or lack thereof), HMOs, hospitals, patients' rights, fitness, nutrition, workplace safety, smoking, exercise, medicine.

ENVIRONMENT – air, water, and noise pollution (and prevention), suburban sprawl, parks, fish stocks, natural habitat, global warming.

MAJOR FIRES/ACCIDENTS – must include deaths or major damage (at least $1 million damage in a small community and at least $10 million in a metro region).

WEATHER – forecasts, storms and their aftermath, droughts short of a natural disaster, minor flooding.

TRANSPORTATION/HOUSING – highway, bridge, rail, bus, transit, and airport issues; housing supply, costs, insurance, construction quality, employment, regulation.

CONSUMER REPORTING – information designed to help consumers make wise choices; must name retailers and products, and must use critical (not promotional) tone and evidence to support its conclusions. (Especially valuable is comparative information about prices and quality, including consumer price index and gasoline and housing price indices.)

MILITARY – armed forces, wars, foreign terrorism, budgets, exercises, peace treaties, alliances. (Care of veterans goes under "health.")

SCIENCE/TECHNOLOGY – physical and social (nonmedical) science discoveries, theories, computers, gadgets.

SOCIAL TRENDS – serious issues that don't fit in more specific categories, for example, discrimination, family composition, population, and immigration.

*Peripheral stories* concern the following topics:

CELEBRITIES – sports and entertainment stars' lives, deaths, marriages, breakups, new shows, and arrests. Put similar stories about current, and former politicians in "politics/government."

MINOR FIRES/ACCIDENTS – nonlethal incidents, mishaps, pipe breaks, and electrical outages where damage is less than $1 million for small communities and less than $10 million in metro areas; includes traffic reports, lost travelers, minor snafus, and earthquakes or other natural occurrences that cause less than $1 million in damage.

LIFESTYLE/POPULARCULTURE – seasonal celebrations (e.g. July 4th and the annual county fair), food, restaurant and theater reviews, home and garden, fashion, style, travel, arts, TV and entertainment listings, fads, boats, cars, and new homes. (Stories about products, like autos or wine, that fall short of the standards for consumer reporting in the core section go here. Reviews of fiction books go here, but put nonfiction reviews under whichever category best matches the content. Treat reviews of documentary films like nonfiction books.)

SPORTS – scholastic, Olympic, amateur, and professional competition, hobbies, and recreation. (Stories about performance-enhancing drug scandals go here, but if they address health effects for large classes of athletes, such as high school or college players, place in "health.") Put stories about the business of sports – revenues, stadium construction, public subsidies – in "economics/business" or another core category.

NOVELTIES – lost and found pets, giant or weird vegetables, reunions, emotional stories about animals, unusual or ironic events, humorous encounters.

OTHER – topics that don't fit elsewhere.

*Instructions for Question #2 – Social impact:* For stories about *core* topics only. Give each such story a score from 1 to 4 based on its potential to orient people to reality and its potential to excite empathy for everyday people in need. Stories high on both dimensions merit a 4; those high in orientation but low in empathy get a 3; those low in orientation but high in empathy get a 2; and those low on both dimensions get 1. In deciding between low and high on a dimension, be guided by the explanation below. If all the criteria for orientation are met, mark high. If the story contains information that allows you to identify with others or share their joys or pains, mark high along the empathy dimension.

*Explanation*

Why only core topics? If the primary purpose of socially responsible journalism is to orient us to reality, articles about peripheral topics contribute little, no matter how much information they contain, how interesting they are, or how much they may tug at our heartstrings.

I realize some will chafe at this exclusion. If you pay attention to news to keep up with celebrities or sports, for example, I may have blown my credibility with you. But before you toss this book in the recycling bin, ask yourself whether you are using the news to entertain yourself or to make sense of the world around you. As I argued earlier, socially responsible journalism makes use of entertaining elements only as a means, not an end in itself. To be responsible, news has to go beyond amusement. So even if everyone is talking about the story (perhaps a celebrity scandal or sports event) or if you're elated or depressed for a few days about a championship game, skip this question and move on to number three.

The most important function of socially responsible journalism is to maximize public understanding of those issues and events of the day that have the greatest impact on the largest number in the community that a news outlet serves. So we'll rate articles based on whether they are likely to have a direct and more-than-momentary impact on the knowledge of at least 10 percent of those within the primary circulation area of a newspaper or magazine, the broadcast radius of a radio or TV station, or the audience a Website aims to serve. If so, rate them high in orientation potential. Journalism's secondary purpose is to move us to care about others in need, both in our community and in the wider world. If a story has this impact on you, rate it high in empathy.

*Orientation:* By direct impact, I mean, the information in the article has the potential to change people's understanding of the world. Such a news story might affect their decision-making by alerting them to an opportunity or adjusting their opinion of a politician, a school or school district, a company, a product, what's healthy, what's dangerous, or what's valuable. A useful way of measuring orientational value is to ask yourself: "What, if anything, do people need to know about this issue or event to make sense of it?" Mark the story high if much of that information is provided; low if it's not.

By lasting, I mean something that matters for more than a few days. Let's set one month as a minimum. A traffic or weather report, for example, may have a direct impact on people's lives, but its value passes very quickly. So if the information a story imparts is of fleeting value, rate it low in orientation.

Why must 10 percent of the community served be affected to count as high in orientation? In daily journalism, few stories affect everyone in the community the news outlet serves in a direct and enduring way. Exceptions would include news of an impending natural disaster, the launch of a war, a state or national election, an economic boom or recession, and events of similar reach. But most news affects smaller groups of people. They could be residents of a particular school district or a city within the circulation or broadcast range of a news outlet (or the target audience of a website). They could be people working within a particular industry, like construction, computers, oil, mining, or agriculture, or within a sector of the local economy, such as government employees or service workers.

Selecting 10 percent as the cutoff places greater value on news directed at significant chunks of the audience than on news that might have a direct and lasting impact only on smaller groups. An exception to the 10 percent threshold makes sense when the community a news outlet, such as NPR, network TV or *Time* magazine, serves is national. Then an appropriate minimum ought to be a number – 1 million people affected.[2]

Event-oriented stories – those about a particular incident – generally carry less orientational value than issue-oriented stories – those about the ideas that connect events and those about causes, effects, solutions, and trends. "Big picture" stories – those about the forest rather than the tree – usually provide more resources for making sense of our environment, and they affect more people. (Of course, reports of cataclysmic events, such as the 9/11/2001 terror attacks, have enormous orientational value.)

Lots of prominent news stories won't meet these orientation criteria. For example, if you live in a metropolitan area, it's likely that someone within that area will die every few days from an accident or crime. Every death has enormous orientational impact on the friends, family, and perhaps the neighbors of the victim. But those affected are not likely to constitute 10 percent of the residents of the area. (If the metro area has one million residents, the death would have to affect at least 100,000.)

Such stories may rate high on the empathy dimension if they touch our hearts. But they probably won't change the way a significant number of residents make sense of the world. They might affirm a prior decision not to drink and drive or to avoid a certain part of town at night or to lock the doors, but their mental picture of the world will remain about the same. In a small community, however, where deaths from accidents or violence are uncommon and where everyone knows each other, a death might easily affect 10 percent of the population.

Even in a large metro area, almost all stories about politics and government exhibit orientational value, even "boring" stories about government meetings. That's because governments protect us, pick up our trash, pave our streets, and provide education and clean water. They also tax us. Most such stories will rate high in orientation.

*Empathy:* Stories written with empathy evoke concern for others in the community served or the wider world. They remind us that we are interdependent, that we need each other to flourish as humans.

Such stories often call our attention to others in need. Examples include articles that show us the suffering of those afflicted by illness, crime, war, or natural disaster. Empathic stories can also reflect joy. Such articles help us share people's sense of accomplishment or good fortune. Any story that helps us to identify with others, to understand what it is to walk in somebody else's shoes, generates empathy. Examples include stories in which people speak with emotion about the impact of news events, "slice of life" narratives, and when one person's or one family's experience is explored as a microcosm of a wider issue.

Every core story can be placed along each of the dimensions. It will end up in one of four quadrants below. Point values recognize that orientation to reality is the primary purpose of socially responsible journalism, and empathy is its secondary purpose.

In the upper right quadrant will be stories with the greatest social value, those that contain orienting information with a direct and enduring impact on at least 10 percent of the population served and are presented in a way that makes you care about the people involved. They are both important and empathy-building.

The second most valuable quadrant is the upper left. Stories there provide orienting information but are not presented in a way that builds empathy for the people involved. They are informative but dry and unemotional.

The third most valuable quadrant is the lower right. These are stories that engage your sympathy for the people involved but do not impart significant information to 10 percent or more of the community served. In metro areas, much crime reporting fits in this category.

The least valuable quadrant is the lower left. These are stories that address issues and events of consequence to few or no members of the community and do not move you to care about those involved. Such stories may be very interesting, even fun to watch or read. They may even be a hot topic at the water cooler, because they involve quirky or humorous behavior.

Note that if a story is unclear, illogical, or disorganized, if it lacks evidence for its conclusions or if it quotes sources who are not well informed or if it gets the facts wrong, people are not likely to learn much or be moved by it. Mark it appropriately.

*Instructions for Question #3 – Number of named sources*: After reading the explanation below, give each regular named source in a story half a point and each independent expert one point. Add the points for the story up to as many as three points, and write that number on the line. Separate one story total from another with a comma. After grading the last story, add all of the story totals, and place the sum in the space marked "total points" at the right.

*Explanation*

Sources literally make the news. In general, the more there are and the more diverse their viewpoints, the better. Identifying sources is also important. It allows you to decide how much to believe their information. It also tips you off about their biases.

Count the number of human or document sources that are (1) identified at least by name or source of document and (2) directly quoted (at least one remark is in " " marks). In the case of documentary sources (for example, court papers or government or academic studies), we'll treat statistics taken from them as if they were direct quotes.

We'll divide sources into two types – low and high scores on at least two of the three PIE criteria described in chapter 8. Finding an independent expert is valuable because it can lift reporting beyond "he-said-she-said" coverage that often leaves the audience confused.

Consider expert someone who either has long experience with the subject of the story or has formally studied it. An expert need not have an advanced degree in the area if s/he has a great deal of familiarity with it. Thus a longtime resident might be a neighborhood expert and a farmer might be an agriculture expert. Because no one is absolutely neutral, disqualify an expert only if there's a clear conflict of interest.

*Exceptions*: (1) If a named source refuses comment, we'll still count that person as a source, since the reporter tried to include him/her. (2) Ignore anonymous sources, with one exception – those whom the reporter explicitly grants anonymity to protect them from some type of harm, such as retribution for breaking the rules that forbid discussion of some issue.

Why cap sources at three points? To level the playing field between broadcast on one hand and print and Web on the other. Because time in a broadcast is more limited than space in print and on the Internet, we stop counting at a level achievable by any news medium.

*Instructions for Question #4 – Fairness*: (Only for stories that describe a controversy.) Place a mark to the right of "No" if only one side of a controversial topic is offered the chance to make its case. Mark "Yes" if more than one side is represented, even if just to refuse comment. Subtract two points for each "No" story, and enter the total points after the minus sign. These will be subtracted from the overall quality score. "Yes" stories gain no points because fairness is expected, not optional. If there is no controversy, skip this question.

*Explanation*

Whenever there's a controversy, journalists are expected to get each side's best arguments. Consider as a controversy any story in which (1) a named person or institution is associated with crime or behavior that reflects poorly on them in the eyes of the community or (2) someone claims as fact something that many in the community would disagree with; or (3) a conflict or contest between two or more parties (other than a sporting event) is involved.

Note: Neither time nor space for different views must be equal (because the evidence may be stronger for one side than another). Sometimes, a story may present more than one controversial issue. If so, rate the story based on the principal or most serious allegation (which will usually be high in the story).

*Exceptions:* Leave blank if:

- The story concerns a day in a trial when only one side testifies, or the other side cannot be reached – for example, when police are searching for the accused or when a subject of the story is dead. (Arrest reports, however, should mention an attempt to get a statement from the person in custody, a family member, or an attorney.)
- The story profiles a single political candidate, as long as other candidates get about the same exposure within a reasonable time, or the story covers a demonstration or public speech where only one side is available onsite.

*Instructions for Question # 5 – Gender diversity:* For each story, divide the number of female sources by all named sources to get the proportion that is female. If it equals or exceeds 40 percent, put a hatch mark after "Yes." Otherwise, put a mark after "No." Give one point for each "Yes" in print, half a point for each "Yes" in video, and no points for each "No." Add up the points and put the sum after "total points." Exception: If a story focuses on just one gender, such as a women's or men's sports team, mark "Yes"; it's not appropriate to penalize such a story for gender imbalance.

*Explanation*

As we saw in chapter 4, men and women often see things differently. Reporters should try to include this diversity when they choose who shall have the privilege to speak through the megaphone of mass media.

Sources are usually identifiable by gender because of pictures and audio or the use of honorific titles, pronouns, or first names. If you can't tell, don't count that source for this question. Keep track on a scratch pad. If sources can't be identified in question 3, don't include them here either.

Why set 40 percent female sources as a threshold? News has to reflect the real world, but it need not reinforce its prejudices. Because news appropriately reports on the expression of power, and power is not equally distributed by gender (or race or ethnicity), some mismatch in favor of males (and Euro/Anglos) may be expected. But since those upon whom power is exercised are also newsworthy and usually far more diverse, a ratio more than 10 percentage points out of balance with the proportion of a demographic group in the community served is suspect.

Why half a point for video stories? Because diversity in video will be measured by gender and apparent racial or ethnic identity, each measure is worth half a point. The latter cannot be measured in print, unless the reporter identifies the source by ethnicity or race.

*Instructions for Question #6 – Racial and ethnic diversity:* (Only for video stories.) Put a mark to the right of the appropriate racial or ethnic category for each named on-camera source that you can. For each story, calculate the proportion of Euro-American sources the same way you calculated female sources above. If 40 percent or more of all named sources are not Euro-Americans, put a mark next to "Yes;" otherwise, mark "No." Give half a point for each "Yes" and no points for each "No." Add the points, and put the sum after "total points." Exception: If a story focuses on just one racial or ethnic group (for example, an ethnic neighborhood, business, school, or sports team, or a racially uniform society), mark "Yes." It's not appropriate to penalize such a story for imbalance.

*Explanation*

You can use visual cues and sometimes characteristic names to categorize sources who appear on screen. We can only score *apparent* identity because names and appearances may mislead and most sources are not identified by ethnicity. Race is also a poorly defined category, particularly in a diverse population where people intermarry.

So why bother? Racial and ethnic identity can powerfully affect viewpoints. Journalists who interview diverse sources are more likely to capture these perspectives. An imprecise measure is better than none. If you can't tell, mark that box.

Note that the table also allows you to check the diversity of the entire edition. And it indicates who is being excluded from the powerful role of source.

*Instructions for Question #7 – Extra credit*: Apply only to core topics.

a.) Depth: Add two points to text stories that are 40 paragraphs or longer and to broadcast or video stories that are four minutes or longer.

b.) Investigative report: Add three points for each such story in which the news-provider's own journalists uncover illegal or incompetent behavior on the part of named individuals or institutions. Reporting on another news organization's investigation, or one by a government or corporation, does not count. Important: story text must be 40 paragraphs or longer, and videos must be 4 minutes or longer.

c.) Vivid presentation: Add one point for each story with informational graphics attached (such as tables, graphs, maps, summaries of key points), with a photo or video of an event, or with natural sound from the scene in radio or Web.

*Instructions for Question #8 – Overall score*: For a single story, add up the points on the right margin. Find the average score for a whole edition by dividing the sum of all point totals by the number of stories analyzed.

Since we're only evaluating the top stories of the day, the quality of the news – like children in Lake Wobegon (www.prairiehome.publicradio.org) – ought to be above average. On the other hand, news media may need to produce some "cotton candy" stories simply to attract audience. The wide range of passing scores, from 60 to 100, addresses both concerns.

Don't be surprised if a few articles are difficult to neatly fit into the quality evaluation tool. Use your best judgment and the logic of earlier chapters, especially chapter 7 on journalism standards, to inform your choices.

## An example of how to use the news scorecard

On Feb. 12, 2008, the NBC-owned-and-operated station in San Jose, California (KNTV) opened its 11 p.m. newscast with live coverage of a controversial debate taking place 50 miles to the north in Berkeley. Let's look at the lead of newscast's top story. Here's how it began:

[Sounds of crowd noise and women screaming; video of a burning poster; voice of anchor Jessica Aguirre] A burning debate tonight in Berkeley. Hundreds are arguing whether the city can kick the Marine recruiters out of town. [Voiceover, co-anchor Lisa Kim; video of city council chambers] And you are looking live inside the city council, which is working late into the night to decide what to do. [Aguirre] Stream of people after people making their opinion heard. Tonight's top stories in the first 11 minutes start right now. I'm Jessica Aguirre. [Kim] And I'm Lisa Kim. News 11's Jean Elle is live in Berkeley tonight. Jean, we watched this all day and all night long, certainly triggering a lot of emotions on both sides here and across the nation. [Jean Elle] Very emotional debate, Lisa. And right now hundreds of people are still here, waiting outside and inside for the council to make a decision and right now the city council is considering emotional testimony.

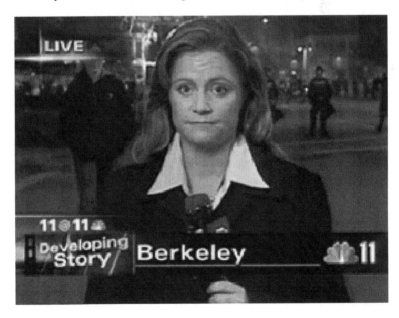

[Source #1, an unnamed white woman; video of previously recorded speaker inside council chambers]: "I don't want my kids friends recruited for an illegal war based on a thousand lies, a war that enrages the world and does not make us safer"

[Source #2, an unnamed white man; similar pre-recorded video] "This is ridiculous! You're not the Supreme Court. You can't pass judgment on the war.... I think it's great that they're going to pull federal funding now from city councils and county governments who actually go out and violate the law."

The premise of the story is a city council debate over whether Berkeley ought to ban Marine recruiters from operating within its borders. For people to make sense of this issue, they need to know answers to some basic questions: (1) Why does the city want to do this? (2) What are the likely consequences of such an action? (3) Can a city legally ban military recruiters? (4) What are the major arguments for and against such a decision? Now let's continue to see what answers the story provides?

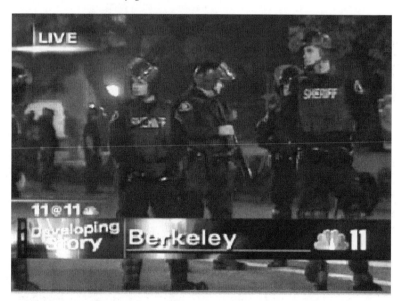

[Video outside of chambers; voice of reporter Elle] Police are here in riot gear to make sure this protest and counter-protest remain safe. This controversial issue has created some tense moments outside the meeting.

[Pre-recorded video of chanting, flag-waving crowd] "Shame on you! Shame on you!" [Voice of Elle] People on both sides of the issue face off with Berkeley police standing in the middle, trying to keep things peaceful. [Voice in the crowd] "What does that have to do with anything...?" [Voice of Elle] While heated debate raged, someone set fire to the sign pointing to Berkeley's Peace Wall. Anti-war activists want the Marine recruiting center out of Berkeley. Military supporters say the idea is a slap-in-the-face to active troops.

[Pre-recorded video of white woman wiping egg off her jacket; voice of Elle] Gayle Massingale took an egg in the face and still stood tall supporting her Marine sons. [Source #3: Massingale] "It's a fabulous organization and we're very proud of it. we're proud that they're a part of it. We're ashamed of Berkeley and California."

[Pre recorded video of source #4, a white woman; voice of Elle ] This is Marianne Vanasupa's first protest. Fighting back tears, she says Berkeley is out of line. [Voice of Vanasupa] "And I wonder about the tolerance, in this city that's known for being tolerant."

[Video of anti-war protesters; voice of Elle] But anti-war protesters support Berkeley's controversial position and say it's time to end the war in Iraq.

[Pre-recorded video of source #5, a black man, Harry Johnson] "I support the U.S. military as far as defending the U.S. borders, but I do not defend U.S. troops in other people's countries."

[Background voice] "It's my country!" [Voice of Elle] Many hope this war of words will make a difference. [voice of source #6, a white man, Mike Moroney, carrying sleepy son] "If there's any chance that it furthers the question throughout the country, and then through this coming election, then 100percent, it's helping."

[Voice of Elle; live video of continuing debate in chambers] The debate continues. This is a live look again of that city council meeting. So the question now is will the council go ahead and send the Marines the controversial letter or back down. If the decision is made during this newscast, we'll bring you an update. Reporting live in Berkeley, Jean Elle, NBC 11 news.

Now let's fill in the news scorecard:

## News Scorecard

**Date** presented _2/12/2008_ News-provider_KNTV-NEWS11_
Newscast/Web **time or edition**____11 p.m.

**1. Story topic?** Put a mark next to the single topic that best matches the primary subject of the story:

**Core Topics**

| | |
|---|---|
| Politics/Government*:                     \| | (1 ) |
| Natural disaster: | ( ) |
| Education: | ( ) |
| Economics/Business: | ( ) |
| Crime/Justice: | ( ) |
| Health: | ( ) |
| Environment: | ( ) |
| Major fires/Accidents: | ( ) |
| Weather: | ( ) |
| Transportation/Housing: | ( ) |
| Consumer reporting: | ( ) |
| Military: | ( ) |
| Science/Technology: | ( ) |

*Add 1 bonus point for each story in this category.

Total core topic stories _1_

Total points (2 points each + bonus points) _3___

| Peripheral Topics | |
|---|---|
| Celebrities: | ( ) |
| Minor fires/Accidents: | ( ) |
| Lifestyle/Pop Culture: | ( ) |
| Sports: | ( ) |
| Novelties: | ( ) |
| Other: | ( ) |

*Total peripheral topic stories =* _____

*Total points (1 point each)* _____

**2. Social impact?** (*Apply only to stories about core topics*)
Rate the story on two dimensions: (1) whether the story provides information at least 10percent of the community can use to make sense of an issue or event of consequence (orientation) and 2) whether the story made you care about the people in it (empathy). Put a mark next to the appropriate quadrant for the story.

1:__|_____( 1 ) 2:_____( )
Low on both                    Low orientation, high empathy

3:_____( ) 4:_____( )
High orientation, low empathy    High on both

*Total points* _1_____

**3. Number of named sources?** Give ½ point for each named source, up to a total of 3 points per story. But if a source is high in PIE, give 1 point for each. Points per story:_2_____

_____
_____.

*Total points* _2__

**4. Fair?** Does the story involve a *controversy or accusation?* If no, skip ahead to the next question. If yes, are two or more sides presented? Put a hatch mark in the appropriate space.

Yes:_|_____(1 ) No:_____(
) Subtract 2 points for each "No."

*Total points subtracted* -_0__

**5. Gender diversity of named sources?** Are 40percent or more of named sources in the story female? Put a hatch mark in the appropriate space.

Yes: ____|_____( 1 )
No:_____( )

1 point for each "Yes" in print, ½ point for video, 0 points for each "No."                          *Total points* _0.5_

**6. (Video only) Apparent racial or ethnic diversity?** Place a mark for each named on-camera source in the story.

| | |
|---|---|
| African-American:        \| | ( 1 ) |
| Asian-American: | ( ) |
| Euro-American:        3 | (3 ) |
| Hispanic-American: | ( ) |
| Native-American: | ( ) |
| Other/Couldn't tell: | ( ) |

Are 40percent or more of named sources in story *non*-Euro?

Yes: _____( )
No:_|_____(1 )
Give ½ point for each "Yes," 0 points for each "No."

                          *Total points* _0___

**7. Extra credit questions:** *(Apply only to stories about <u>core</u> topics)*

a) *Depth?* Put a hatch mark for text stories 40 paragraphs or longer or for video stories 4 minutes or longer. Number of in-depth reports:_____( )

Multiply each by 2 for *total points* _____

b) *Investigative report?* Put a mark for each original investigation. (For text stories, must be 40 paragraphs or more; for video stories, must be 4 minutes or longer.) Number of investigative reports: _____( )

Multiply each by 3 for *total points* _____

c) *Presentation?* Put a mark for each story with on-site audio, video, or informational graphic:

|_____( 1 )

1 point for each; *Total points* _1____

**Overall quality score:** Add point totals for questions 1–7
_7.5_ ÷ number of stories ___1___ = ___7.5___

This story earned a C+. It rated 3 points for being about government. The topic was important to a significant part of the Bay Area community because if Berkeley banned Marine recruiters, other cities might follow suit. Obstructing the Marines' ability to recruit while the nation was prosecuting two wars also could have national significance. But the treatment focused on the noisy confrontation outside more than the debate inside (evidence of commercial bias). Notice the emphasis right from the start on emotion; the word itself is used three times in the first minute.

The reporter seems more interested in capturing feelings than facts. The comments recorded seem random. We're given no idea of what Berkeley hoped to accomplish with the ban, whether it would be legal, or what the repercussions might be for such a ban. Some empathy was stirred by the passion of the speakers, but not enough to qualify as high in empathy because the sound bites were so short.

The four named sources added 2 points to the total. The story was fair, with two sources for and two against banning the recruiters. On-site camera work added 1 extra credit point. In sum, the story signaled something important was going on, but provided little useful information for viewers to make sense of it.

## Evaluating news can improve its quality particularly if you act in concert with others

*What to do with your evaluation?*

For starters, never ask this question of an editor or blogger whose product you've criticized!

At Grade the News, we found the saying that editors are thin-skinned right on target. To be fair, the people in charge of newsrooms have much less power at most American media than you might suppose. Executives at corporate headquarters can impose budgets that straightjacket editors and news directors. Some prominent newsroom leaders have quit rather than accept such restraints.[3]

If your scorecard identifies a quality news-provider, you have important information to share with the community. Whether that outlet is mainstream, an established alternative, or an entirely new provider, your analysis can contribute to a consumer report on local journalism. If you evaluated several news-providers head-to-head (during the same news-gathering cycle), ask those that performed well to report on your findings. Show your study to community leaders or local journalism groups (perhaps a regional chapter of the Society of Professional Journalists or a city press club or the League of Women Voters). Seek the assistance of local high school or college journalism or political science departments in replicating or circulating your results.

*Always* send your evaluations to the news-providers assessed, even if you risk an angry reaction. With this scorecard, you have the advantage of evaluating their work on the same standards they claim to apply to it. If you scored them highly, congratulate them. Everyone appreciates positive feedback.

If they earned a low grade, politely ask them to respond to problems you've identified. Unless the news-provider has a designated public editor or ombudsman, send your evaluation to the executive editor at newspapers and the news director at broadcast stations and affiliated websites. Send it to the most important-sounding person on the contact page of new online news sources.

Asking to open a polite conversation about the quality of coverage or partisan bias is the respectful and right thing to do. Most news media say they welcome such a dialogue.

## Seek allies

But from a practical standpoint, you are just one customer among many. Particularly if your complaint identifies coverage flaws that would cost money to remedy, you are likely to have to recruit allies – the more influential the better.

Complainers with high status, who often have extensive experience dealing with the media and skill in articulating complaints, were able to get the newspaper to respond. Other kinds of complainers, though, had difficulty doing so.

~ Purdue professor Neil Nemeth, describing his study of a Bloomington, Indiana newspaper.[4]

In his 2000 book, *Holding the media accountable: Citizens, ethics, and the law*, David Pritchard concludes: "Despite the often pious pronouncements of news industry leaders about their concern for the public, ordinary citizens do not seem to be taken very seriously by the news media." (p. 186)

The simplest remedy for poor journalism is to change your media habits and select other providers. Scan the Web for new local voices. But given the scarcity of new sources and the unprecedented concentration of media ownership currently underway, you may have little choice for local news. You and your community may have to deal with the local news monopoly.

The best place to look for allies in making a complaint to news-providers is among those who feel aggrieved: community groups ignored or victimized by poor quality or biased journalism. If you can attract more than one such group to your complaint, so much the better.

Finding an ally or champion on the faculty of a local high school or college journalism or political science department or from a local press club or chapter of the Society of Professional Journalists, or League of Women Voters will give your complaint greater authority.

If you go to the trouble of seeking allies, you'll obviously be more persuasive the more carefully you have documented the news-provider's inadequate coverage. Getting several people – perhaps a journalism or political science class – to analyze coverage over a week or longer, using the form above, will add credibility to your case. (I worked with journalism students at Palo Alto High School with good results.)

Recognize that a key element of the news scorecard – social impact – is highly subjective. What's informative to you may be already well known to another. So the greater the diversity of the group analyzing the coverage, the more reliable the findings.

If your critique of coverage is disregarded, consider going to alternative media with the results of your analysis. Few news media report on their own exercise of power, though the codes of journalism ethics require them to. So don't expect a news-provider you have critiqued – or any others owned by the same company – to carry news of your analysis.

Alternative media include weekly papers, local college newspapers, public radio stations, and websites dealing with local issues. If your complaint is one that might be true of many news-providers, you may even be able to prompt a story from professional media critics at *Columbia Journalism Review*, NPR's On the Media, FAIR, or other organization.

There are, of course, other remedies to consider. The law provides protection against libel – reports that unjustly harm your reputation – or invade your privacy. The Federal Communications

Commission takes complaints about broadcast and cable, but not print or Web operations. At times, groups have tried to boycott media whose reports they believed to be harmful. But these have rarely succeeded, except when joined by major advertisers. We saw in earlier chapters how when a critical mass of advertisers leave, even as big a money-maker as Fox's Bill O'Reilly, can lose their jobs. Let money talk and even the stars will walk.

If evaluating news and asking for improvements seems burdensome, consider the alternative. To ignore inadequate reporting and misleading opinion-writing or to give up on the news is to surrender your opportunity for informed participation in government. Omissions and distortions by the media can have very serious consequences for the whole community, because the media have so much ability to define reality. In a democracy, if you snooze, you lose.

## End Notes

A story, for our purpose, is an account of a particular issue or event prepared by one or more reporters. In print and Web, it usually has a headline and the reporter's name or wire service name under the head. On TV, stories are usually introduced by an anchor and "tossed" to a reporter, but they may be simply "reader" articles with just the anchor reporting. If there's a "team" of journalists reporting a particular event or issue on TV, count it as one larger story.

Sometimes news media will cluster brief articles under one heading, perhaps "International News" or "Police Report," or a columnist will write about several disconnected issues or events, or answer letters from readers. On TV, it could be a summary of brief stories from around the nation or the world. Treat each article as a separate news story if it describes a different event or issue than other items in the cluster. I suggest excluding stories shorter than 20 seconds or 10 square inches from analysis.

[2] To answer this question, you must have a general idea about the size of your community and its other characteristics, such as major industries. U.S. Census and Chamber of Commerce summaries are helpful in this regard. These will enable you to provide an informed estimate, which is all you need. Knowing something about your community is necessary to evaluate the orientational value of a mass medium that bundles news for consumers with differing information needs and interests. When you assess the story's empathic qualities, by contrast, you need only rely on your own reaction. That's because all normal humans possess the capacity for identification with our fellows. (And I'm assuming you're normal!)

[3] Gene Roberts of the *Philadelphia Inquirer*, Jay Harris of the *San Jose Mercury News*, and Jon Carroll and Dean Bacquet of the *Los Angeles Times* come to mind immediately. To be fair to corporate CEOs, they often must answer to distant investors who pay much more attention to profit than public service. As we saw in chapter 2, lately there has been little profit in newspapers and many of the large chains are staggering under enormous debts their CEOs undertook when they bought newspapers from previous owners.

[4] David Pritchard (Ed.) (2000) *Holding the media accountable: Citizens, ethics, and the law.* Bloomington, IN: Indiana University Press, p. 52.

# Index

# Acknowledgments

Here are some of the people who shaped this book as well as the earlier editions: Reneé Hobbs, professor and founding director of the Harrington School of Communication and Media at the University of Rhode Island; Larry Jinks, former executive editor of the *San Jose Mercury News* and senior vice president of Knight Ridder; Stephen Lacy, associate dean for graduate studies at Michigan State University Department of Communication and School of Journalism; Dr. Faith Rogow, founding president of the American Media Literacy Association; and Dr. Deborah Gump, director of the journalism program at the University of Delaware.

Professors Bella Mody and Michael McDevitt of the University of Colorado offered advice as did Professor Marilyn Greenwald of Ohio University and Professor Doug Underwood of the University of Washington. Professor John Durham Peters of Harvard University added his insights as did Professor Stephan Russ-Mohl of Università della Svizzera italiana. Prof. Judy Muller, former ABC and NPR journalist and now professor of journalism at the University of Southern California, offered comments on the second edition. So did three friends: Shiloh Ballard, author Paul Bendix and attorney Pamela Cohen, the queen of commas.

Professor Charles D. Feinstein of Santa Clara University helped shape the chapter on truth, as did Swedish journalist Torbjörn von Krogh and Professor Theodore L. Glasser of Stanford. Professor Chris Paterson of the University of Leeds helped me think about ideology. Prof. Arthur Asa Berger of San Francisco State University assisted on visual literacy. Cognitive scientist George Lakoff of the University of California, Berkeley taught me about framing. The late Dori J. Maynard, director of the Maynard Institute for Journalism Education, alerted me to the "Fault Lines" bias analysis pioneered by her father Robert Maynard. The late William F. "Bill" Woo helped me become more sensitive to the value of human interest in news during the time Grade the News was at Stanford. Credit is due them all, but blame is mine alone.

# About the Author

A former journalist and communication professor, John McManus writes and lectures about changes in news media and their impact on democracy. His 1994 book, *Market-Driven Journalism: Let the Citizen Beware?* won the annual research award from the Society of Professional Journalists. So did his 2009 college textbook, *Detecting Bull: How to Identify Bias and Junk Journalism in Print, Broadcast and on the Wild Web*. In 2000, he founded GradeTheNews.org. Using *Consumer Reports* as a model, the project scientifically sampled the most popular newspapers and newscasts in the San Francisco Bay Area and rated them head-to-head on seven yardsticks of journalism quality. Grade the News was funded by the Gerbode, Knight and Ford Foundations and received both national and regional awards.

Made in the USA
Columbia, SC
15 June 2017